Islands in the
Chaotic Ocean of Life

By

Shawn P. Sullivan

© 2017

DEDICATION

This book is dedicated to my family and friends, and to the readers of the Sanford News.

Thanks for your support! Best wishes!
Shaun P. Sull...

The following material first appeared in the Sanford News, a weekly newspaper in Southern Maine, in issues published between 2006 and 2014. George J. Foster & Company, of Dover, New Hampshire, owned the Sanford News during this time and its publisher, Patrice Foster, gave this book her blessing. The author is grateful.

TABLE OF CONTENTS

Introduction

A few years ago, I lugged two footlockers up from the basement and set them in front of the couch in my living room. I sat down and popped them open.

I emptied their contents onto the floor and sifted through them, spending a few moments with some things and glossing over others. I threw out most of what I found. What remained I condensed into a small plastic container the size of a junk drawer.

Maybe I'm sounding a bit cavalier here, as though I completed this task so efficiently and dispassionately that it took all of a few moments. Not so. It took me a full Saturday afternoon. The items in these footlockers were artifacts from my past, and I knew in discarding them that I was electing in the future either to rely on my memory or forget about them altogether.

And that's fine. I lingered a moment over the airline pass I used when I flew from Portland to Tallahassee to begin my sophomore year at Florida State University on New Year's Day in 1992, but I thought nothing about tossing movie and concert ticket stubs. *I* know I saw Bruce Springsteen in Boston in 1999. Do I really need an old stub reminding me so?

I threw out a lot of cards. Milestones. Birthdays. Holidays. I appreciated getting those cards, but it's a safe bet their senders do not even remember sending them. I kept a few cards from friends who offered encouragement during challenging times; they remain a nice tribute to the people with whom I've surrounded myself over the years. I also kept one card each from loved ones who are no longer with us; it will be nice, for example, to see my Memere's signature once in a while.

I went years without peeking inside these footlockers, so many of the items in there surprised me. Some of them made me laugh.

I found a patch of blue vinyl that I tore from the seat of my friend's car when we were in high school. He had gotten into an accident, and the ol' gang and I gathered around his wrecked car in a lot one Friday night and eulogized it. One of us played "Taps" on a trumpet. I'm sure one of us said a prayer. Then we all reached inside the car and took pieces of it with us as keepsakes.

I also discovered a handwritten note that read, *"Shawn: All set! No prob. I'll explain it to Linda. Talk to you later. Heather."*

I have no idea who Linda and Heather are. Nor do I know when, where or why the letter was written. Why did I decide to keep it?

I laughed when I found a progress report that my high school chemistry teacher sent home to my parents when I took his class as a junior back in 1989. "Shawn has not passed a test or quiz for this quarter," he wrote. He noted on the report that I seemed interested in the subject and appeared to try but needed to take a "more serious approach." He recommended that I prepare for class better and seek after-school help. Yeah, chemistry was not my best subject. French was.

Other items tugged at my heart.

I found two old letters that my Grammy sent me. She passed away in November of 2008. I ran my fingertips across her handwriting and kissed the tops of both letters. Then I tucked them into that small container.

I also came across a stack of postcards that my parents sent me when I was in college. During my first semester as a freshman, they mailed them every week, just to say hello. Dad wrote some, Mom wrote others. The love, humor and support in each of them made a difference as I began to make my own way in the world, often with mixed results.

I took those postcards and wrapped them tightly with a rubber band. At the time, my father was struggling against an incurable illness. I knew those postcards he sent me twenty years earlier would eventually mean even more to me in the future. I resolved to keep them.

I also found notes, cards and letters that my wife, Valerie, sent me, either while we were dating or during the earlier years of our marriage. I'd like our daughter, Madeline, to be able to see them some day.

As well, I uncovered letters and poems written and sent to me by my childhood neighbor, Mrs. Dunfield, during my college years. She was in her nineties at the time. She typed those letters, or "ditties," as she called them, on small notepad paper on her antiquated typewriter.

I tossed out small or peculiar items that I somehow felt the need to stash when I was young.

A red checker from the summer camp where I was a counselor.

Rusted keys to forgotten doors.

A wrapper from a York Peppermint Patty that I bought for an old girlfriend during a Valentine's Day date back in college.

I found a chunk of the Berlin Wall, sent to me by my cousin who was in Germany when it came down in 1989. I kept that, of course. I also kept a few news magazines that were published after the terrorist attacks on September 11, 2001.

As I went through these items, I was reminded of a long-gone child who became a teenager and then a young adult. He was confident and brash, silly and prankish. He certainly had that *joie de vivre*. I liked much about him but was glad he matured. He's a grown man now, blessed with the foundation of his own family. He's a lot more serious but still a seeker of fun times.

I'm sure it sounds like I had enough things in those two footlockers to make even the most fanatic pack rat blush. But here's the thing: I'm not a pack rat. That's my line, anyway, and I'm stickin' with it.

I just had these two trunks, see, and when I was younger I opened them just enough to stuff sentimental items in there. I rarely opened these footlockers over the years. If anything, I used the oldest one as nothing more than a coffee table when I was single. I'd plop down on my couch, kick my feet up on it, and watch TV.

Why did I keep all those things? Some of them, I know why - - that's why I got that small container for everything that survived the cut.

But what of that other stuff? The candy wrapper? The movie tickets? The red checker?

Not sure. I'll leave it up to you armchair analysts out there.

All I know is that I finally felt it was time for all of it to go.

But maybe I've cheated here. Perhaps I'm taking advantage of a loophole, something that allows me to have that proverbial cake and eat it too. After all, I have these columns, the ones you will read in the pages ahead and the hundreds of others that did not make it into this book.

Truth be told, this book is filled with infinitely more memories than both of those two sizable footlockers could hold together. Maybe, then, you've noticed a nimble trick I've pulled here. I may have thrown out that red checker, but I also recorded its existence here. In other words, the checker hasn't gone anywhere. It's still here. So to speak.

In 2006, I became the editor of the Sanford News, a weekly newspaper that covers my hometown of Sanford and its surrounding communities in Southern Maine. I delivered the paper when I was ten years old, so I guess that means I've circled back to the first place ever to give me a job.

I enjoyed that paper route, but I drove my father crazy when it came to managing the money that it generated. He tried so many times to get me to follow the basics in that department.

"Okay, the paper costs a quarter, right?" he'd begin.

I'd confirm that it did.

"And of that quarter, you owe 15 cents to the Sanford News, right?"

I'd confirm that he was correct there too.

"And you keep the dime that's left over, as well as the tips."

I nodded yes.

"Right. So, what you do, after you collect all your money, is take the number of papers you deliver and multiply it by point-one-five. That's what you owe the Sanford News."

"Uh-huh."

"Then you take the number of papers you deliver, and you multiply it by a dime. You know, point-one."

"Uh-huh."

"The amount there is what you get to keep. That and the tips."

Sounds simple enough, right? Dad wanted me to be methodical and thorough. I took another approach. I took all the money I collected on Tuesdays, paid my bill on time and in full at the Sanford News office, and kept the rest. If I ran out of money, I'd go to the customers who still owed me and collected. For example, on the way to the movies one evening, I'd stop at so-and-so's house, collect the money, and head to the theater.

That looseness, that lack of specific accounting, drove Dad crazy. At the time, I never understood why, as I responsibly paid my bill and had money left over to do what I wanted: go to movies, buy the latest compilation of "Garfield" comic strips, save up for Atari games, you name it. I know now that Dad was trying to develop in me a rock-solid business sense and an ability to manage money. I so frustrated my father on this issue that, one time, when I resisted his efforts to teach me, he threw up his hands and said he wanted to get a tee-shirt that said, "Parenthood Sucks!"

So it was a big deal when, more than two decades later, I became the editor of the Sanford News. This development in my life filled my folks with happiness and pride. One night, though, shortly after I started as editor, Dad ribbed me about those days in the early Eighties when he tried to teach me to manage my paper route money. He mock-lamented over how unteachable I had been on that subject.

"But Dad," I retorted. "Now I'm the *editor* of the paper. Clearly, I've turned out all right!"

Dad smiled and had a twinkle in his eye.

"Yes," he conceded, "but notice they did not put you in charge of the paper's *budget*."

Vintage Dad. He loved teasing those he loved. As an Irishman, that was how he showed affection. You'll see more of that in the pages ahead.

What follows is a collection of slice-of-life columns that I wrote for the Sanford News between the years 2006 and 2014. These columns were written under a deadline. This book was organized at my leisure. As a result, I've tweaked a few of these columns, essentially giving them an extra edit if I came across something that may not have worked well the first time around or discovered a clearer and more effective way to say something. One piece, "Extraordinary People," actually combines part of one column, written in 2006, with another, written in 2007.

I've organized the columns inside this book so that they have the flow of a novel; for all of the "stand-alone" pieces that you'll find in the pages ahead, there are a few story arcs too. My daughter's progress in the world and my father's departure from it are two of them.

Back in 2006, I named the column "From the Editor's Desk." There was, I admit, a part of me that thought I was *supposed* to name it that. After all, I'd be writing these columns from the desk of an editor. It's not a fancy title, I'll grant you that, but it shoots straight enough.

The title of this book, "Islands in the Chaotic Ocean of Life," is not as easily grasped as "From the Editor's Desk," but I assure you it is appropriate. On the cover, that's my father at 40 years old, keeping one foot firmly planted on land while dipping the other into the Gulf of Mexico during a family trip to Florida at Christmastime in 1985. That picture, taken by Mom more than 30 years ago, embodies a remark Dad would make decades later - - a remark, in fact, that would provide the theme and the title of this book.

Think back to the beginning of this introduction. By any chance, did you nod your head with recognition as you read about that afternoon when I emptied out my footlockers? Did you smile and think of the time when you sifted through the relics of your own past and did a little downsizing as well? Were you reminded of the people in your life? The places you've been? The things you've done?

If the answer is yes, then this book is for you. Thanks for picking it up.

The pages ahead are filled with all the things that comprise a life. There are stories of family and friendship, joys and challenges, follies and hard times, and love and loss and grief and healing and new beginnings. There are tales of holidays and travels and books and movies and songs. If any of them prompt you to recall your own life, with smiles and laughter, with recognition, with a newfound peace toward the challenges you have faced or are facing, then I will have accomplished what I've set out to do. We are all bound by universal truths, and, as the old expression goes, we're all in this together.

When you reach "An Island in the Chaotic Ocean of Life," the last column in this book, you'll find that much in life falls into one of two categories that, together, capture life as a whole.

For such clarity, credit goes to a father and his chair.

Islands in the
Chaotic Ocean of Life

Dog Days

I recently took Molly, our Cairn terrier, to the vet for her annual checkup.

Molly's blind and needs drops in her eyes to keep them from drying up, and she's also three pounds overweight. Overall, though, she's doing quite well.

Not bad for an old girl. She's 98 in dog years.

My wife Valerie and I welcomed Molly into our lives eight years ago, in the fall of 1999, when we were newlyweds living in a shoebox-sized apartment in Massachusetts. At the time, Val's cousins were getting ready to move from Boston to New Hampshire, and they were wondering if we'd like to take their dog.

"They're moving *from* the city to the country," I told Val. "Don't people sometimes give away their pets when they're moving *to* the city?"

"Yeah, well, this dog has a . . . social problem," Valerie explained. "I guess they don't want to deal with it at their new home."

"What problem is that?"

"She tinkles when she gets excited."

"Okay," I said. "No biggy. I know some very nice people who have the same problem. When does she get excited?"

"Every time someone comes home."

"*Every* time?"

"Pretty much."

"I dunno, Val. I come home a lot. Many times a day, actually. I leave, and then I come back. Is this going to happen every time?"

"Shawn, do you want the dog or not?"

I did. I started stocking up on rolls of paper towels.

I liked Molly right away. I came home from work one day to see Molly running from our front door quicker than a greyhound to meet me. She rolled onto her back and went belly-up when I began ruffling her fur. Then she tinkled on my sneakers.

And she kept tinkling, whenever Valerie and I came home from anywhere. I didn't mind after a while. I really liked the hero's welcome. Molly always raced to the door to greet me, wagging her tail and kicking back onto her hind legs and waving her front paws in the air.

You would have thought that I had been spending my days building churches or rescuing orphans, or something. I didn't have the heart to tell Molly that I had just been at a desk all day, tapping away on a keyboard and trying to get bunches of words all in the right order.

Molly and I became fast friends. We'd go for walks in the evening, watch movies on our couch, and take rides in our car. Molly would sit on Valerie's lap, rest her chin on the window, and let the wind whip her fur back while I drove.

Molly opened up a whole new world to me. She's a short dog who barely reaches your knees, a far cry from Shannon, the large, beautiful collie my family owned when I was a kid.

Shannon and I went everywhere together. He was such a handsome devil that local store owners would forget about the "No Pets Allowed" signs hanging in their windows. They'd invite Shannon into the stores with me, and they'd stroke his back, play with his ears and rub underneath his chin.

With Molly, though, I got quickly used to living with a small dog. There are benefits to owning a dog of short stature. They can't create awkward moments by nudging their noses in unfortunate places when guests visit your home, for instance.

And it's not like Molly's one of those lap dogs, so tiny and wispy they may as well be cats. No, Molly's a stocky little sausage, wide and rugged, but teddy-bear-faced and fluffy.

She's also clueless about her size. I've seen her go nose-to-nose with the meanest dogs.

"You *do* realize that's a pit bull?" I once asked Molly, as I prayed the bigger dog's owner would come and take him away.

Molly didn't care. She'd stand with her furry chest out and with her tail at straight attention. She'd stare right up into her opponent's darkest eyes and growl. She'd sound like an angry Ewok from one of the "Star Wars" movies.

That was years ago. These days, Molly's slower, quieter and more cautious, as she relies on her fading sense of smell to compensate for her blindness. She also gets scruffier after her baths more quickly these days; as she ambles along our wooden floors and occasionally picks up dust-balls, I'm sure she feels like the canine equivalent of a Swiffer.

Molly's 14 years old, so such change is inevitable. She started slowing and quieting down, however, when my daughter, Madeline, was born in 2003. Molly ceded the spotlight with enormous grace, but you could tell she didn't quite know what to make of this new little person who kept us awake at night and needed constant feeding, changing and cradling.

In time, Molly warmed up to Maddie. Now they get along famously. Maddie pats and hugs and feeds Molly, and drapes her dresses over her back to make it look like she's wearing little-girl clothes. At night, Molly sleeps on the floor near Maddie's bed.

It's all good. It's all there to be enjoyed, cherished and savored now because Valerie and I know that day might come for us when we will have to make The Decision.

When I brought Molly to the vet's recently, I saw a man there who had brought his dog to be put to sleep. The dog rested quietly at his feet. The man stood there, holding up well, looking around stoically, and bending down once to rub his dog's belly.

He seemed a private, strong type, not prone to expressing emotions.

Soon, though, he began turning away a bit and looking at his feet. He started shielding his eyes with the brim of his hat and wiping them repeatedly. Eventually, he picked up his dog and carried him into another room to have a bit of privacy.

My heart went out to the man. I wanted to say something to him, to attempt to offer him some comfort, but it's difficult to reach across the divide that exists between strangers.

I thought of Shannon. During the first week of school in 1983, I knelt down and gave him a strong hug and said goodbye. My parents, red-eyed and silent, took him by his brown leather leash and led him away. He'll no longer be in pain, they told my sister and me. His suffering will be over.

After the man vanished into privacy with his beloved dog, I looked down at Molly as she sat at my feet. I smiled weakly, filled with love but aware of the responsibilities of caring for an older pet.

I bent down and petted Molly on the head, smoothing back her little ears.

She looked up and wagged her tail.

Don't Forget the Lens Cap

My favorite photograph shows my family and me sitting on our front steps a couple of hours after we closed on our first home.

In the picture, Valerie and I are sitting beside each other with big smiles on our faces. We were a couple of proud new homeowners. Madeline, who'd turn two the next day, is sitting on Val's lap. I'm holding Molly, our Cairn terrier, who's looking away from the camera at something that has caught her attention. Probably a chipmunk, knowing Molly.

I keep this picture framed on my desk at work and on our bookshelf at home. It's also the image on our computer's desktop. It's a nice picture.

"We should take another picture on the front steps," Maddie suggested to me the other day.

What a great idea. We'll do it on the night before her fifth birthday this spring. And then we'll do it again next year. And the year after that. We'll look back on these photos and marvel over how much Maddie has grown.

Photographs preserve memories, of course, even ones you forgot years ago.

Last fall, my friend Jen sent me an old picture in the mail. It was one of me on my nineteenth birthday. I'm at her house, smiling for the camera and holding up a chocolate cake. Jen found this picture while cleaning her home in Massachusetts and thought she'd send it my way.

Memories long gone returned. The photo had been snapped after midnight on a Friday night. My birthday had fallen on Good Friday that year, and my Catholic friends and I had dutifully fasted between meals. Once that clock struck midnight, though, we carved into the cake.

I looked at that picture. I recognized the shirt and chuckled. I barely recognized myself. I was scrawnier then. Had a full head of hair too.

I showed the photo to Maddie.

"Do you know who that is?" I asked her.

"It's you, Daddy," she replied.

Phew. I guess I'm not *that* much older.

Another one of my favorite photos - - well, I get a kick out of looking at it, anyway - - shows the living room of my childhood home under renovation in the 1970s. Unless you know where to look, there's nothing special in the picture. If you have a whiff of archaeology in you, though, there are plenty of artifacts to appreciate.

In the corner, I can see the old color television we had. Then there's the tacky-colored, boat-sized automobile seen through the front-door window, parked at the neighbor's house across the street. Tucked between the cushions on the couch, there's a miniature baseball helmet that I bought filled with a Slush Puppy from Tony's Variety up the street.

Nothing's more meaningful, though, than pictures of people we know and love, especially those who are no longer with us. It's bittersweet to look at these photos. We look at these snapshots - - of a friend, a grandparent, or a classmate, for example - - and our emotions are mixed. We're grateful to see them at a moment when they were happy and healthy, but we know what fate awaits them. We know how, and when, their stories end.

We used to keep our photos in albums, of course. Maybe you still do. At home, our photo collection reflects advances in technology. Most of our pictures from the past few years are stored on CDs after being uploaded onto our computer from our digital camera.

Valerie and I still have a couple of boxes in our basement of the pictures we took or collected before we got our first digital camera. I'm glad those old-school pics are there.

Last October I was also glad to discover that some people still even use a Polaroid. When Valerie and I took Maddie trick-or-treating, our neighbor took two pictures of the three of us with her Polaroid. Maddie had fun watching the photo as it developed and the image of the three of us swam into view. I have these two Polaroids at my desk at work.

And then there are those photos that never quite happen. A thumb gets in the way. We forget to use the flash. Everything looks blurry.

Seconds after Maddie was born, our doctor held her up to the clock on the wall, so that I could snap a picture and record the exact moment when we welcomed our daughter into the world. The doctor told us this was a tradition at the hospital.

I pointed my camera in Maddie's general direction. There was my daughter, held up to the clock, red-faced and crying for her first bath, at exactly 1:30 in the afternoon.

I snapped away, pressing the camera's button as quickly and repeatedly as I could.

Pressed for time, our doctor whisked Maddie away to be rinsed off and given her shots.

I turned to Valerie and smiled.

"You forgot to take the lens cap off, Shawn," she smiled back and told me from the operating table.

Val said she tried to tell me about the cap while I was snapping away. Apparently, she kept repeating *"Shaaaaaaaawn"* in a soft, medicated drawl to get my attention.

Val said the doctor tried to tell me too. I didn't hear him. I was caught up in a whirlwind of excitement.

I looked at the camera. Oops. Biggest moment of our lives, and in my euphoric first seconds of fatherhood I completely forgot to remove the lens cap when taking our first picture of our daughter. It's my favorite picture I never took.

Patriotism Run Amok

Some parents leave a fortune to their children in their will. My father and mother are leaving me a portrait of my sister and me that was professionally taken days before the Fourth of July Bicentennial in 1976.

In the picture, my sister Kelly is wearing a colonial dress with an apron that my Aunt Jo-Ann made. She's also wearing a bonnet. She was one year old at the time, so she looked cute.

I was four in 1976. In the portrait, I'm wearing a costume made by my grandmother that consisted of a colonial vest, a lace shirt, knickers, shiny black shoes, and a cheap department store-bought hat that George Washington might have worn if he too had parents with a misguided sense of humor. And if they had K-Marts back in the early 1700s.

I also am wearing tights in the photograph. White ones.

"You did *not* like putting those tights on," my mother recently told me.

All throughout my childhood, my parents kept that large, imposing portrait on the wall of my family's den. My friends never stopped laughing when they saw it; my friend Denise, in fact, would laugh so hard she'd cry.

One day, early into my college career, I went home and noticed that my parents had finally removed the portrait from the wall. Obviously, the picture had served its purpose; with me away at college, and my friends gone too, Mom and Dad must have figured they had humiliated me enough.

According to Mom, Legere's Studio took the portrait shortly before the Fourth of July in 1976. Days later, on Friday, July 2, Mom and Dad dressed Kelly and me up again and brought us to the office of the Sanford *Tribune* up the street. A photographer snapped a picture that later appeared in the paper.

I am smiling in this newspaper photo, but my lips are pursed and my cheeks are tight. Surely this moment was the beginning of a lifelong habit of grinding my teeth during uncomfortable situations.

That Sunday, Kelly and I suited up yet again and went to watch the Fourth of July parade on Main Street at noon. I remember very little about the occasion, although I recently looked at old newspaper clippings and learned it was 100 degrees that day. I *do* recall a younger kid standing behind me and pointing at me in my colonial garb and asking his mother, *"Mommy, is that George Washington? Is that George Washington? Is he, Mom? Is that George Washington?"*

According to Mom, a lot of people attending the parade got a kick out of Kelly and me and took a few photos. If you were around back then, and you sat in front of the old Crabapple Bookstore at the Village Shoppes to watch the parade, you might want to check your family album. There's a very good chance that I'm in there. Look for the kid grinding his teeth.

Mom also told me the owner of Legere's Studio kept the portrait of Kelly and me in his store window for quite some time following the holiday. Mom stopped by the studio one day and asked him what he planned to do with the picture once he was done displaying it. He told her he planned to throw it out.

Now *there* was a plan.

Alas, Mom had other ideas. She bought the portrait for $80.

I'm not sure what $80 in 1976 money would be worth today, but I do know it was big bucks for my parents back then. Still, when you divide into that $80 the total number of hours my friends spent laughing at the picture, I'm sure it paid itself off thousands of time over.

"You know your mother," Mom told me the other day. "Everything's a celebration. We had to dress you and Kelly up then because your father and I won't be around for the tri-centennial."

Then, to assure me of my own mortality, she added, "Neither will you, Shawn."

So, according to Mom, the intent of the portrait was to celebrate the bicentennial. Dad sees it differently.

"The intent was to embarrass you," he said.

Patriotism always has run amok in my family. This infamous portrait is just one example.

One time, back in the 1970s, my father pulled out all the stops and belted out "God Bless America." He figured it was safe to do so because no one was home and he had the house to himself. Unfortunately, he didn't have the whole neighborhood to himself too.

Two weeks later, Glenna, our neighbor, knocked on our front door. Dad answered. Glenna told him she had a bone to pick with him. Confused, Dad asked her what he possibly could have done to offend her.

As it turns out, Glenna was sitting on her porch that day Dad gave "God Bless America" his all, and she heard every word. She laughed so hard at his off-key vocals that she hurt her stomach somehow and had to go to the hospital. She needed stitches.

Ever since, my father has boasted that his singing causes actual physical pain.

Also during the 1970s, my father decorated his study with red, white and blue wallpaper that had hundreds of American bald eagles on it. Clearly, Watergate and Vietnam had not left my father disillusioned about our country.

He kept that tacky wallpaper up until the late 1990s, by the way. He let me use his study as my bedroom when I was home for the summer during college because it was bigger than the room I had growing up. Sure enough, when my friends visited, they laughed when they saw all that dated patriotic overkill on the wall.

Of course, Dad only removed that wallpaper once I graduated from college and eventually moved out of the house for good.

All right. Enough. Here's the truth: I have inherited my father's patriotism and my Mom's belief that practically everything in life is worth celebrating. And there's no occasion like the Fourth of July to bring those two attitudes together.

That doesn't mean I'm going to dress up my daughter like Martha Washington one day. It's bad enough that she'll look at the portrait of her father and her Auntie Kelly and think that's the way people dressed back in the "olden days" of the 1970s.

That 25% is 100% Irish

I have this book at home called "Being Irish." It's a collection of essays written by artists, politicians, businessmen and average folks from Ireland who share what it means to them to be Irish.

Occasionally, I'll pick up the book and read a particularly moving essay about famines, economic strife, prejudice, discrimination and bloodshed. Sometimes I'll pause, put the book down on my lap, and contemplate what it means to me to be Irish.

So far, I haven't come up with anything.

All I know is that I'm proud to be Irish. There's no other group of people who can laugh at themselves so easily and invite others to laugh along with them.

The Irish also are on a short list of people who do not take stereotypes to heart. Not that we all fit those stereotypes.

For example, I don't like potatoes. Well, the ones my father makes, anyway.

All throughout my childhood, my father would mash those things and put them on my plate. Every night, for 18 years. It didn't really matter what else we'd be eating.

"But Dad, mashed potatoes don't really go with spaghetti," I'd object.

"Your father likes his mashed potatoes," my mother would reply. What an enabler.

I'd go to great lengths to get out of eating those potatoes. I'd mash them down when my parents weren't looking, to make it look like I at least ate *some* of them. I'd feed them to our collie, Shannon. I'd dump them into my napkin and crumple it up.

One time, I tried to make those mashed potatoes disappear by dropping them into my glass of milk, hoping they'd disappear into the whiteness, where my parents wouldn't see them. Then Mom and Dad told me to finish my milk.

My Dad's one of the best cooks I know, but to this day I skip eating his potatoes whenever I have dinner at my parents' house. I spent 18 years eating them. There are only so many potatoes a man can eat.

I wonder what my ancestors would think of me. They risked their lives to cross the sea and come to America from Ireland because there were no more potatoes over there.

One day I hope to make it to Ireland. That's my dream trip. I've never been there.

Actually, that's not completely true. My parents took their honeymoon to Ireland when my mother was five weeks pregnant with me. So sure, I was there, I guess. Lousy view, but the room and board were good.

One day during their trip, Dad held Mom by the ankles and dangled her upside-down over a drop so that she could kiss the Blarney Stone. That kiss gave me a lifelong excuse for my loquaciousness; as legend has it, the stone blesses those who kiss it with the "Gift of Gab."

I'm thinking my parents would probably appreciate it if I told you here that their wedding was not one of, shall we say, "necessity." After all, most newlyweds take off on their honeymoon the day after their wedding, and there was Mom, five weeks along with me, when she and Dad went to Ireland.

Nah, Gary and Lorraine got married in June of 1971, thought me up in July, and took their honeymoon in August, so that Dad could spend the earlier part of the summer finishing up his Master's degree.

That's what Mom has always told me, anyway. Dad just likes to say Mom had morning sickness on their honeymoon, and he leaves it at that.

Most people I meet assume I'm 100-percent Irish. With a name like mine, it's no wonder. Shawn P. Sullivan. And the "P" stands for Patrick, no less, although I've had a few adversaries in life who've insisted it stands for something else.

I have news for you. Despite my name, I'm really only 25 percent Irish. The rest is French.

My memere and pepere, my mother's parents, hailed from Quebec. Grammy, my father's mother, is all French too. My father's father, though, was completely Irish; he gave my Dad half of that Irishness, and my Dad gave me a quarter. You know how it works.

Come to think of it, I know quite a few married couples in which one's Irish and the other's French. And three very close friends of mine are completely French. The two heritages go well together. What's the common factor at work there, I wonder? A shared history of differences toward England?

My wife, Valerie, constantly reminds me that I'm not 100-percent Irish. It's her mission in life to always be there to set the record straight if she thinks I'm laying it on a little too thick with the Irish stuff.

She should talk. She's the one who married a Sullivan. Who wants to pass for Irish now?

At least there's always St. Patrick's Day. That's when we're *all* Irish for a day.

Even you, Valerie.

The Pork Gravy Incident

My younger sister Kelly and I stared at our supper as a certain queasiness began to swell in our bellies. We were sitting in our living room at the time, watching a rerun of "The Brady Bunch" on Channel 56. We were probably around eight and five years old at the time.

"I don't want to eat this," I said.

"I'm not hungry," Kelly stated.

Mom was not home that evening. Maybe she had to work late or attend a ceramics class, or something. Dad stopped at a local supermarket on the way home and bought a can of pork gravy. When he got home, he heated it up and slathered it on some leftover pork from another dinner earlier that week.

You know those 30-minute meals that Rachael Ray prepares on television? That night, Dad's special dish, "Pork Remnants Au Jus," was more like a 30-second meal. That's all the time my sister and I needed to take a bite, chew a little and conclude that our taste buds would never trust us again if we kept eating. Years later, even Dad finally confessed that this meal was "awful, just terrible."

I watched the pork gravy turn cold and mutate into a mucous-like Jell-O and asked Kelly what she thought we should do. As she chipped the gravy off her pork with a fork, we both agreed to go tell Dad we wanted to pass on supper.

We carried our plates into the dining room, where Dad sat eating alone. Kelly had been leading the way, ready to do her part, but at the last moment I swept past her and took charge.

"I'm not going to eat this slop!" I declared with great drama and indignation. I tossed my plate onto the table, and it clattered to a stop.

I wonder how far my father's voice traveled that night. Pretty far, I'm sure. My friend Richard grew up around the corner, and from his home he frequently heard Dad read me the riot act while I was growing up. "What did that kid say *now*?" Richard asked himself each time.

Dad's message, unleashed with red-faced furiousness, was loud and clear: I had been ungrateful, and once again I had failed to think before I spoke. He had rushed home from work to put food on the table, and I had the nerve to throw it back at him.

Eventually, Dad finished reading me that riot act. Afterward, my sister, who had *led the charge* to the dining room, held up her plate of pork like it was a prized pig, smiled and told our father, "Mmmmmmm. Dad, this tastes *goooooood*."

She then went back into the living room and finished every bite.

I thought of this memory when I read a recent article in *USA Today* that stated, "Scientists have found that first-born children are smarter than their brothers and sisters."

According to the article, Norwegian scientists conducted a study that led them to believe that first-borns have slightly higher IQs than their siblings and are more likely to rise to the level of CEO in the world of business.

USA Today conducted its own survey of 155 CEOs throughout the nation. As many as 59 percent of them were first-borns, 18 percent were the youngest in their families, and 23 percent fell somewhere in the middle of their family's totem pole.

USA Today found that first-born children rise to the top for a number of reasons. As children, they had their parents' undivided attention until their younger siblings came along. And, by virtue of being the oldest sibling, first-borns also felt greater pressure to fulfill certain responsibilities and meet expectations.

According to *USA Today*, first-born children are "more extraverted, confident, assertive, authoritarian, dominant, inflexible, conformist, politically conservative, task-oriented, conscientious, disciplined, defensive about errors and fearful of losing position and rank."

"Sound like someone we know?" Dad asked me after I read him that description.

Easy for him to say. He's the third-born in his family. No pressure there.

And sure, I look at my daughter, who for four years now has had the undivided attention and adoration of her parents. One night, several months ago, Madeline made Valerie, my parents and me sit in our living room quietly and watch her dance. If we talked, she stopped mid-pirouette and told us she couldn't concentrate. If we clapped, she wagged her finger at us and told us she wasn't finished yet.

I remember commenting at the time that Maddie's likely to grow up to become either a CEO or the ruler of a small country.

But I dunno. I'm skeptical about this study. Maybe I can't dispute that first-borns tend to become the world's CEOs; the figures seem to be there. I doubt, though, that sharper intelligence is one of the factors.

If the subject is making one's way in the world, which is really what matters, I would think that younger siblings have the edge. They get to watch their older brother or sister make mistakes and flounder. As a result, they can take notes and proceed more smoothly. Look at the way my sister sized up my performance when we took our pork dinners to Dad that evening.

It's a touchy subject, I suppose, for it pits siblings against each other. But even if it is true that first-borns are smarter, this first-born can't get too cocky, anyway. I told my Dad about this study that said first-borns have higher IQs.

"Oh, you mean we never told you?" he replied. "You have an older brother somewhere out there."

Pepere

Pepere hadn't been expecting me when I showed up at his workplace that summer afternoon. Without missing a beat, though, he greeted me with a special, grandfatherly pride that made me feel like my surprise visit was the highlight of his day.

He smiled, placed a hand on my shoulder and introduced me to his coworkers while giving me a grand tour of York County Community College Services. He was in charge of maintenance there. He worked there under the Green Thumb program, which helped retired people find jobs.

When we passed through the break room, Pepere stopped at the soda machine and treated me to an ice-cold can of Pepsi. My visit must have wrapped up shortly afterward, for I remember still sipping that soda on my walk home to Shaw Street.

It was sunny and pleasant that day, July 15, 1981. I was nine years old and much of the summer remained ahead of me. The fourth grade at the Sanford Middle School seemed a lifetime away, and I had a full afternoon to do anything I wanted to do. You were a kid once. You remember those days.

For some reason, I had decided to head up the street to visit my grandfather at his office on Main Street. I had never done that before, so I'm not sure why the idea struck me. Surely, there was a neighborhood baseball game somewhere. Certainly, there was a bike ride that needed taking. All I know is that paying Pepere a visit seemed like a good idea. It later proved to be a wise and lucky one too.

At 5:30 the next morning, my mother got the call that something was wrong with Pepere. She and my father sped to the hospital, while our neighbor, Mrs. Driscoll, took care of my sister and me and tried to keep us busy so that we didn't worry too much. I remember coloring in a coloring book at our dining-room table.

Less than an hour later, my father returned. His eyes were red; his expression, grim. He sat my sister and me down on the stairs and explained as well as you could to a nine-year-old and a six-year-old that our grandfather had passed away.

Arthur Bourre died in his sleep, in the way that most of us would prefer to go when our time comes. He was 65.

I share these experiences with you not to publicly mark the twenty-fifth anniversary of my family's private loss, but instead to suggest how fortunate we are when we are given a chance to say goodbye to someone we do not know we are seeing for the last time.

I will never understand what compelled me to visit my grandfather at work on that particular afternoon, especially since I had never done so before. I've always believed something nudged me up the hill that day.

Somehow, I had been afforded one last moment with my grandfather just hours before his life ended. I've always been grateful for that opportunity, and as I've gotten older I have tried to heed its message. When you think of it, we are all promised a fulfilling farewell to our loved ones, if only we appreciate and enjoy each moment we are with them.

I remember a lot about my Pepere. He was a great grandfather, a fun prankster who'd fool me into looking in the wrong direction after he tapped me on the right shoulder while he sat to my left in church. On some days, Memere would take care of me while I was sick and out of school; he'd come home with treats from McDonald's and sit in his chair and smoke his pipe and watch "The Price Is Right" with us on TV.

My mother remembers her father as having a no-nonsense confidence. She and her sisters would sit on the floor in their living room as children, quaking in fear from a suspenseful show on television, and Pepere would just shake his head, smile, and say, "Where do you think the camera is?" Pepere knew it was all make-believe. There was no fooling him.

Twenty-five years is a very long time. The older I get, though, the clearer I seem to remember Pepere and the more I think I know him. After all, our friends and loved ones never leave us. They smile at us from family albums and old videos, they live in our minds and hearts, and they show up as we get older, resemble them and take after their ways.

My office at the Sanford News used to be a funeral home. My desk sits exactly where Pepere's casket rested during his wake in 1981. I sit and work where I saw him for the last time.

I'm not quite sure what to make of that. Call me odd, but I think I'm beginning to find it comforting.

Dad's Chair

While I was growing up Dad had a chair in the corner of our living room that he claimed as his throne. I remember how proud he was when he bought it back in the early eighties.

"I have this new recliner," he'd tell his friends. "It's really comfortable. It should come with a tag that reads, 'Warning: Chair could cause drowsiness'."

It was a light brown La-Z-Boy recliner, the plush kind in which you plop down, crank up the attached hassock, and lean back for a light snooze or a night of your favorite sitcoms.

Many a night Dad sat in that chair. Many a time he kicked me out of it.

It was never an issue when I was a kid. I'd be relaxing in his chair, watching MTV, and Dad would walk into the room. Very softly, he'd say, "Can I have my chair?" It was one of those questions that's not really a question.

Every father has his chair. I may be the one exception. There is one seat in our house where I can sit alone and relax and catch up on some reading and contemplate life, but I'm hardly in charge of it. The chair has a lid, and my wife's always telling me to keep it down. And now my three-year-old daughter is even claiming it as her "potty."

Still. "Dad's Chair" is not something to be messed with.

I learned that the hard way.

It was a hot July afternoon many years ago. Jimmy Stewart had died a few days earlier, so I thought I'd give one of his old films a look. I picked "Mr. Smith Goes to Washington." I stuck the tape in the VCR, eased into Dad's chair and settled in for a feel-good Frank Capra classic.

I was about half way through the movie when Dad walked into the room. He decided to watch the movie with me and "asked" me to give him his chair.

"But I'm comfortable," I told him.

He smiled as though I was kidding. To keep things light, he motioned to the couch across the room and told me its luxury could all be mine for the bargain price of a few short steps in the right direction.

I dug in my heels and quietly insisted that I was comfortable. He gave me a funny look, something half way between a frown and a smile. Basically, the look said, *C'mon. Stop fooling around.*

Seconds later, I was sitting on the couch. I had lost a battle for Dad's chair. My clear view of the movie was gone. In its place was the sun's bright reflection on the screen, coming in through the living room window. There was a blinding ball of light right where Jimmy Stewart's head was supposed to be.

I tried watching the movie from that angle, with the sun's obstruction, but I couldn't take it. After a few moments of sulky silence, I let Dad know that I was upset about the whole chair thing. He let me know that he paid for the chair and could sit in it any time he wanted. I let him know I paid for the movie, and I ejected it from the VCR and walked off with it.

We didn't talk to each other for the rest of the day.

This is just a hunch, but I'm willing to bet that's the only time in the history of film that two guys broke out into a heated argument while watching a feel-good Capra movie. One with Jimmy Stewart, no less.

Okay. So maybe I acted like a punk. But here's the thing: I was in my twenties and I guess I just resented being kicked out of a chair at that age. That's all. I figured I should be able to sit in a chair if I had it first.

The truth is, I should have learned by then that Dad's chair was just that. His.

I'm sure all of this sounds like a bad lost episode of the sitcom, "Frasier."

Forget for a moment that Dr. Frasier Crane thinks his father's chair is an ugly affront to his tastefully decorated Seattle apartment. Can you imagine the sparks that would have flown if Frasier started sitting in his father's chair and refused to get up? Ol' Martin Crane would have been commanding his dog, Eddie, to sic Frasier's shins in no time. It'd be a sweeps-week gold mine.

Earlier this week I asked Dad about his philosophy regarding his chair.

"A man with a wife and two kids has nothing to himself," he told me. "A father's chair is an island in the chaotic ocean of life."

He reminded me that my sister and I used to tip over his chair when we were kids and shake it down for loose change.

"If it was not for my chair and my shallow pockets, you guys would have gone completely without while growing up," he told me. "No movies, no candy, nothing."

Guess what, though? Last week my parents bought new furniture for their living room, and they gave Dad's old chair to me and Valerie. We now keep it tucked in a corner in our living room. It fits nicely with everything else we have in there, and it'll do the trick until we get a new set of furniture for ourselves.

Even when that moment comes, though, I think I'll keep that chair right where it is. I like having it there.

It's the chair where my father used to sit and help me with my homework.

It's the chair where he used to sit and listen to my sister and me whenever we shared our worries and concerns and problems and sought his advice.

It's the chair where he used to sit and watch the evening news and laugh during all of the sitcoms we watched together while I was growing up.

It is also the chair in which he sat when he told us he had been diagnosed with Lou Gehrig's disease. My mother and sister and I gathered around him afterward and consoled him and wept with deep sadness and fear.

Yeah, I'll always keep that chair around. It reminds me of my father, the man who, in the end, graciously, lovingly, let me win the battle for Dad's chair.

Extraordinary People

May, 2006

Dad was diagnosed with ALS in December of 2004 and has spent much of his time since fighting for a cure.

He now walks slower, with the help of two sleek braces that wrap around his lower legs. Climbing stairs is a challenge, and he can no longer run.

He speaks just fine, but he's growing more convinced that the raspy crack in his voice is not simply caused by stress or talking too much.

He tastes his food less, due to medication he takes that slows the progression of his condition and gives him more energy but diminishes his ability to enjoy his favorite sweets or a well-cooked meal.

He stays up well past midnight, figuring it's the expected insomnia and not his lifelong inclination to catch the 11 o'clock news or the late-night comics on television.

He wakes up at night, too, sometimes when his muscles twitch too aggressively, other times when his fears of the future will not give his mind a rest.

Along the way, he has made one concession after another. Retiring prematurely from his career. Wearing those braces. Buying a cane. Attaching a handicapped license plate to his car. Spending thousands of dollars to remodel his home to make it more accessible for the inevitable wheelchair.

ALS, or amyotrophic lateral sclerosis, is a progressive neurological disease that affects nerve cells in the brain and the spinal cord. Basically, as the disease runs its course, motor neurons degenerate and the brain becomes unable to control all muscles in the body. Eventually, ALS patients are paralyzed from head to toe.

Here's the cruelest part. No matter how badly the disease progresses, the mind is hardly affected. People with ALS completely lose their ability to move and function without a caregiver, but most of them retain as sharp a mind as ever. A patient's thoughts, memories, and feelings, not to mention the natural human desire to communicate them, remain intact.

I used to compare the disease to a custodian who at the end of the night turns off every light in the warehouse, one at a time, until the entire building is dark. I recently saw a movie, however, that provided a more fitting analogy when a character with ALS said all parts of her body were acting like stubborn teenagers who won't do as they're told.

***

33

May, 2007.

Greetings from Washington.

This week I am attending the ALS Association's annual national conference in the nation's capital with my father. This is the first father-and-son trip Dad and I have taken in years; he and I probably have not gone off somewhere together since he took me camping up in Bangor almost 25 years ago.

Dad and I are here to meet with Maine's senators and representatives to urge them to pass the ALS Registry Act, which would authorize the Centers for Disease Control and Prevention to establish and maintain a single, nationwide registry of those who have ALS, or Lou Gehrig's disease, after the famous New York Yankees legend who had it. We'll also be urging them to support ALS research at the Department of Defense, so we can determine why it is that our military veterans, who already put their lives in jeopardy to defend our freedom, are twice as likely as others to be diagnosed with ALS.

Dad and I left for this trip on Sunday. As excited as we were about this journey, we figured out before we even made it through the terminal at the Portland jetport that Gehrig's ghost would be following us everywhere.

Believe it or not, this week's trip makes my first time on an airplane since the September 11 terrorist attacks. At the terminal I knew that I would have to throw everything I owned into a tray, take off my sneakers, and shuffle through the metal detector to get to the other side. I had on a clean pair of socks, so I was fine.

Dad was another story. He wears two braces that cradle his feet and come together with straps fastened just below his knees. For someone with ALS, whose fingers and hands are losing their strength, putting on these braces can be a major production. Dad explained to the security guards that he was wearing braces with metal snaps on them, in the hopes that they'd understand he had an illness and lacked the strength to remove his sneakers and supports with any ease.

One of the security guards took Dad off to the side, instructed him to spread his arms, and began to pat him down from head to toe. He examined Dad's feet, shoes and braces, and then swabbed his hands completely clean, perhaps to see if he had the residue of an explosive powder on them.

The whole experience lasted roughly 5 to 10 minutes. At first I found it amusing, looking at Dad and smiling in a *can-you-believe-the-age-we-live-in* kind of way. He smiled back too.

As the pat-down continued, though, I started to get frustrated. I know the search is for security's sake, and on that level I guess you have to appreciate the extra care taken. At the same time, though, Dad has a disease that has pretty much taken his legs on its brutal, slow and steady mission to completely paralyze him. It did not make sense to me that the very person who needed the most care, accommodation and accessibility ended up being the one most poked and prodded and inconvenienced while trying to get on a plane.

When he was free to go, Dad smiled, joked and took the whole thing in stride. But he did say that he couldn't remember the last time a frail, 62-year-old guy with Lou Gehrig's disease had strength enough to take over a plane or blow one up.

You have to have a sense of humor if you're going to spend the rest of your life fighting ALS. You can either laugh, or you can cry, curl up and die, Dad says. There are no other choices.

Fortunately, everybody here at this ALS conference in Washington seems to agree. I'm astonished by the number of ALS patients and their advocates and loved ones at this event who are upbeat, optimistic, motivated and filled with humor.

They're advocates, of course, here to take their fight to the most powerful chambers in the United States, so it's no surprise they're so focused, determined and robust, despite their physical limitations and their psychological burdens.

But make no mistake. These people *choose* to be positive. They're tired and they're dying, but they choose to get up, get out and get involved.

There's Dad, for example.

There's the woman from California, who stood up during the roll call on Monday and said she has lost 30 people in her family to ALS.

Thirty.

Then there's the man from Michigan, who talked about his friend, who succumbed to ALS, but not before he fulfilled his lifelong dream of cruising the whole way across Route 66 in a Corvette. His friend didn't just cross Route 66; he led a convoy of Corvettes through it, in a fundraiser he organized to raise money for the fight against the disease that ultimately would take him.

There are the people who hopped on a plane and traveled thousands of miles to attend the convention by themselves, lone voices representing their states, Davids to the disease's Goliath. A woman from New Mexico has made such a trip. So has a man from Wyoming.

Finally, and most importantly, there are the ALS patients here at the conference who sit silently, motionlessly, in their wheelchairs, taking charge of their own destinies when the easy thing to do, the understandable thing to do, would be to go home, close the door, and wait sadly, defeated, for the incurable to become the inevitable.

These are extraordinary people.

"We could all die tomorrow," people tell my father, in their efforts to relate, to understand, to console. "We could all wake up tomorrow and get hit by a truck."

We all say that when we're trying to acknowledge the fragility of life, usually for the benefit of one who's suffering.

There is darkness, for my father and others who share his disease. There is despair. There are drawn shades, shed tears, cold fear. All things the outside world rarely sees. All things that come naturally, with cruel, effortless ease.

But there are the jokes too, the self-deprecating throwaways, the gallows humor, the irreverent jabs that cut the mighty disease down to size. There is laughter, expressed with smiles, chuckles and boisterous peals. And there is activism and advocacy, in which you take what's happening to you, turn the tables on it, and lead the charge.

Those are the things the outside world sees, but they do not come automatically, naturally, easily.

Instead, they're choices, conscious efforts, decisions made on one's own terms.

They're exactly the tools needed in the fight against ALS. And wielding those tools, right here in Washington this week, from all 50 states, are some truly extraordinary people who have the hope, the courage, and the strength to strike out Lou Gehrig's disease.

'When My Is Done'

Did you know cows have four stomachs?

I did not. I admit I knew very little about cows before my three-year-old daughter taught me about them. I knew they tasted good at McDonald's, and I knew it was fun to honk and wave to them while driving down a country road, but I didn't know they have not one, not two, not three, but *four* stomachs. No wonder they're out there grazing all day. They have all those chambers to fill.

One day I was sitting at the computer and my daughter called out to me from the other room and said, "Daddy, cows have four stomachs."

It was such an out-of-the-blue statement, delivered without context, that the best I could do was say, "Really?"

Sure enough, when my wife got home, I asked her if cows have four stomachs.

"Yes," Valerie replied. "Why?"

I explained. Neither of us knew where Maddie picked up that tidbit about cows.

I have been learning a lot from my daughter. I really have to be on my feet lately because the lessons are coming out of nowhere, like a pop quiz. One night I was driving down River Street and my daughter made a statement from the back seat.

"Daddy, condors don't like to fly at night," she said.

We had not been discussing the nocturnal preferences of birds, but, unlike the comment about the cows, I was quick and ready with a response.

"Why is that, Maddie?"

Sure enough, she explained why condors stay put after the sun sets.

I already know some of the things Maddie has told me: Firefighters help people. Schools are where kids go to get smart. Caterpillars turn into butterflies. It's nice to know that Maddie knows these things too.

It is true, however, that as my daughter's imagination develops, I have to distinguish between the facts and fictions of what she says. For example, the other night, my mother called while I was reading Maddie a bedtime story. I gave Maddie the phone so that she could say hello to her grandmother.

"Mem, last night I went outside while Mommy and Daddy were sleeping and I saw an owl in the tree near the side of the house," Maddie told my mother.

Not true. While Maddie was talking to my mother, she was looking at a picture of an owl in a tree in the book I had been reading to her before the phone rang.

"Why was Maddie outside?" my mother asked me, practically accusing me of negligence.

40

"She wasn't outside, Mom."

"She said she saw an owl."

"She's *looking* at an owl in a book we're reading. That's why she mentioned an owl. We lock the doors at night, anyway, so nobody's going anywhere," I said.

"But she said she saw an owl," my mother insisted. "She's a smart girl, Shawn."

"Mom, there's no owl."

And it seems my wife and I are rampant smokers. Maddie says so, anyway.

I took Maddie to see her doctor the other day because she had symptoms of an ear infection. After hearing my description of Maddie's cough, stuffy nose and ear ache, the doctor asked Maddie if anybody smokes in our house. I knew the answer, and I waited confidently for Maddie to give it.

"Yes," she said.

It was the owl-in-the-tree all over again. I had to correct Maddie and insist to the doctor that my wife and I do not smoke, and that nobody else who visits us lights up, either. There's no smoke anywhere in the house.

See? I have to sort out the fiction from the facts. It's not that easy because grandmothers and pediatricians apparently are more apt to believe a three-year-old than some guy in the newspaper business.

There are other things Maddie has told me that I swear she made up; she has told me that a dinosaur bit her, that she patted a tiger, and that she went for a ride in a kangaroo's pouch.

It's nice to see, though, that my daughter is always trying to learn new things, whether by looking at the words and pictures in a book, drawing pictures, or balancing on one of those concrete slabs at the front of a parking space.

Her new thing is to say "in a minute" whenever I ask her to do something other than what she's doing. Everything's "in a minute." She used to say "When my is done" before we taught her to say "When I am done" instead.

"Madeline, it's time for dinner," I'd say while she's drawing.

"In a minute."

"Bubbaloo, it's time to brush your teeth and get ready for bed."

"In a minute."

"Maddie, aliens are coming to take over the planet, so we need to go hide in a bunker 500 feet below ground *right now*."

"In a minute, Daddy."

Sometimes I have the patience to wait that minute. Sometimes, admittedly, I do not, and I end up giving her a lecture about how she needs to listen to Daddy. I'm sure I sound to her like all adults do in those Charlie Brown cartoons on TV. *Wuhhhk, wuhhhk, wuhhhk, wuhhhk, wuuuuuuuhhhhhh.*

42

If I give the moment some thought, though, I find that the world will not end if I grant Maddie that minute to continue to stop and smell the roses.

One day, my wife and I are going to bring Maddie to college for her first day there. There's going to be that moment, after she has walked us back to our car, when she's turning away and heading back to her dorm. Then *I'll* be the one who says, "In a minute."

I'm going to need an extra hug goodbye. By then, after 18 years of my daughter saying "in a minute," I'd like to have earned the right to say that too.

Gazing Upon a Summer Moon

On Monday night I sat on the couch and stared at the list of shows I had recorded on TiVo and tried to pick one to watch before I called it a night. My wife had turned in early, exhausted by her first day of teaching summer school. My daughter had gone to bed maybe an hour earlier after taking her bath and washing off the day's sweat and dirt and the ice cream that smeared her cheeks.

Should I watch the "Saturday Night Live" repeat from the other night? Catch a bit more of that Clint Eastwood western? Check out one of the four episodes of "My Name is Earl" that I have yet to see since recording them earlier this spring?

My friend Richard called a little after nine and solved my problem.

"Look outside," he said. "You have to check out the moon."

I went outside, stood in my driveway, and looked east. No luck. The moon had not yet risen above the trees in my neighborhood. Richard, who had just finished teaching driving school, said he was standing in the parking lot of the Midtown Mall two miles north of me and had a clear shot of the moon. He said it looked full and orange and reminded him of Halloween. He recommended that I head toward Main Street and try to see it from there.

I told him I'd call him back. I put on my sneakers and headed down my street to the corner of Route 109. I looked east, and there it was: a large, completely round, rust-colored moon, the kind that tells you the next day is going to be a scorcher.

Such a moon was to be expected. An hour earlier, the setting sun had been a perfect sphere in the sky, hot and red and full with the threat of a humid summer day to follow.

Richard was right. The moon, low in the hazy night sky, did make me think of Halloween. It resembled not only a pumpkin, but, with its timeless face, a jack-o-lantern too.

I called Richard back and thanked him for the literal heads-up. Then I called my parents, who also went out into the middle of their street and noted they had never seen the Man on the Moon appear so vivid.

There have been a few nights over the years with other full moons I will never forget.

There was that moon I saw, looking large and perfectly round and white beyond the Boston skyline as I crossed the bridge over the Charles River one cold night in February of 1997. Best of all, there was that perfectly timed, eclipsed moon that darkened overhead during the last half of Game 4 when the Red Sox beat the Cardinals to finally win the World Series in October of 2004.

I remember one full moon during my senior year of high school. My girlfriend and I were standing in her driveway and we both looked up and commented on how extraordinary the moon looked. We stargazed for a few silent moments.

Across town, a friend of mine saw the same moon and felt inspired to write a whole poem about it for the school newspaper. I remember how much he had impressed me with his writing. I looked up at the moon and likely said nothing more than "wow." He looked up at it and responded with a full page of perfectly placed verses.

On Monday night I let my tired wife sleep, but I did pick my three-year-old daughter Maddie up from her bed and head outside. I walked down the street, carrying her as she slept with her head on my shoulder. I returned to my post at the corner of our street and Route 109 and looked at the moon once more. I pointed to the moon and whispered into my daughter's ear, in the hopes that she'd lift her head and open her eyes enough to see the night's main attraction. Nothing happened. The kid was out like a light. I was disappointed, but I still thought it was special to stand out there on a hot summer night in July, holding my daughter and savoring the sight of a moon that reminded me of autumn.

Just minutes earlier, I had been looking at a long list of shows on my TV screen and had been spending too much time trying to pick something to entertain me.

My friend Richard saved me from such brainless, couch-potato indecision. He encouraged me to look to the skies, and I did. What I got was the best show in town.

Sleep, Interrupted

Does anybody know how to reach the guy who invented the "snooze" button on alarm clocks? I'd really like to have a word with him.

I have waged a war against the "snooze" button for most of my adult life. I think the problem dates as far back as college, when there were some days in which my classes started later in the morning and I turned staying up well past midnight into an art form. Only within the past year have I started winning battles against that nasty little button, which serves no purpose other than procrastination.

Don't get me wrong. I love mornings. If only I could wake up for them.

I enjoy waking before dawn and getting a jump on the day. Something's lost when the sun comes up and everyone else in the world rises with it.

When I delivered the *Maine Sunday Telegram* as a teenager, I used to like walking down the middle of the street, under the moon and stars, claiming the peace and quiet as my own. I appreciated the quaint flickers of bluish light that came from the living room windows of neighbors who fell asleep in front of their televisions. I cherished the sound of the Angelus echoing throughout downtown Sanford from St. Ignatius Church at six.

These days, I enjoy heading to work in the dark on production day and writing and editing articles that are due for publication in a few hours. The mind is clear. The whole day's ahead of me.

A paper route and a busy day at the office, however, are catalysts for getting me out of bed early. Take away those responsibilities and leave me to my own devices and, well, that's where the "snooze" button takes over, and over, and over . . .

Seriously. I set my alarm clock for a good hour before I really need to wake up because I need that time. I envy people who hear the alarm, shut it off, and swing their feet onto the floor. I want to know their secret.

I have tried everything.

I have removed my alarm clock from my bedside and locked it down across my bedroom, so that when it cries out its shrill, annoying beeps I would have to physically get out of bed, shuffle across the floor, and shut the thing off. Ideally, there I'd be, on my feet, vertical, halfway to the bathroom, ready to wash up and launch into the day.

That has never worked.

I have switched the alarm from that grating, high-pitched *beep-beep-beep* to the radio, so that hard rock blares into my ear when the morning comes. That would be enough to wake the dead, right? No dice. The alarm goes off, I hear an old Quiet Riot tune from the 1980s on WBLM, and then I laugh and hit the "snooze" button and fall back asleep.

I have even tried *two* alarm clocks, one here and one there. That does not work, either. All I end up with is a nerve-wracking alarm-clock equivalent of the Battle of the Bands.

You're probably wondering where my wife is when all of this is happening. Some mornings, she's on the couch, trying to sleep out of earshot. Other mornings, she's in a hotel across town, attempting get as far away from the lunacy as she can.

Oh, all right. I'm just trying to protect Valerie. The truth is, she's no different. She presses "snooze" too.

Yeah, mornings are fun in the Sullivan household.

My mother-in-law knows I have a problem with the "snooze" button, so she handed me a magazine article written by a "performance-energy consultant." I'm not pulling your leg here. This guy's an actual energy addict who counsels everybody from football players to bankers.

Anyway, this consultant advises against pressing the "snooze" button because doing so cuts short a sleep cycle and makes you groggy when you finally do wake up. "Snooze" button-pressers already know this, thank you.

Now I'm going to tell you something that I did once, and I want you to take into account that I was a college kid when I did it. You know college kids. They do the darnedest things.

Once, in college, I pressed the "snooze" button for *nine* hours.

This is the truth. I went to bed the night before as an idealist, a young and ambitious lad determined to wake early the next morning and seize the day like Ferris Bueller. I woke up hours later as the real me, a college kid who stayed out too late the night before and had no concrete plans for the following day.

At least I meant well.

Nine hours. I slept *nine hours* in increments of *nine minutes*. That means I pressed "snooze" *sixty times*.

Yes, I *know* that's disgraceful. I *know* it shows an alarming lack of discipline and motivation. I *know* that's what we do to detained terrorists who we want to deprive of sleep until they tell us where they plan to strike next.

It just occurred to me, only now, that perhaps I could solve my problem by getting an alarm clock that does not feature the "snooze" button. I wonder why I never thought of that before.

Knowing me, though, I'd probably just end up repeatedly resetting the alarm clock for hours on end.

Pardon My French

I think I witnessed the death of quality customer service this week.

It was not a scandalous, messy, tragic downfall, forced by a glaring Shakespearean flaw. No, it was a quiet passing, like the kind for which we all hope when we are old and fast asleep. The proverbial thief in the night, silently slipping in through the bedroom window, comes to mind.

I went to the supermarket to pick up "Things We Need," which is the name of the sparse, economical, practical list of items handed to me by my wife. What my wife did not know is that I also had with me a list that I created called "Things We Do Not Need But I Will Get Anyway." This means my basket was filled with ice cream, chips and salsa, in addition to the spaghetti sauce, meatballs and a loaf of Italian bread needed for that night's dinner.

As I approached the express lane, I glanced at my basket and made sure that I had fewer than 10 items. When I looked back up I saw the cashier subtly roll her eyes and shift slightly to let me know she was annoyed that I had come along and squashed her solitude like a world-class party-pooper.

I almost had gone through the self-checkout lane. I usually do. I like the self-sufficiency of that option, even though I sometimes botch my own transaction. I'll place an item on the counter and the friendly computerized voice will tell me that there's an "unexpected item in the bagging area" that I need to remove. I'll remove the item and then the voice will tell me that there has been an "item removed from the bagging area" that I need to put back. A shift leader with a special key usually has to step in and solve the problem.

So much for the self-checkout.

The cashier who rolled her eyes bounced back a bit when she politely explained to me the procedure by which I could get cash back with my debit card. She dropped the ball again, though, once she handed me my receipt and turned to the next customer.

She did not turn on the conveyor belt to shuffle my three plastic bags of groceries to the end of the counter, so that I could scoop them up and be on my way. My bags sat to her left at the top of the belt, and I could not get to them without awkwardly reaching over the ATM pad or slipping my arm around the little shelf where you write out the checks.

The whole transaction did not upset me. I knew I was dealing with a teenager who probably did not feel like working and still had not polished her work ethic. However, I could not help but sigh and think, "Sheesh, you know, it's too bad friendly, quality customer service is not always guaranteed."

53

I once pulled up to the speaker at the drive-thru of a doughnut shop out of town. I asked the scratchy, nearly indiscernible voice on the other end what flavors of iced coffee were available. I had been prompted by a cheery sign that said, "Ask us about our new coffee flavors."

"Well, we have regular," the employee replied.

There was an awkward pause.

"Are there any other kinds?" I asked.

"Well, um, yes. We have . . . what we have."

I didn't get frustrated. I just laughed at the ridiculous service. But all I got was a regular iced coffee.

I'm not picky. A waiter, for example, really has to treat me rudely or do something awful like sneeze in my dessert or pull the wrapper off my straw with his teeth before I have a mental image of his tip flying out the window. If anything, when my wife and I go out to eat with a couple that's too demanding or easily dissatisfied, I'm the guy who ends up feeling bad for the waiter and giving him a hefty tip.

Is it too much, however, to ask for a smile? For politeness, patience and respect? For a transaction free of any inconvenience?

For the record, I have worked on the other side of the cash register, so now is a good time to admit that I was not always on my best behavior. There was that time I unintentionally asked a customer to sleep with me in front of her husband.

Hold on. Wait. Don't stop reading. Hear me out.

I was a cashier at a supermarket out of town, working to save money for college in the fall. I was working my shift in the express lane, and I had a long line of customers that reached all the way back to the shipping and receiving dock in the rear parking lot.

I had been having a completely pleasant conversation with an older couple when the time came for me to ask them what they had in their bakery bag so I could ring it up.

For some reason, my question puzzled them. They either did not hear me or figured that what they picked up at the bakery was not my business.

I asked them again. Twice more. The confusion persisted.

I thought I'd try something amusing. The supermarket was located in the heart of one of Maine's biggest tourist spots known for attracting practically the entire population of Quebec during the summertime. I speak French fairly well; it was my strongest subject in school. Just for kicks, I thought I'd ask the couple in French to tell me what was hiding in that bakery bag. You know, treat the locals like tourists.

I wanted to say "Qu'est-ce que c'est dans le sac?" For those of you who took Spanish instead, I believe that's close enough to "What is inside the bag?"

Instead, inexplicably, I said to the wife, "Voulez-vous couchez avec moi ce soir?" Translated: *Do you want to sleep with me tonight?*

Earlier in my shift, my co-workers and I cracked a few jokes when we heard the 1970s disco song named after that very French question on the store's sound system. You've probably heard it; maybe you even danced to it back in the day. Now that I have mentioned it, you probably will have it stuck in your head for the rest of the month.

I can't tell you why I said that to the poor woman. I can't. I don't *know* why. The words just came out. I only know that I had been joking about that song beforehand.

I'm not sure the woman with the mysterious bakery bag understood what I said. The handful of Canadians behind her in line, however, were enjoying a good laugh.

"I *don't* speak French," the woman snapped.

"I know," I said, sounding apologetic. "I just . . ."

I drifted off and opened the bag myself. I think they had two doughnuts. *Deux beignets.*

So as you can see, I'm not really able to throw stones at the cashier who rolled her eyes at me this week. I'm not trying to become something like the Phantom Gourmet of supermarkets and doughnut shop drive-thus.

I would, however, like to see a smile, a willingness, even an eagerness, to help when I patronize an establishment. That's all.

And I'll keep my end of the bargain. I'll tell you what's in my bakery bag.

Take My Junk . . . Please

There's something galling about yard sales.

Think about it. You empty your house of all its junk and plunk it down on blankets and flimsy card tables on your front lawn. Then you welcome complete strangers onto your property and expect them to *buy* things you'd *pay* to get out of your life.

For example, take the . . . the . . . you know, I don't even *know* what that thing was my wife and I tried to sell when we had a yard sale a couple of weekends ago. All I know is that it belonged to my brother-in-law before my sister married him and brought some decorative sense into his life.

"Oh, you're having a yard sale?" my sister asked me. "Here, take this."

Basically, the thing looks like a giant hornets' nest. Maybe you're supposed to stuff some flowers on top of it and stick it in the corner of your living room. I suspect it's really something cranky old people can stick on their front lawn to scare away little children who won't stop playing on their grass.

"What's that thing?" someone brave enough to approach the monstrosity asked me.

"It's a conversation piece," my wife interjected, saving me from my own blank stare and a major brain cramp.

The customer grimaced and headed back to her car. So much for conversation.

I think I'm going to bar my brother-in-law from contributing to the annual Sullivan family yard sale. Valerie and I never did sell that hornets' nest. By not selling it, we have inherited it. Now it sits in my garage, terrifying my three-year-old daughter whenever she goes in there to get her tricycle.

Both my wife and I do things to drive each other crazy during yard sales. My wife puts out things that I'd still like to keep. Last year I retrieved a mug that I bought during a weekend trip to North Conway. I never drink from it anymore, but hey, it has my last name printed on it. This year I took back the Mickey Mouse doll that I bought my daughter when she was six months old.

As for me, I will sell some things so dirt cheap that it's a wonder why we bothered putting a price sticker on them in the first place. For $1.50 I let a guy walk off with enough aluminum flex-hose to run across town from the clothes dryer in his basement. I even helped the guy load all of it into his truck.

This is not the first time I have failed to properly assess merchandise.

I once forked over $35 for a two-foot wooden giraffe while my wife and I were on our honeymoon in Jamaica. We were walking along the beach at our resort when a native called out to us from his boat on the water.

I believe the guy's name was "Dr. Jim." If Dr. Jim was a doctor of anything, it was love. He told us he had 29 children, not all with the same woman. He did not look a day over 30. Dr. Jim's a busy guy.

Anyway, Dr. Jim was selling homemade souvenirs. One of the things that we actually could buy from him and not get arrested was the hand-carved giraffe. I paid $35 for it, thinking I was a hot ticket because I told Dr. Jim that was all I had to spend, even though I really had $50 in my pocket.

Afterward, Valerie told me that the giraffe was probably worth no more than $5. Feeling like a sucker, I tried to rationalize my purchase.

"Dr. Jim has a lot of kids," I said. "He needs all the money he can get."

At the very least, I had a souvenir from Jamaica, and I enjoyed having the giraffe around the house until my daughter accidentally broke its head off five years later.

Back to our yard sale.

My friend Brian stopped by the house that morning and caught me in the act of reselling something that I picked up at his family's yard sale last summer - - a DVD of the movie "Santa Claus Conquers the Martians." I even kept the $4 price tag that he had slapped on it.

Brian laughed and wished me luck selling the movie. Now I know why. By the end of the afternoon, I had sold all but two of the 40 movies that I put out for sale. "Santa Claus Conquers the Martians" was one of them.

I guess nobody shares my appreciation for awful movies that are so bad they're fun. Perhaps the yard-salers who stopped by our house had logged on to rottentomatoes.com and had read reviews of the Santa movie.

On that website, the movie's score, culled from critical consensus, was 27 out of 100. One critic says the movie is "shot in that hopeless, bad filmmaking style, with the delayed, artificial rhythm of a trans-Atlantic phone call." Another critic described the movie as "White Christmas" on a red planet. My favorite critical blurb said that the movie is "about as heartwarming as a documentary about reconstructive bowel surgery."

I don't know. Maybe it's the title that doesn't work. After all, it's called "Santa Claus *Conquers* the Martians." Where's the suspense in that? You know who wins. If the movie instead had been called "Santa Claus *Versus* the Martians," then maybe the outcome would feel less certain.

I brought the movie back to Brian when he and his family held their own yard sale a week later. He and I now have a running joke; we'll keep bringing the movie back and forth to each other's yard sales until finally somebody takes it off our hands. This could go on for years.

Unless some wise yard-saler knows a deal when he sees one. Next year, I'll sell "Santa Claus Conquers the Martians" at the marked-down price of one buck.

I'll even throw in the hornets' nest to seal the deal.

The Pen's It For Me

So there we were on Saturday morning, five guys with our sleeves rolled up, pushing my friend John's boiler across the dirt floor in his cellar.

It took a lot of might and muscle to force that thing across the uneven ground of John's basement, and as I threw all of my weight into the effort I couldn't help but think I was not contributing any strength to the task at all.

Has that ever happened to you? Have you ever felt you were one pair of hands too many as others sweated, grunted and pushed a piano up a flight of stairs or unloaded a marble dining room table from a U-Haul truck?

Both of my hands were on that boiler Saturday. I leaned into that thing, which was as tall as a fridge but heavier, and I pushed, and I just *knew* it was the other four guys who were actually getting it from point A to point B.

I'm not implying that I lack strength. I'm saying that I'm never quite sure how to apply the right strength and smarts to get grunt work done.

Saturday's a good example. By the time I showed up at John's house, the other guys had the boiler on its side and were sliding it along a trail they blazed with planks of smooth wood with long steel pipes underneath to roll things along.

I'm not sure I would have figured out that whole thing with the planks and pipes if the task had been left to me. I think I would have simply pushed the boiler across the dirt floor, applying as much brute, dumb force as I could as the rocks, pebbles and coarse sand on the floor scuffed up the boiler even worse than it had been. It was an old boiler.

I can cut myself *some* slack. I wasn't responsible for the jagged split that ran up the wall of John's living room when the guys accidentally slammed the boiler into a support beam in the cellar below. That happened *before* I showed up.

We did finally put the boiler where it needed to go, on a small, steel platform at the other end of the basement. As we all congratulated each other on our manliness, I couldn't help but notice I didn't bear the same scars as my brothers. They all had grubby lips and teeth. I did not.

I first noticed the grime on my friend Scott. As he talked there was a black smudge on his teeth. I just thought to myself, "I wonder what he ate. Should I tell him he has something stuck on his teeth?"

Then I noticed the other guys had black smears on their lips, and I thought, *"Wow, what did these guys all eat for breakfast?"*

Then I figured it out. They had dirt on their lips and teeth.

I knew all along that plenty of dirt and dust had been kicked up as we pushed the boiler across the floor because I inhaled most of it through my nose. Somehow, though, my pearly whites stayed pearly.

John and his wife, Denise, appreciated my "help," so they treated my family and me to a pizza. I thanked John but told him the gesture was disproportionate to my actual contribution to the effort, which I insisted was minimal.

"Yeah, you looked kinda lost," he agreed, "but you showed up to help, and that meant a lot to me."

John's a good guy.

He told me I reminded him of him. He used to be clumsy on matters of grunt work and home improvement as well.

Yeah, I have never been handy. When I was a kid I used to take things apart - - my bike, a miniature pinball machine I once had - - but I never quite figured out how to put them back together again.

Last winter, my father and his friends knocked down a wall in my parents' house to start building a whole new room. They put me in charge of prying the nails from all of the wood they tore out. I was outside in the driveway, alone with my hammer, away from the power saws and drills and Sheetrock.

Part of my problem is that I admittedly have never shown interest in such work. I'm not a tinkerer. I was always outside playing whenever my father was redoing a room when I was a kid.

Patience is another problem. My wife and I painted a few rooms in our new house, and I managed to get paint all over our hardwood floors because I didn't patiently apply the roller to the walls. I rushed the job.

As a result, we needed a sander to get all that paint off our floors. My parents got us one for Christmas. I still remember when they handed us the present. It had a tag on it that said, "To Valerie, From Lorraine and Gary."

Would it have *killed* my parents to put my name on the gift too?

My Dad got a new power saw. You clamp it to a table, and it cuts wood with absolute precision and shoots all of the saw dust into a tiny cloth bag that's attached. One day, Dad told my brother-in-law, Jay, that someday he'll inherit the saw.

Puzzled, Jay looked at Dad and said, "What about Shawn?"

As in, you know, *your son*?

"Well, I don't want Shawn to cut off his hand," Dad said, remembering the time he asked me to open a storm window and it came crashing down on my fingers with the full force of a guillotine and I needed to go to the hospital for stitches.

Ha, ha. Funny guy, my father. That's all right. I need my hand. My fingers help put food on my family's table.

I'm not the guy to build your garage, do your taxes, program your computer, stop that annoying clunky noise under the hood of your car, or represent you in a court of law. If, however, you need something written, I'm your man.

That said, if you're moving something really big on Saturday, I'm still available.

As we pushed that boiler last Saturday, one of the guys said, "Hey, Shawn, you should write a column about this morning."

Not a bad idea.

Halloween

This Halloween's going to be fun. My three-year-old daughter's starting to figure out what the holiday's all about.

I'm not sure that was the case last year. Maddie was a toddler then. She understood Halloween enough to want to dress up as a ladybug, but she didn't like it one bit when my wife and I didn't allow her to gobble up each piece of candy upon receiving it at the houses where we trick-or-treated.

If Maddie had her way, all candy would have followed a direct pipeline from the person giving her the treats to her belly. Her plastic pumpkin goodie bucket would have been for decorative purposes only. It would have been like an empty pocketbook with an orange smile on it. I'm not even sure she would've even taken the wrappers off the Tootsie Rolls and miniature Snickers bars.

As you'll see by Maddie's response, a child in the throes of the terrible twos has no concept of the future - - that point in time when they *can* have the candy, for example.

"Let me get this straight," she demanded. "All of these people are giving me candy, and you're telling me all I can do is walk around with it in my plastic pumpkin goodie bucket, or whatever you call this stupid thing?"

Well, okay, no, she didn't really say that. All parents of toddlers, though, become proficient in "toddlerese," so I had no problem understanding Maddie loud and clear when she turned red-faced with anguish and wailed and used her limited command of vowels to rail against the injustice of it all.

Needless to say, we only went trick-or-treating to four houses last year.

So you can heave a sigh of relief. That wasn't a dangerous wolf baby you heard howling angrily at the moon last Halloween night. It was just my daughter, begging for a Gobstopper that her little, brand new teeth couldn't handle.

Things lightened up a bit afterward. Maddie sat with me on our front steps and helped me hand out candy to the trick-or-treaters. I wasn't quite sure what to tell her when a 13-year-old girl showed up on our doorstep dressed as a prostitute, but I had an easy enough time explaining who Batman was.

This year will be different. Valerie and I will probably loosen up and let Maddie snack on a few treats while we make our rounds, which, hopefully, will include more houses and people who aren't just related to us.

Maddie's going to be a witch this time. Make that a purple witch. Everything's got to be purple with Maddie. It's her favorite color. Valerie and I aren't sure what a purple witch looks like, but I'm sure we'll figure it out. I bought Maddie a witch's broom at Walmart last weekend. It's black, but I bet by Halloween it'll be spray-painted the same color as Barney the Dinosaur.

This Halloween also should be more fun because Maddie is starting to appreciate the art of a good, safe, fun scare. Last weekend I bought a huge fake spider and hung it from a branch on the giant oak tree in our yard.

"Maddie, wait till you see the giant spider in our tree," I told her when I picked her and Valerie up at the house where they had been babysitting our friends' triplets.

"How do you know it's going to be there when we get home?" asked Valerie, always having to be the one who "keeps it real."

I gave her a look that said, *"It's not a real spider."* I don't like those kinds.

When we got home, I picked Maddie up and carried her over to the fake spider hanging from the branch from an elastic. The look in her eyes told me it's going to be a fun Halloween. She had a certain wonder in those baby blues of hers. She looked like she could be a bit scared if she wanted, but she seemed to be enjoying a spooky thrill that superseded everything else. She smiled.

"See?" I asked. "It's a friendly spider. You know, like Charlotte in *Charlotte's Web*."

I love Halloween. I always have. It's not the most important and meaningful holiday, but like the Fourth of July it's just plain fun. There's very little pressure. There's no turkey to cook, no presents to buy and cards to send, no need to make sure you're out there doing something memorable and sociable when the clock strikes midnight and the new year begins.

You just do whatever you want - - carve a jack-o-lantern, watch scary movies, visit a haunted house, take a scary hay ride, and dress your child up in a costume and go trick-or-treating. It's all fun stuff, with a slightly cathartic side that makes us confront such fears as the boogie man underneath our bed, the loud bump in the night, or Jack Nicholson, all wild-haired and demon-eyed, chasing you with an ax through a hotel during a snowstorm and screaming, *"Heeeeeeeeeeeere's Johnnny!"*

Not that I'm sure if I'll put on a costume this year. For a guy who likes Halloween, I tend to show very little imagination in this department. I get a kick out of parents who become Dracula or the Bride of Frankenstein for an evening while taking their kids house to house.

As a kid it was easy. I remember suiting up as a king, a robot, Mickey Mouse, King Kong, Darth Vader, Spider-Man, a cowboy, a pirate, a punk rocker, and one of the "Saturday Night Live" bees made famous by John Belushi in the 1970s.

As an adult, I've rarely struck gold. I did go to a party a few years ago as Harpo Marx, complete with a curly wig, top hat, baggy overcoat, horn and clashing shirt and tie. That was fun.

And there was another time when I won "best costume" at a party by simply dressing in reverse; I put a pair of jeans, a shirt, a tie and a ball cap on backwards and painted a goofy face on the back of my shaved head. Didn't wear my sneakers backwards, though. That would've hurt.

And then there was another party, shortly after I graduated college, in which I dressed as a reporter. Now I do that every day for my job, so there goes the novelty of that idea.

Maybe this year I'll simply take my daughter's cue.

I'll be a Purple People Eater.

It's Frosty Outside

Frosty the Snowman is sitting on my front steps.

I "inherit" all sorts of things from my family. Recently, my father gave me his beloved chair. Last summer, my sister stuck me with a plant holder that looks like a giant hornets' nest after I couldn't sell it at a yard sale. Earlier this year, my parents presented me with a portrait of my sister and I dressed as colonial folks for the bicentennial parade in 1976.

Now I have the four-foot illuminated plastic snowman that for years sat on my parents' front steps every Christmas.

You see what's going on here. My house has become a dumping ground for things my family no longer wants. The snowman's just the latest giveaway. All the same, I like seeing Frosty on my front steps. My daughter Maddie does too.

Valerie finally likes him as well. She had to warm up to him at first. She thought he was a little . . . dated.

Well, she's right about that. My parents bought Frosty 35 years ago at King's or Grant's or another one of those big department stores that no longer exist. At the time, he cost $19, which in 2006 dollars comes out to roughly $1,599, according to my parents. They had no money back then.

So, yeah, it's true: Frosty's a little long in the tooth. The early seventies were a long time ago. We may as well have Lawrence Welk propped up on our front steps.

He's a pleasant fellow, though. He sits on our steps, all white, round-faced and pudgy. He wears a top hat, mittens and a scarf and smiles at the people who drive down our street. Frosty, that is. Not Lawrence Welk.

I never understood why kids put hats and mittens and scarves on snowmen. They're made of *snow*. Are all those clothes supposed to keep the snowmen warm?

I was a bit startled last week when I ventured into my parents' cellar to pick up Frosty and take him home. I had expected him to be taller and heavier, a nuisance to drag up the stairs, stuff into my car and unload when I got home after a busy, tiring day at work. Instead, he was pretty light.

Then I realized something. *I* was the one who was taller and heavier. I hadn't picked up Frosty since I was a kid.

Last Wednesday, my father offered to light up Frosty after we all went out to dinner. He wanted to do the honors for his granddaughter.

It should have been a simple task. Go to the store, get an adapter for the light socket outside our house, hook up the snowman, and flick the switch. You've seen "National Lampoon's Christmas Vacation," though. Nothing goes that easily.

We set everything up, no problem. We hooked Frosty up to the socket inside the lamp that is attached to our house, a couple of feet over our heads, next to the front door. When we flicked the switch to light up Frosty, though, we were greeted with darkness. We couldn't understand it; we had just tested the bulb inside of Frosty moments earlier. We repeatedly flicked the switch on and off, expecting a different result.

When that didn't work, we decided to check the fuse box downstairs. Since the fuses are not labeled, this led to a spectacular show inside my house, as various rooms would light up and then go dark and all digital clocks and the answering machine were set back to midnight.

When that proved fruitless, we unscrewed a light bulb in our bathroom and tested the one that went dark outside. My father dropped the bathroom bulb, which would have shattered loudly and dangerously in the sink had it not fallen plush into the cup my daughter uses to rinse after she brushes her teeth. The bulb didn't break inside the cup because Madeline had left it filled with water, like the kid in the movie, "Signs." My father took credit for saving the bulb.

After a few minutes, my father finally had a theory about our problem. Dust and dirt had fallen into the outdoor socket when we unscrewed the bulb. We needed to vacuum the socket, which was inside that lamp high over our heads, and clear the way for the bulb again.

Maybe two grown men should know better than to go sticking a nozzle in a socket. In any event, we were safe because my father spent nearly a minute vacuuming inside the socket of the outdoor light before we both realized that the hose was never connected to the vacuum cleaner. We may as well have been playing Charades.

During this time, my mother sat in our living room with a look of heroic patience that has taken decades of marriage for her to perfect. Valerie, who has only had eight years with me to hone that look, clearly wanted Dad and me to wrap things up so that Maddie could see Frosty all lit up and go to bed. It got late, though, and Maddie had to go to bed, anyway.

Eventually, Dad and I did light Frosty. I woke Maddie up so she could see him. She was a bit groggy - - my father had to explain to her that he, not Frosty, had knocked on our front door to get her to open it and see the surprise.

Maddie went back to bed, my parents headed home, and Valerie and I settled down not for a long winter's nap, but for an episode of "The Sopranos" on DVD.

At around 9:30, we heard rustling in our front yard. When you're watching "The Sopranos," and you hear someone rooting around outside your home, you can't help but be a little concerned. I got up from the couch and opened the front door, hoping not to see a hit man pointing a gun with a big silencer on it. I saw my father, stringing holiday lights in our bushes. He had

75

parked on the street and crept up to our house, in an attempt not to disturb us.

Self-consciously, I suggested to Dad that I really should be decorating my own house, and that I was planning to do it that weekend. He just smiled and said he personally wanted to decorate the house for his granddaughter.

It was a sweet gesture, yes, but it was an ironic one too.

He had given us Frosty and the Christmas lights because he didn't want to have to put them up anymore.

Resolute About Not Making Resolutions

Well, here it is, more than half way through January, and I have not yet broken any of my resolutions for 2007.

There's a reason for that. I didn't make any.

Usually I do. Maybe it's because I write for a living, but I see the start of every new year as a fresh chapter in the book of life.

My life, anyway. Maybe your new chapter starts on your birthday. Or the first of the month. Or Mondays. Or tomorrow, if you like to procrastinate.

Actually, I cheat. If I fail to capitalize on a new year during its first three months, then I seize upon my birthday at the end of March as a chance to kick off that new chapter.

There have been more than a few years in which I sat down during the first few days of January and knocked off a list of things I'd either like to start or stop doing.

Sometimes the list is a concise acknowledgement that its goals will go unmet. A new year often reveals itself as just another quick 365-day run of an ordinary life with routines and responsibilities that take precedent. Other times the list is ridiculously long and filled with fantastic, outlandish goals - -

even a new party in power in Congress would know better than to set such a lengthy agenda during its first 100 days.

I have a friend who keeps it simple. One year he resolved to eat a mango. He had never tasted one before. As that year drew to a close, I asked him if he had eaten one. Indeed he had. He declared his year a resounding success.

On the other hand, I had written off that year as a complete miss, for I had not written a book, traveled to Europe, taken up an instrument, stepped into a boxing ring, taught the nation's children how to read, built an orphanage, gotten my own talk show, landed on Mars, and won a million dollars from one of those scratch tickets you get at the gas station.

Yeah, I was young, optimistic and idealistic then. Still am. Optimistic and idealistic, anyway.

This year, however, is different. I just decided to let the new year begin. I'm trusting that if I stay busy, keep family first, pay the bills and listen for the knocks of opportunity and fun, then 2007 will take care of itself.

Now that I've given up making resolutions, though, my wife has started making them for me.

The other night Valerie and I were watching the season premiere of "24" on TV. There was Kiefer Sutherland as Jack Bauer, beaten and bruised after years of captivity in China, brandishing a gun and running with great speed and authority from Plot Point A to Plot Point B.

Out of nowhere, as my fingers rummaged through a bowl of potato chips, Valerie turned to me and said, "You could be like that."

I set down my glass of soda and asked, "Like what?"

But of course I knew "like what." The key word in her remark was "could." As in I *could* be like Jack Bauer if I laid off the chips and went to the gym.

Val answered anyway, telling me that somewhere within me is the physique of an action hero waiting to burst through the onset of middle-aged love handles and . . . well, not exactly save the world, I suppose, but at least achieve some heroic feat of strength. Like finally hauling that Frosty the Snowman off our front steps and putting him back in the garage for storage, now that the holidays are over.

I think my wife meant her remark to be a compliment of sorts. Actually, I think she likes Kiefer Sutherland. *That's* what I think.

Can you imagine if the shoe was on the other foot? Somehow I think things would go differently if a couple was watching, say, "Grey's Anatomy," and the man turned to the love of his life and said "You could be like that" when that nurse with the nice figure and blonde hair appeared onscreen.

That guy would have his New Year's resolution made for him too. It'd be "find a new apartment." Or "sleep more nights on the couch."

Here's the thing. Whether we're trying to get in shape or stop being such a drag to our family and friends, we don't need a new year to start the effort. We just need one day, the same day, over and over again.

Just like the movie "Groundhog Day." Bill Murray plays this weatherman who's an insufferable jerk. He becomes a better person - - physically healthier, smarter, more skilled, talented, patient, thoughtful and positive - - after he is forced to repeat the same old February 2 for decades until he gets its right.

That's what we need. And, when you think about it, that's what we have.

If there's one thing I have learned, it's that the opportunities to improve ourselves do not exist in the lists we make or the fresh starts of a new year. They can be found in the routine of everyday life. They emerge when we grow tired of the sameness, when we have had it with a bad habit that needs dropping, when we have a good run of energy, when a light bulb sparks to life over our heads and we have a great idea or see a better way to do something.

Which brings me back up to the top. I'll just keep doing what I'm doing. Keep busy in 2007. Put family first. Pay those bills. Listen for those knocks of opportunity and fun.

I bet Jack Bauer wishes he can take a day off from the stress and exhaustion of repeatedly saving the world. I bet he would look at a guy like me and say, "*I* could be like that."

Linus Before Her

I approached my daughter's cubby at her preschool and could not believe my eyes.

There it was, her blanket, draped over her duffel bag and other belongings like a purple shroud.

"Aw, man, what is this?" I whispered to myself.

It's not just any blanket. It's Maddie's biggest one. It's thick and heavy and large enough to cover her entire bed. You could raise that thing on poles and have a circus underneath it.

My daughter likes to bring things to preschool. Her white, fluffy kitty slippers, for example. Her little frog-shaped pillow. A few stuffed animals. A couple of books. Her favorite CD. That's never been an issue with me because I know the other kids bring their creature comforts to day care too. I also remember that I used to bring things to school: a favorite "Star Wars" figure, a huge box of crayons, a cassette I hoped my teacher would play during indoor recess.

There was something about that purple blanket, though, that bothered me. It seemed a little over the top, an overindulgence of a child's need to bring mementos from home into the outside world. Seeing it there, among my daughter's other things, I couldn't help but think the only thing she left home that day was her bed.

Thankfully, she *did* leave her bed at home. I know because I checked under the blanket and did not see it.

Oh, all right. I'll just come out and say it: The blanket made me think of Linus. You know, the "Peanuts" character who carries around a security blanket.

My wife had brought Maddie to school that morning. I asked her if she really wanted to let Maddie get into the habit of bringing a blanket with her.

"What about a smaller blanket?" Valerie asked.

I suggested that size was not the issue. It could have been a facecloth we were talking about, and I'd still be concerned that our child would develop an attachment.

Valerie agreed that we should keep an eye on the matter, but also felt that I was overreacting. It took me a few moments, but eventually I came around to her way of thinking. I figured it was best just to let the matter play out. One day, Maddie will head off to preschool and won't even notice that she forgot her king-sized blanket.

I just felt like Michael Keaton in "Mr. Mom," I guess. Remember that scene after Keaton tries to get his son to toss his "woobie" into the fireplace in an attempt to free him from a lifetime of dependence and insecurity?

"I understand that you little guys start out with your woobies," he tells his son. "You think they're great, and they are, but pretty soon a woobie is not enough. You're out on the street trying to score an electric blanket, maybe a quilt, and the next thing you know, you're strung out on bedspreads. That's serious."

The kid flees, clutching his woobie. In the next scene, though, he agrees to surrender his woobie to his father for a couple of days, to see if he can shake the habit once and for all.

"Can I have a moment to myself, please?" he asks his father, seeking a moment alone to ponder his new life in a woobie-free world.

If the son had stuck with the woobie, it would have lived to see another day, but my hunch is that it would not have lived forever. Something tells me the kid eventually would have given up the blanket, hopefully by the time he entered junior high.

And this gets me to thinking about Linus. Maybe it speaks volumes about me that I'd take the time to contemplate the life of a fictional character in a comic strip, but work with me here.

When you think of it, Linus was probably the only "Peanuts" character who grew up to enjoy a successful adulthood.

Take Lucy, for example. She probably ended up tipsy on a barstool somewhere, telling stories about her glory days of swiping those footballs away from Charlie Brown.

Schroeder? He probably lived in abject poverty as a failed pianist, a victim of his parents' unreasonably high expectations and a culture that does not adequately support its artists.

Pig Pen? Perhaps he choked to death on the dusty haze of his own filth.

But Linus? I bet Linus did all right. He was the smart one in the bunch. He was the level-headed diplomat. The thoughtful ear to Charlie Brown's woes. The man of faith who staked out the pumpkin patch. The kid who cited Scripture from memory during rehearsals for that Christmas pageant.

And I doubt he dragged that security blanket around with him throughout his applauded career at the United Nations.

Just like my daughter does not carry her blanket around at preschool. She just uses it during naptime, is all. And at home she's completely free, a bright, imaginative, joyous, energetic child who's completely untethered by a security blanket or anything else as she runs, jumps, dances and climbs around the house.

Yeah, I guess I did overreact about the purple blanket. I think I was just taken aback by seeing the sheer size of it out of its element. It's a whole lotta blanket to haul out of the house.

My daughter has since been content to bring a smaller one to preschool. I can hear her now.

"Dads. They can be *such* a wet blanket sometimes."

Mary Pettibone Poole Had It Right

I woke up laughing the other night.

Who knows what I was dreaming. It must have been pretty funny, though. I'll say that much.

This happens to me every two months or so. I'll be fast asleep, well into a good night's rest, and then the sound of my own laughter snaps me awake. Sometimes all it takes is an amused snort. Other times it's a chuckle.

My daughter tends to laugh in her sleep too. I'm glad I passed that gene on to her.

There are many things in life for which I am grateful, and laughter's near the top of the list. I'm the kind of guy with whom you can strike pay dirt with a particularly good joke or witty, off-the-cuff remark. Tell it right, and I'll be laughing about it hours later. I'm an easy audience.

One morning, a coworker told me a funny joke, the kind you can't wait to share with friends the next time you see them. Hours later, the receptionist heard a snicker from beyond the partition that separates his office space from mine.

"You're still laughing at that joke, aren't you?" he asked me.

Yup. I was.

As an adult, I have never completely learned the social etiquette of restraining laughter. I'm not talking about the kind of laughter that would be inappropriate, rude or unfortunate, given whatever circumstance. Instead, I'm referring to the kind of laughter in which you unwittingly call attention to yourself.

Some people know how to keep in their laughter. They feel the surprise or joy or rush of a funny moment during a movie, a conversation, or a fleeting observation, but they keep it to themselves. Maybe they'll smile, and you'll see a twinkle in their eyes, and you'll know it's circus-time in their head.

It's a smart trick. It keeps unwanted attention away from you in a movie theater or a restaurant or a meeting. My wife's got this move down pat.

Alas, I do not.

Sometimes I blame "Mad" magazine. I love sophistication, subtlety, sharp satire and wit, but I also laugh at the kind of things that probably should have gotten their last guffaws from me when I was in the third grade.

I'm not talking about knock-knock jokes here. Give me *some* credit. I'm referring to the kinds of things I used to find inside old issues of "Mad," depicted in their comic strips, scribbled in their margins, found in their twice-folded back covers.

Do kids still read that magazine? I sure hope so. I believe I caught every issue from 1980 through 1988. Formative years, those.

"Now why did you think *that* was funny?" my wife usually asks me after, say, a character in a movie would make a most unfortunate, yet completely natural, bodily noise.

I can't explain it. Nor do I feel the need to defend it. Quite simply, people with broader senses of humor laugh more. If you respond only to the most highly developed wit, delivered with the driest subtlety and the quietest, sharpest edge, then you're not going to laugh as much as the guy who laughs at that *and* at something more obvious and easy on the other end of the spectrum.

"He who laughs, lasts."

That's the quote I put underneath my picture in the high school yearbook during my senior year. I got it from a quote book.

Mary Pettibone Poole said it. Do you know who she is? Apparently, she was an author. I only found that out last night when I "Googled" her name on the Internet. I went seventeen years without a clue as to who she was. But I like what she said.

I always have liked that quote, and all of these years later I am pleased that I chose it. Nothing haunts you more through adulthood than a poorly chosen yearbook quote. Just ask anyone who put something by the Bee Gees underneath their picture.

"He who laughs, lasts."

It's true. If God had not equipped us with laughter, then we would have needed to invent it for ourselves.

Laughter's there for you. There are moments in life when it quietly hits you with stark, unnerving clarity that the world is frequently sad, frightening and unjust. Laughter's our reprieve, our escape hatch, our bond with each other.

Laughter's a gift that keeps on giving. It's like interest in the bank; it builds on itself, doubling, tripling, quadrupling your joy, so that it can linger, echo, and be fondly recalled and shared with family and friends. You can laugh at something in the moment, and then laugh about it again, years later.

Laughs last.

Boo-Boo the Parrot

I opened my front door this morning and hoped to hear birds in the trees, but they weren't talking. Obviously, they're taking this unseasonably cold weather to heart, just like the rest of us.

I had birds on the brain this morning because my daughter had to bring something related to our feathered friends to show-and-tell at preschool today.

I've always had a complicated relationship with birds. Most of them are beautiful and wondrous, and they certainly do strike the best notes when it comes to nature's music. However, I have always been wary of birds and have kept them at a distance.

It's not that I've ever been "bombed" by a bird, if you know what I mean. My car, though, that's another story.

And it's not that I'm freaked out by "The Birds," that Hitchcock classic in which hordes of winged terrors set out to peck away at the human race and achieve world domination. I liked the film but found it nothing more than darkly comic; for me, it did not do for pigeons what "Jaws" did for sharks. If memory serves, there was not a bird in the movie that bit Robert Shaw in half.

No. My issues with birds date back to my teenage years, when my Uncle Don used to ask me to feed his pigeons while he and Aunt Noreen took off on a trip somewhere.

He owned dozens of pigeons, you see, and he'd race them. When they weren't speeding through the friendly skies in competitive bids to be the first ones home, they'd all hang out together in his backyard, in a coop no bigger than a phone booth.

To this day I still twitch when I think back on all those pigeons. I always entered their coop with tremendous caution, with my head bowed and my shoulders hunched, as though this defensive crouch would be enough to shield me from their fecal blasts.

These pigeons were everywhere, to the left, to the right, straight ahead, up above, bobbing their heads as though in a constant search for something to peck, staring at me with such wide, unblinking eyes I had to wonder if Uncle Don had put caffeine in their bird baths.

What I remember most, though, is the sounds they made. Their loud, collective, guttural coo. Their feet clawing at the wires surrounding their cages. All of those flapping wings.

Somehow, I made it in and out of their coop without suffering a direct hit, but that's not the point. It was the *threat* of the direct hit, the tense anticipation of one, which made me a wreck.

Not all birds set me on edge. Many of them have managed to make a difference in my life, in their own small way. They sing beautifully during spring mornings, for starters. And there are these sparrows that have a nice little routine of perching in the bushes outside my office window.

There was even a time when birds made more of a difference for me than they could have possibly known.

Go back six years ago, for example. None of us laughed or smiled much in the weeks that followed the terrorist attacks on September 11, 2001. During that dark, despairing time, however, there was one familiar sight on which I could rely to provide a moment of comfort and a fleeting assurance that life as we knew it would continue.

Back in those days, I'd drive by the same standing puddle on the side of the road on my way to work, and I'd see a family of small birds there, taking a bath. They'd hop across the water in that nimble way of theirs, and splash each other. They'd dip their heads, and then they'd dry off with lightning-quick flutters.

I'm not sure how many days in a row that I saw them. I do know that I looked for them every morning that sad September, just as I started taking the slight curve in the road that brought me past their puddle.

They were there just long enough, I guess. There came a day, finally, when I drove past the puddle without realizing it. And then a later day came when I drove past the puddle and did not see them at all.

I've always wondered if other drivers saw these birds and depended on them for even the slightest hint of normalcy and consistency during that time.

Those are the kinds of birds I like. They're not like the other kinds that make me wary and suspicious. Those birds are for the birds.

I blame Boo-Boo the Parrot. He was my wife's cousin's parrot. He liked to sing "I Left My Heart in San Francisco," and he'd roll his eyes and say "Oh, brother," if you tried to sing it with him.

Boo-Boo stayed with my wife and my mother-in-law for a week back in 1997. Valerie and I were dating then, and I drove down to Massachusetts to visit.

Valerie needed to leave the house for a moment, so I stayed behind with Boo-Boo to hold down the fort.

At one point, I was washing my hands in the bathroom sink. Boo-Boo sat in his cage in the living room and watched me. I shut off the faucet and dried my hands on a towel.

I took a moment to look in the mirror, and Boo-Boo let out a loud shriek in that ridiculous, Polly-want-a-cracker voice all parrots have down pat.

"Pretty boy!"

I was stunned. And I know I looked that way because I could see my face in the mirror.

I had no idea what to think. Had I just been mocked by a parrot? I wasn't sure. I had never had a pet make fun of me before.

Boo-Boo and I stared at each other for a long time after he made that remark. I kept searching his jaunty little face for a sign, any sign, that his wisecrack was really just a coincidence, a random blurt unintentionally well suited to the moment.

"Come on, Shawn," Valerie said when she returned. "Do you really think he did that on purpose?"

"I'm telling you, Val, the bird was sticking it to me," I insisted, jabbing a finger in the direction of Boo-Boo's cage. "Just look at him. Look at his face. He knows *exactly* what he's doing."

In my head, I could hear Uncle Don's pigeons laughing.

Fathers on a Walk

I wonder how many of the world's problems would be solved if we all just took a walk and kicked things around in our heads for a while.

Those of you who prefer to talk out loud to yourselves could be my guests. I know you're out there. I hear you when you walk by my office window on Main Street.

We all could just set about our preferred routes, whether they're through our neighborhoods, nearby parks and forests, or favorite vacation spots. Sorry, treadmills wouldn't count.

When we'd return, we'd report back to each other with our answers and solutions.

No, I don't really think a worldwide teleconference among billions of people who have just taken walks would truly pry the collective thorns from our sides. The issues of terrorism, war, illegal immigration, health care and who should win every season of "American Idol" are a bit more demanding than that.

Nonetheless, I think I'm on to something. I've taken a few walks in my life that have completely transformed my approach to certain matters or handed me answers to problems as clearly as though they had dropped on my head from the sky.

I have taken walks for as long as I can remember. Sometimes I walk completely for the exercise, whipping around the two-mile loop of my neighborhood at a good clip.

Other times, though, I take my time and do my thinking. Maybe I'll tackle a problem or an issue that's causing me some worry. Sometimes I'll get caught up in pleasant memories, particularly when I pass the house where my grandparents once lived. And there are those occasions when the weather's perfect and I just take a walk on principle. Can't waste a nice evening, you know.

Something usually happens when I take one of my more contemplative walks. I start out giving a certain matter much thought, but at some point everything becomes about the walk itself. As I make some distance, I pick up my speed without realizing it or purposely striving to exercise; when this happens, trains of thought or preoccupations slip away, the mind becomes clear, and I'm in the moment.

By the time I get home, there's a chance I may not have solved anything or thought my way through something, but the ol' head's been wiped clean and I can start fresh with my inherent optimism and appreciation for my blessings.

It's a great thing. But there's something even better: Walking with a friend or loved one.

Valerie and I have started taking walks with our daughter. Now that Madeline is older, she can keep up and no longer asks me to carry her home if we stray too far for her little feet.

That's a wonderful thing for a family to do, of course, but recently it occurred to me that these walks are filling a void for me.

My father and I used to take walks all the time. We'd go everywhere: around the block, up and down Main Street, along Number One Pond, you name it. We'd talk about all sorts of things, from politics to religion to movies to memories of family and friends. As I made my way through high school, and then college, and then the earlier years of the so-called "real world," I also asked Dad for a lot of advice during our walks.

Dad and I no longer get to take walks. ALS has given him a third leg, a cane, but has made even the shortest distances most exhausting and challenging for him. We still talk about all sorts of things, of course, but our conversations now take place in our living rooms, at our kitchen tables, during our rides in the car, and over the telephone.

I miss those walks. But in a way, I'm still taking them.

The other day, Maddie and I played a little baseball in our driveway. At one point, I paused mid-pitch and said, "Hey, Maddie, do you wanna take a walk?" I was thrilled when she said yes.

I took her by her little hand and we ventured into our neighborhood. Maddie talked about all sorts of things, and I asked her follow-up questions. She told me that tigers lived inside the woods near our home. She didn't seem afraid of them, so I let her believe it. Why impose a boring truth on a child's wild and free imagination?

As we walked I felt enormous peace and satisfaction. I knew, just *knew*, that there was no other place I wanted to be at that moment. There was absolutely nothing else that I wanted to be doing. Maddie and I were taking a walk. Everything else either did not matter or would need to wait.

I looked at Maddie and realized something reassuring. I have picked up where my father has left off. A father and his child are still going for walks. My tradition with Dad literally marches on.

Brand New Wheels

Maddie got a brand new bike for her birthday.

Valerie and I knew that was the bike for our little girl when we saw it at Toys 'R Us on Saturday night.

It's purple, to begin with. Everything has to be purple when it comes to Maddie, whether it's her clothes, her blanket, her backpack, her teddy bear, or now, her bike. Prince didn't even have this much purple back in his "Purple Rain" days. When I look around my house and see purple everywhere, I feel like my head's stuck in a violet.

This is a good, straightforward bike, shiny, sleek, and large enough to last Maddie until she's about seven years old. It even has a pouch strapped to the handlebars that holds a bottle of water.

And it's not one of those "theme" bikes, either, with Barbie or Disney decals plastered all over it. There's nothing wrong with those bicycles, I suppose, although Valerie and I did shudder when we saw a pink one with stickers of the obnoxious "Bratz" girls slapped all over it.

Valerie and I enjoyed watching Maddie on Sunday, pedaling up and down our driveway on her new bike, tottering slightly to the left and right on its training wheels. She was wearing a helmet, of course. And, yes, it was purple.

Wearing a helmet is mandatory, smart and safe, but my friends and I never wore one when we were whipping around town on two wheels. Times were different back then.

On Sunday I watched Maddie climb on to her bike and fearlessly work the pedals. Something tells me that Valerie and I will be prying the training wheels off that bike before Maddie turns five next spring. That would put her way ahead of her old man.

My parents took the training wheels off my first bike at just about the right time, but it was a great deal longer before I could ride smoothly and avoid falling off and braking on the pavement with my knees or my face.

Actually, I was high as a kite when I finally learned to ride my bike.

I better explain that.

I had a bad summer cold, you see, and Mom gave me a spoonful of cough syrup. Maybe the bottle said to give me a teaspoon, and maybe Mom gave me a tablespoon. Perhaps I had one tablespoon too many. Nobody knows, nobody remembers. Either that, or Mom's not saying.

Here's what we do know. Hopped up on codeine, I jumped on my bike and took right off. I put all anxieties and inhibitions in my bike's rearview mirror, you could say.

My father came home from church that evening and saw me zipping around the neighborhood like I owned the place.

"We've been trying to teach him to ride that thing all summer," he told Mom. "I've only been gone an hour. How did you do it?"

Mom shrugged. Maybe it's the cough syrup, she said. All that codeine.

Don't worry. I didn't learn to drive a car the same way.

I got that bike for my birthday when I was five, by the way. It was a red one with swooping chrome handlebars. It did the trick . . . when I was five, six, and seven years old. By the time I was eight, I was starting to outgrow it. By the time I was ten, I was ditching it in a bush and walking the last block to baseball practice because my teammates were having a field day picking on me about it.

I got a new BMX for my eleventh birthday, in the spring of 1983. This new bike was the real deal, its bars wrapped with blue foam pads to ensure the continuation of my family's name if I had to slam on my brakes without warning.

And it was a huge bike, too, pretty much the size of one of Arnold Schwarzenegger's gas-guzzling Hummers. Obviously, I chose this bike to compensate for the previous five years spent tooting around on the smaller, childish red one.

I got a 10-speed in high school. Then I got my driver's license when I was 16, and, regrettably, I have not ridden a bike since.

Actually, that's not completely true. Ten years ago, Valerie and I rode on mountain bikes from Waltham to Cambridge, Massachusetts. My muscles screamed at me the whole week that followed.

Now that Maddie has a bike, Valerie and I should get ones too. I always like it when I see parents riding their bikes with their kids. I wonder, though, if kids today feel the same way I felt when I rode my bike at their age. One of my favorite childhood memories harks back to a warm summer evening in May of 1984. I was 12 years old, and I was riding my bike home from baseball practice at the high school.

I took my time that evening, choosing the back roads along Number One Pond rather than the straight route home provided by Main Street.

I stopped at a service station. I bought a Pepsi. It came in a glass bottle and cost 27 cents.

I drank that Pepsi on the rest of the ride home. I remember feeling such freedom and independence.

I was a 12-year-old kid without a single care in the world, riding his bike and drinking a soda.

Now I'm a father. If I saw a kid riding his bike without a helmet while drinking from a glass bottle, I'd say that's a disaster waiting to happen.

To this day, though, I can feel - - not simply recall, but actually *feel* - - the faint echoes of that freedom and independence during that evening in May back in '84. It's a feeling, a sensation, a revelation, that belongs to children. Adults, with their fears, responsibilities and worn self-sufficiency, cannot experience its newness, its innocence, its grace.

I hope Maddie experiences that freedom as she learns to ride her new bike. If she's like me, she will. And if she's like her mom, she won't need the cough syrup.

May I Have My Hand Back Now?

I have thought a lot over the years about what should and should not go into a handshake.

It started when I was a freshman in college. A friend and I were sitting in the front seat of my car in her driveway when she looked up and said, "Looks like my dad's coming out of the house to meet you."

"All right," I said. "He seems like a nice guy."

"He is, but listen," my friend said. "He has a thing with handshakes."

"Handshakes?"

"Yes. He thinks all you need to know about a guy you can learn from the way he shakes hands."

"I get it," I said. "No problem."

"I mean it," she said. "Shake his hand *real* hard."

So I shook her father's hand, real hard, just like she told me to do. The problem is, she didn't tell me how long I should go on shaking it.

The father came to my car window, smiled and said hello, and stuck out his hand for a shake. I grabbed it and pumped it a few times, and then I made my biggest mistake.

I let go. Or rather, I tried to. The guy wouldn't let go of my hand. He ended up holding my slack hand and limp fingers in the palm of his tightly gripped fist for what felt like an eternity.

He kept smiling, of course.

"What kind of jerk judges a person solely on the way they shake hands?" I asked my father when I told him about the incident during dinner the next night.

"Well, isn't that what you're doing?" he asked me.

"What?"

"Judging a person solely by the way they shake hands?"

I could never get anywhere with my father while growing up.

The bottom line is, my friend's father didn't have to hold on to my hand so long. I wasn't even trying to hold his *daughter's* hand because we were just friends, so there was no reason for him to go on squeezing my much-needed typing fingers.

Handshakes should be simple. Lock hands firmly with the other party, give two solid pumps, and let go. And remember the eye contact. This is the way it should be done with everybody.

Except old ladies, of course. I really felt bad that time I heard a woman's knuckles and joints crack when I shook her hand. Sometimes, when I look back on moments like these in my life, I just shake my head and wonder what I was thinking.

People manage to screw up a handshake all the time, especially if they think it's a mammoth power struggle instead of a formal greeting. For example, there are those people who grab your hand and then pull you into them. The only time anyone needs to do that with me is if I've been tossed over the side of a boat and need someone to pull me back on board.

The hand-shakers who really get under my skin are the ones who come at me from an odd angle. I extend my hand straightforwardly, and they swoop down from above and end up grabbing only my fingers.

What an awkward moment that is. I'm there, ready to give a strong, firm handshake, one of strength, confidence and unimpeachable manliness, and this guy holds my fingers like he's helping me off the steps of Cinderella's carriage.

I used to wipe my hands after a handshake. I never even knew I was doing it until somebody pointed it out to me. I would shake someone's hand, and then I'd twice skim one of my palms over the other. You know, like you do when you're done with a task. Or, unfortunately, like you do when you've had it with someone and you're figuratively washing your hands of them.

It was a shy tic, is all, something I'd do when I'd first meet someone and I was waiting for the ice to break. You know, it was something to do with my hands, rather than just have them hang at my sides, doing nothing.

Try telling that to the wrong person, though.

"What? You think I have germs or something, wiping your hands like that?"

"No, not at all, not at all."

"You think maybe I don't wash up after I use the john? Pick my nose, maybe?"

I can't remember who told me to stop doing that with my hands after shaking someone else's. I'll bet you a nickel it was my wife.

Here, let's shake on it.

Childhood Romance Is Fleeting

There's a new kid at my daughter's day care. Let's call him "Billy."

"I think Billy wants to marry me," Madeline told Valerie and me.

We were eating at Wendy's at the time. I was drinking my lemonade and paused mid-sip when Maddie broke the news. I looked up at Valerie, with my straw clamped between my teeth.

Billy's an older man, five years old to Maddie's four. He seems like a great little fellow. On his first day at the day care, he helped Maddie on and off the slide in the playground. He also makes a point to wish her goodbye when I pick her up to take her home.

He's a gentleman, really. I haven't met his parents yet, but I bet they're nice folks.

Still, we're talking about my daughter here. There's a little part of me that wants to sit Billy down for a heartfelt chat.

"Now look, son," I'd say. "I was five once. What are your intentions here?"

Poor Billy would probably be stuck for an answer. At least the talk would give me practice for when Maddie's a teenager

107

and some guy with a pierced lip and a driver's license shows up on my doorstep with a dozen roses.

Actually, that's the great thing about little kids. They don't *have* any intentions. They just know it when they like someone, and that's that. If anything, I'd have to warn Billy and steer him away from inevitable heartbreak. Little girls have a way of . . . moving on.

When I was in kindergarten I liked a girl we'll call "Esther." That seems like a safe name to pick because I don't know anyone under the age of 90 who has it.

Anyway, Esther and I got along famously. We hung out all the time. We sat together in our classroom, played together during recess, you name it.

Each morning, I'd surprise her by sneaking gifts into her cubby, whether it was dandelions, toys I wouldn't miss, or pictures I drew. In turn, she'd help me tie my shoes or zip my coat because, well, I was a late bloomer when it came to that kind of stuff.

Our courtship lasted much of the school year. Then June came around, and summer vacation followed.

In September, we bumped into each other in the playground on the first day of the first grade. We smiled awkwardly and looked down at our shoes. She whispered hello. I grunted. Then we both went our own ways.

More than two months had passed since we graduated kindergarten and last saw each other. Our pint-sized romance had not survived the gulf of time. It was not meant to be.

It would be years and years before Esther and I spoke again. We went to the same schools, but we made a point never to cross paths. We had forged an unspoken pact, designed to prevent us from ever again duplicating that awkward moment on the first day of school in the first grade.

The pact worked until high school. That's when we had a class together for the first time in ten years.

We had no choice. We would have to face each other.

At first, we did not speak. Then, as the semester progressed, we loosened up. I'd say hello. She'd laugh at my jokes. I had no illusions that we'd ever work back to what we had during that blissful year of 1978, but we did seem to be forging a comfortable friendship, without the shyness that had driven an awkward wedge between us.

That June, we even swapped yearbooks. I signed hers and waited with great anticipation to see what she wrote in mine.

"To Shawn," she wrote, and then added, "a nice guy I met this year. Have a nice summer. I hope we have another class together next year. Your friend, Esther."

I stared at her words. A nice guy she met this year? As in *this* year? *1988?*

What about kindergarten? All of those recesses we spent together? The surprises in her cubby? The inspired conversations over chocolate milk during snack time?

I walked over to Esther.

"You don't remember, do you?" I smiled and asked her.

"Remember what?" she asked.

"You and me? Kindergarten? Mrs. Davies' class?"

She looked at me blankly.

I couldn't believe it. She had completely forgotten me.

Gone. I had been completely wiped from somebody's memory. Wow.

"Obviously, you made a great impression when you were five," one of my friends later told me.

Unbelievable. The awkwardness of those ten years we went without speaking to each other was *all in my head.*

So, Billy, if indeed you do kind of like my daughter, the chances are regrettably slim that she will remember you when you're a little older. It's okay. It happens.

By the way, I didn't tell you the whole story about that night at Wendy's.

"I think Billy wants to marry me," Maddie said. But then she added, "But he doesn't like kissing."

I heaved a big sigh. I'm in for a long ride.

Mrs. Dunfield

One of my dearest friends, Mrs. Dunfield, passed away during the summer of 1997.

I frequently think of Mrs. Dunfield, especially when I look at my daughter and hope that she'll have someone like her in her life.

Mrs. Dunfield lived next door to me while I was growing up. Our houses on Shaw Street were so close we could hear the television shows we each watched while our windows were open on summer evenings.

Well, come to think of it, we could hear *her* TV shows. She had the volume turned up because she couldn't hear well.

My family and I never minded, of course. These days, people need their privacy and define their success by how much space exists between them and their neighbors. Back then, however, we seemed to welcome, or accept, such neighborly proximity. My family especially liked it when Mrs. Dunfield put a Christmas candle in her living room window that was hardly ten feet away from ours. She did it for my sister and me.

In a way, Mrs. Mildred Dunfield was my first friend. She was there in the beginning, before school started, before my best friend moved into the neighborhood, before I was old enough to cross the street and meet the Bemises up the hill. She and her husband, Harry, would invite me over for sticks of rhubarb that they'd grow in their garden and I'd dip into bowls of sugar. We'd play games and watch television, and they'd let me read the comics in their issues of "Grit" magazine.

Mr. Dunfield passed away in the spring of 1985. On the afternoon he died, Mrs. Dunfield came to our house to break the news. When I walked into the kitchen to meet her, she was giving my father a sad hug.

I think she was the one who reached out for the embrace. She was, by nature, quite formal and stoic, so my father probably respected her reserve and initially held back to take her cue instead.

The hug surprised my father. Mrs. Dunfield used to yell at him something fierce when he was a kid, when he and his friends would steal apples from the tree in her backyard.

In the years that followed, however, Mrs. Dunfield softened, and I proved particularly blessed because she bestowed most of this new warmth toward me. I was a busy teenager, but I found time occasionally to watch "Wheel of Fortune" with her or stop by and introduce her to my girlfriends.

She fascinated me. She was born in Sanford on December 20, 1900, and she had lived in that white house on Shaw Street since she was eight years old. I came into the world decades later, in 1972. Growing up, I'd listen to her talk for hours about the dusty, unpaved roads of my neighborhood and the nearby empty lots where she played before houses and businesses were built there.

We even stayed in touch after I graduated from high school and left Sanford to attend college. I wrote her letters. She'd write poems - - little ditties, she'd call them - - and send them my way. They'd be perfectly paced rhymes, typed carefully in single spaces on her old typewriter. She usually wrote poems about me, the boy next door who became a man and ventured out into the world to explore its possibilities.

On the day I graduated from college, I stopped by her place to see her on the way back to Sanford from Massachusetts. She was living at an assisted-care facility out of town at the time. I got out of the car and put my cap and gown back on before I went inside to see her.

She returned to Sanford a few months later, but she did not live much longer. She stayed at a rest home on the east side of town, and you could just tell she had never quite adapted to life away from Shaw Street.

In June 1997, she took a turn for the worse and spent her final days at the Newton Center at Goodall Hospital. I visited her frequently, and when she stopped talking and started laboring for each breath I looked into her fading, opaque eyes and knew the time had come to say goodbye.

One month later, on a warm July evening, I packed up my car with everything I owned, bade farewell to my family, and headed down to Massachusetts to start a new life. While I was excited by the opportunities before me, I felt pensive that evening, so I took the quiet back roads out of town. I stopped at Oakdale Cemetery on Twombley Road and spent a few moments at Mrs. Dunfield's grave. Once more, I said goodbye.

Five years later, Valerie and I were married and expecting our first child. We were living in a small apartment outside of Boston at the time, and we didn't really know anybody in the community.

In this remote environment, in which Valerie and I knew few people and had no roots, I worried about what our child's quality of life would be like. To me, quality of life is defined by those who surround us; basically, I wondered if Valerie and I would live in a tight-knit neighborhood and Madeline would have a Mrs. Dunfield of her own.

It seems she might. Valerie, Maddie and I moved back to Sanford two years ago, and we lucked out with our neighbors. We really like them and, best of all, they really like Maddie.

The family next door opens up their pool to her, and it's there that Maddie's learning to swim and cooling off in this summer heat.

The couple across the street invites Maddie over to help them plant their flower garden. They even helped us build the new gym set she got for her birthday. From their living room window, they watch Maddie grow, as she pedals cautiously on her new bike, swings her bat at softballs, and draws with chalk on our driveway.

Our neighbors are nowhere near Mrs. Dunfield's age. One day, though, they will be, and I hope between now and then Maddie listens to their stories, cherishes their neighborliness, and develops an appreciation for and a connection with the generations that arrived before her.

Vaca-Shawns and Val-Cations

I'm going on vacation. Valerie, Maddie and I are heading to Harrison, Maine, where we'll be renting a cottage on Crystal Lake with my Cousin Missy, her husband Chris, and their son Graydon.

I'm not sure yet if this trip will be a "val-cation" or a "vaca-shawn." My wife and I are polar opposites when it comes to taking vacations.

Valerie likes vacations in which you pick one spot, go there, and then do nothing. Nada. Zilch. Squat. You sleep in. You bring a book. You lounge by the pool or on the beach, and that's it. The purpose of the trip is to take a breath and rest, two things you don't get to do at home when you're working a full-time job and raising a child.

In our house, that's what you call a "Val-cation."

I like vacations in which you pack as much into your time away as possible. You drive as many miles, see as many sights, enjoy as many amusements, eat in as many restaurants, and do, do, do as many things as you can.

Sleep in? Rest? You do those things when you get home. Vacations are for exploring, living it up, seeing how others live.

You're away from home, hundreds or thousands of miles from the same old sights that comprise your daily existence. Why experience it all completely from a single poolside?

In 2002, Valerie and I took a five-day trip in which we visited Washington, D.C., Philadelphia and New York City. Our day in The Big Apple ran a curious gamut of emotional extremes; we began it at Ground Zero, paying our respects to those who died on September 11, and ended it at a taping of David Letterman's TV show.

That trip's an example of a "vaca-shawn."

"Vaca-shawns" are for people who can't sit still. "Val-cations" are for people who don't get to sit still at home.

As I get older, I admit I can see the appeal of "val-cations." Growing up, my family took only one such trip. I was ten at the time. We stayed a whole week at my father's coworker's cottage on Wilson Lake in Acton, about ten miles from home. Mom had to work that week, so in the morning she'd leave in our family's one car, and Dad would be stuck with my sister and me.

Dad can't stay in one place with nothing to do, so he went nuts on Wilson Lake that summer. Think of Jack Nicholson in "The Shining," but imagine a small A-frame cottage, not a huge, stately inn. Oh, and leave out all that snow. It was July.

We Sullivans never took relaxing getaways. We made hyper sprints around the country, mixing amusements with American history. If we spent one day riding rollercoasters at Busch Gardens, then we spent another touring colonial

Williamsburg. If we spent one afternoon eating too much chocolate at Hershey Park, then we spent another visiting the battlefields of Gettysburg.

Strangely, though, my family never reminisces about the pure joys and good fortune of the trips we took. These days, we never smile peacefully and say, "Ah, remember that time when we stood shoulder to shoulder as a family and gazed into the awesome wonder of the Grand Canyon?"

Instead, we look back and laugh at moments that play like bad outtakes from the "National Lampoon's Vacation" movies. And we usually end up giving my Dad a rough time because he always filled the Chevy Chase role so expertly.

One time, in 1980, my family visited one of those zoos in Canada where you drive around in your car and the animals come up and greet you. Dad fed a camel that approached our car. He tossed the box of animal food on the floor of the passenger's side when he thought the camel had eaten enough.

Alas, the camel was still hungry. Aren't these the guys who can go days in the dessert without eating or drinking?

The sloppy, foaming beast stuck its head as far into the front seat of our car as it could. It lurched past my father and pinned him to his seat. My sister, who had been sitting in front with Dad, retreated and crouched on the floor of the passenger's side in sheer terror. Kelly hadn't done herself any favors because the box of food the camel wanted was there on the floor with her.

Think of "Cujo," but with a camel. And yes, I'm aware this makes my second reference to a Stephen King horror novel when discussing my family's vacations.

Dad screamed at the camel and wrestled it with all his might. We couldn't hear him too well because his mouth was filled with camel fur. Determined to eat something, the camel bit into our map of Canada. It took a battle of wills, but Dad eventually pried the map from the camel's oversized, slobbery teeth and pushed its head out of our car. He slammed on the gas to get away. He almost ran over a monkey in the road.

Later that day, Dad needed that map when we were stuck and completely lost in rush-hour traffic in the middle of French-speaking Montreal. As Dad kept one twitching eye on the traffic, he watched as Mom unfolded the map and searched frantically for any indication of where we might be.

We were out of luck. The camel had eaten the part of the map we needed. We were on our own. Rising to the occasion of our surroundings, Dad swore in two languages that day.

But that's the good stuff, no? Isn't that why we take family vacations?

We don't take 'em so we can say we've seen George Washington's estate at Mount Vernon, conquered Space Mountain at Disney World, or climbed to the top of the Empire State Building.

We take family vacations so we can have stories that last forever. We did a lot when my family took that trip to Canada, but the memory I cherish most from that trip is of Dad battling that camel.

My sister and I went swimming in the hotel's pool later that evening. There were low-hanging electrical wires passing over the water, and lightning was zapping the sky in the distance, but we jumped into the pool anyway. My parents were too exhausted to care.

Time for a Change

Mom's calling it a career.

She made the decision last week as she drove to work and noticed that the leaves were beginning to change. She didn't want another autumn to escape her. Fall has always been my mother's favorite time of the year.

She reported to work and gave her two weeks' notice. When she got home that afternoon, she quickly shared the news.

Dad lit right up when she told him. He had been pulling for her to make this decision. He smiled and gave her a hug.

I was surprised when I answered the phone at a little before ten that night and heard Mom on the other end of the line. She's usually long gone at that hour; once she has watched that morning's "Regis" and that afternoon's "All My Children" after dinner, she tends to conk out on the couch after a busy day at work.

"I gave my two weeks' notice," Mom told me.

"Really?" I asked, surprised, for I didn't know what that meant. Had she found another job?

She told me about her drive to work that morning. The leaves were starting to show a little bit of color, she explained, and she realized that she did not want to miss the season. When she started talking about her hopes of traveling with Dad in the weeks to come, the reason for her retirement came into focus. Dad's slowing down, and this fall may be the final one ALS grants him to enjoy with ease.

"Well, I think that's great, Mom," I said. "Good for you. You've worked hard for this day."

"Maybe I'll just take the rest of the year off," she said, never one to spoil herself. "Maybe come the new year I'll find a job and work two days a week."

"No, dear," my father objected in the background. "You're retired. That's it."

She must agree. A couple of days later, she wasn't talking about working two days a week. Instead, she was talking about taking a yoga class twice a week.

I remember when Mom first went back to work. She has always said it was one of the worst days of her life because she started it by dropping off my sister and me at the babysitter's house. She had really been proud that she stayed home with me when I was a baby, and she felt badly that she could not do the same for my younger sister. Our family needed the money.

And Mom didn't have a car back then, either. She bought her first wheels many years later, right when her son turned sixteen and got his license and started begging for her car keys. Each morning, when Kelly and I were young, Mom would walk us from our home on Shaw Street to our babysitter's house at the top of Lebanon Street. Then she'd double-back and walk some more to her job at the bank on Main Street. That's a lot of running around - - more than a mile, for sure.

Over the years, Mom worked at banks and credit unions and businesses where counseling and health-care services were offered.

One afternoon, when I was seven, my school bus broke down in front of the bank on Main Street where Mom worked. Another bus arrived to pick us up. As my classmates and I exited the broken-down bus and climbed aboard the working one, I slipped out of line and sneaked into Mom's bank. Nearly 30 years later, Mom says she can still see the top of my head appear over the teller's counter where she sat; I had approached her window and stood on my tiptoes to get her attention. She called my grandmother across town and told her not to expect me to get off the bus that day.

That summer, my friends and I would wait in front of Mom's bank for the bus to come take us to camp at Holdsworth Park in Springvale. Mom always made a point to appear in the bank's bay window to wave hello.

These are the memories, the vivid images, really, that occur to me as I contemplate my mother getting older and retiring. I'm sure Mom, like so many mothers, looked at me during those times and ached to be home for my sister and me. She can rest assured that I got quite a kick out of seeing her at the bank those times.

Well done, Mom. You helped put food on our table, stack presents under our Christmas tree, and send my sister and me to college.

Now's your time. Enjoy the foliage.

Nipping At My 'Knows'

"Daddy, what's all that white stuff on the ground?" Madeline asked me as I backed out of our driveway for our morning trip to preschool.

"That's frost, sweetie," I answered. "Looks like Jack Frost got a lot of work done last night."

"Who's Jack Frost?" Maddie asked.

I had thought Maddie already knew about Jack Frost. She sure knows about the other guys. Santa Claus? Check. The Easter Bunny? Check. The Tooth Fairy? Check that twice; she lost her first two teeth this past summer.

The Great Pumpkin? Skip that one. Last week, Maddie watched "It's the Great Pumpkin, Charlie Brown" on TV and commented that Linus was wasting his time out there in the pumpkin patch.

But Jack Frost? I thought Maddie had already heard of him. After all, she's heading into her fifth winter.

"Jack Frost is the guy that comes around and sprinkles frost all over the place when the nights start getting cold," I explained.

I love that my daughter's inquisitive, but sometimes I get stumped by her questions and come close to revealing to her just how little I know about some things. Like the legend of Jack Frost, for example.

Once in a while, after I answer one of Maddie's questions, I admit it'd be nice if she just skipped the Socratic Method and simply said, "Oh." I'm not betting my paycheck on it happening any time soon.

"How does Jack Frost carry around all of that frost?" Maddie asked as we pulled onto Main Street.

"Well, um . . ."

"Does he have a bucket?"

"He does," I replied, grateful for the assist. "A big one."

We drove a bit in silence, so I figured the issue had passed.

"Does Jack Frost only put frost on the ground?" she asked two minutes later.

"He also puts it on the plants and flowers and trees too," I said. "And cars. Dad really gets annoyed when he puts frost on the car in the morning, and he has to scrape it off. Dad just likes to get in the car and *go*."

At this moment, I wondered when I was going to stop referring to myself in the third person when talking with my daughter. She turns five in April. Do any of you more experienced parents out there know the cut-off age on this subject? You're going to tell me it's supposed to be three, aren't you?

We drove another mile in silence. We turned onto the hill that takes us to Maddie's preschool.

"Hmmm," Maddie observed. "There's a car right there with frost on it."

I looked at the car parked on the right side of the road. Frost covered the vehicle from front to back and glistened in the morning sun.

"Yup," I said. "Jack Frost's a busy guy."

"So, Daddy, does Jack Frost just cover our town in frost, or does he do it other places too?"

I took a moment with this one.

"Well, he covers wherever it's cold," I explained. "He usually stays up here, in the north. He doesn't go down south too much because it's too warm down there."

Mercifully, we finally arrived at Maddie's preschool. I had been enjoying our conversation, but I was also running out of answers.

I helped Maddie hang up her coat and stuff her backpack into her cubby, and then I kissed her goodbye and headed to work. As I drove I wondered if my tall tales about Jack Frost were going to come back and nip me in the nose.

I could imagine Maddie at kindergarten next year.

"Today, we're going to learn about frost," her teacher will say. "Frost is a covering of minute ice crystals formed on a cold surface from atmospheric vapor."

In my imagination, the Merriam-Webster Dictionary is always handy.

Anyway, Maddie will raise her hand and say, "My Dad said frost is the magic stuff Jack Frost carries around in a big pail and spreads everywhere when it's cold at night."

Maddie's classmates and the teacher will laugh, and then she'll be known as "that Jack Frost kid" during the following 12 years she spends in the school system.

I suppose I could have just told Maddie that Jack Frost is a figurative term. After all, there's really nothing to gain by believing in the guy. Santa brings presents, the Easter Bunny brings candy, and the Tooth Fairy brings big bucks. Jack Frost just kills your plants and makes you curse winter as you scrape your windshield.

I like my daughter's imagination, though. I like her capacity for faith and belief.

Later, I hopped online and checked out the history of Jack Frost on Wikipedia, the website where billions of people can have a say in what's true. According to Wikipedia, Jack Frost is an "elfish creature who personifies crisp, cold, winter weather."

Well, I could have told you that.

Wikipedia also says that "those who believe in Viking folklore roots state that the English derived the name Jack Frost from the Norse character names Jokul and Frosti. Another theory is that he is a much more recent import into Anglo-Saxon culture from a Russian fairy tale. In the Finnish epos Kalevala Canto number 30, translated from Finnish into English by Keith Bosley, Jack Frost is the son of Blast, 'Pakkanen Puhurin Poika.'

Other tales in Russia represent frost as Father Frost, a smith who binds water and earth together with heavy chains. In Germany, however, it is an old woman who causes it to snow by shaking white feathers out of her bed."

Oh.

Lemonade

My parents sat in their living room and discussed how they wanted their new wheelchair ramp to look.

"What about a lattice on the sides?" my mother asked.

"No," my father answered. "I don't like lattice."

Depressed by the conversation, I did my best to take part.

"Aw, come on, Dad," I said. "Lattice isn't bad. Just throw some tomatoes, cucumbers and ranch dressing on it, and you'll have a salad."

Most of the time, amyotrophic lateral sclerosis, or ALS, strikes its victims quickly, destroying their motor neurons, stripping their muscles and leaving them paralyzed with ruthless efficiency.

Then there are others, like my father, for whom ALS takes its time, methodically shutting down their bodies with a cruel deliberateness that's like the steady drips of water torture. Concessions are made, one after the other, for years.

First there's the leg brace to help steady the step. Then there's the brace for the other leg.

The handicap license plate is next, literally bringing you to your knees as you stoop down to attach it to your car.

The cane is next. At first you buy a fancy one of elaborately carved wood, in the hopes that people will ask you where you found that cane instead of why you need it. Then the cane breaks, and you settle for an old-fashioned, straightforward one, with plain wood and the curved handle at the top.

The breathing device follows. You strap it over your face and it helps you breathe while you sleep at night. Keeps your poor spouse awake, though.

Then comes the walker. You use it when you're out of town. In the meantime, you work up the courage to appear with it around your family, friends and acquaintances in your hometown.

Eventually, there's the wheelchair. But first you need the ramp to get into your own home.

I started with the "lattice" remark up at the top not to make light of a dark situation or impress you with a silly quip - - we Sullivans proudly embrace bad puns as witticisms - - but rather to show you that humor helps you through.

The humor represents progress. There was no laughter for months after Dad was diagnosed with ALS in December 2004.

Case in point: In November of 2005, Dad's high school classmates and friends spent a Saturday helping our family build a new, handicapped-accessible bathroom on the first floor of my parents' home. As they tore down the kitchen wall, I caught glimpses of my childhood home's past. I saw faded and dusty wallpaper and paint that previous owners had chosen over the past century to make the house homey.

My slight fascination with these secret layers passed quickly. I was too preoccupied with the serious reasons why my parents were overhauling their home of 34 years. It was a rough day.

Now, a little more than two years later, my childhood home has changed again. Over the years, my parents have done a nice job keeping up the outside appearance of their house, but they've done very little to alter it. Fifteen years ago, they planted a tree on the side, but that's about it.

Now there's a long, wide, handicapped-accessible ramp running up the side of the house.

Guess what, though? We all like it.

In addition to humor, there are other perspectives and attitudes that help cope with life and maybe even squeeze some lemonade out of the proverbial lemon.

It's a fine-looking ramp. The carpenter who built it did a good job. It even has a bit of a deck up at the top; Dad's excited because there's enough space there for him to fit a small grill and cook this summer. Mom's glad that she's able to hang her flower box from the ramp.

My daughter, Maddie, likes the ramp, too. She said she's looking forward to pushing her doll up and down it in a stroller this spring.

As for me, the son who reveres his father, I've accepted the ramp's necessity with much better ease and practicality than I felt and showed that day we built that new bathroom two years ago. Plus, there's enough room at the top to set up a few chairs this summer for my family and I to sit and enjoy a few glasses of iced tea.

Or lemonade.

Worldview

The world is an evil place, the talk show host stated on the radio the other day.

The United States must remain vigilant, he added, because countries such as Iran and North Korea and terrorists strive to do us harm.

The caller tried to argue an opposing view, but the talk show host darkly reiterated his point that Americans cannot retreat and risk being caught off guard. The world is an evil, evil place, he repeated.

"Well, that's not true," said someone who begged to differ.

The words came from behind me. My daughter, who had been sitting quietly in the back seat of our car, evidently had been listening to the program. I had just picked her up from day care and we were half way home at the time.

"What's not true?" I responded, not believing at first that my four-year-old had been following a geopolitical discussion.

"It's not true what the man said on the radio," Madeline answered. "The world is not an evil place."

Speechless, I looked at Maddie in my rearview mirror. She stared peacefully out the window as we circled the rotary down by Number One Pond. The little pistol had stunned me, and had impressed me, on at least three levels.

One, I had always figured that Maddie tuned out the blowhards I play on the radio while I drive her home after preschool in the afternoon. That's what I did when my father strained to hear WBZ through the static out of Boston when I was a child.

Two, I appreciated that Maddie had not taken the talk show host's word as gospel. She had thought for herself.

And three, Maddie suggested her view of the world around her. I'd like to think most kids believe the world is a good place, but sadly I know some have the emotional, physical and psychological scars to feel otherwise. As a parent, Maddie's remark reassured me.

I did not pursue the conversation with Maddie. I did change the radio station, though. Now that I knew my daughter was listening, I had no desire to acquaint her with the current volatile state of the post-September 11 world in which we adults live.

I hope Maddie never outgrows her belief that the world is fundamentally good, not predominantly evil. The key is to look within and around ourselves whenever evil does rear its ugly head in this world.

One day, a history teacher will explain to Maddie and her peers that a slight man with a peculiar mustache seized power and killed six million innocent men, women and children because he hated them.

One day, perhaps on a cool September morning, Maddie will see old footage on TV of jets crashing into skyscrapers, exploding into flames and igniting a war without end.

Those are two chapters of our world history that I will not be able to keep from Maddie when she gets older. When the appropriate time comes, she must know about such events, particularly the darkest chapters that reshaped the world and changed the course of the human race. Studying such history informs us and helps us do our part to avoid repeating it.

Evil *does* exist. It is not most effectively confronted and defeated, however, by taking the view that the world itself is evil.

That's why Maddie impressed me when she refuted the talk show host's assertion. She's right. The world *is* good. Ordinary people collectively make it so when they live their lives quietly and focus on their families and their communities. Extraordinary people make it so when they rise to levels of volunteerism and leadership - - in their hometown, in their state, in their country, in the world - - and meet their responsibilities with selflessness, honesty, and decency.

A single evil person can park a truck packed with explosives next to a building in Oklahoma City and walk away. Millions, however, will respond by offering condolences, listening to those who need support, praying, giving blood and finding many other ways to help heal the pain.

It's there in the math. Evil exists, but it's outnumbered.

My wife Valerie and I celebrated our wedding anniversary on Wednesday. Nine years ago, at our reception, we danced to Louis Armstrong's "What a Wonderful World." The song proved a fitting choice because both my wife and I agree that when you add everything up, it *is* a wonderful world.

I'm glad my daughter agrees. Hopefully, she always will.

Not Hard To Swallow

My daughter recently lost a tooth.

I mean that literally. We can't find it.

She must have swallowed it. Maddie and I were visiting my parents the other day and my father offered her a bite of his bagel. Biting into it was not a problem. Taking a bite out of it was a whole different story.

Dad held on one side of the bagel while Maddie clenched down on the other with her teeth. Both tugged in opposing directions. It was one tough bagel.

"Dad, she's got a loose tooth," I warned as Maddie began to rock back on her heels.

Not anymore. Maddie tore off a chunk of the bagel, smearing the sides of her mouth with cream cheese. As she chewed, I noticed her top tooth was missing. When she swallowed, I had a hunch where it went.

Worry not. The Tooth Fairy still stopped by the house that night and slipped some money under Maddie's pillow. She left a dollar. That's considerably less than Maddie got the last time, but that's what happens when the Tooth Fairy forgets to stop at an ATM on the way home.

Fortunately, Maddie didn't notice. She recognizes bills not by their value but by the faces on them. That's George Bush on the one-dollar bill, she'll say, and I'll smile and tell her she's got the wrong George W. She knows Abraham Lincoln's on the five-spot because "he's the one who freed the slaves."

Maddie seemed pleased by her windfall. Somehow, she knew she had cleared more cash than her Old Man did back when he was a kid losing teeth by the mouthful.

"Daddy, did the Tooth Fairy just bring you coins when you were a kid?" she asked me.

I told her, yes, she did. Then we had a long conversation about inflation.

Like most four-year-olds, Maddie usually has a lot of questions. Last fall, she asked me how Jack Frost manages to spread all of those white crystals on our lawns, streets, cars and trees, all in one night. She stumped me with that one. She answered her own question and supposed he carries all of that frost around in a big pail. That's a much simpler answer than I was going to give her. I was going to tell her Jack Frost uses a crop duster, which would have only prompted even more questions, such as, "Daddy, what's a crop duster?"

To date, that bills-versus-coins question is the only one Maddie has asked me about the Tooth Fairy. She takes the Tooth Fairy at the same face value that she does Santa Claus and the Easter Bunny. Apparently, she knows a good thing when she sees it and quits while she's ahead. Magical childhood icons that sneak into your house at night and bring you money, Christmas gifts, and chocolate bunnies are okay in her book. Ones that fly around at night and dump ice on Daddy's windshield, however, are a cause for inquiry.

Maddie has lost three teeth so far, two on the bottom and one on the top, all of them in front. You couldn't carve a jack-o-lantern with a cuter smile.

I'm waiting for her to ask me what the Tooth Fairy does with all of those teeth. My wife and I have not come up with an answer for that one.

This time, of course, Maddie didn't have to ask because she ate her tooth - - with a bagel and cream cheese on the side, no less.

Memory and Memories

My family and I had just about let Cinco de Mayo pass unnoticed on Monday. We had fish for dinner, not tacos, and Valerie and I did not drink margaritas after Maddie went to bed.

If it were not for my mother, Monday would have simply been May 5 in the Sullivan household. How boring.

Mom called, however, and left a simple, quick message on our answering machine for her 5-year-old granddaughter.

"Hi, Maddie, it's Mem," Mom said. "Just wanted to call and wish you a happy Cinco de Mayo."

Then there was a beep, and that was it.

When I listened to the message I realized it exemplified what I like best about my mother. She believes almost everything is a cause for celebration, or at the very least a moment worth noting.

Every April 10, I can be certain that Mom will call and remind me it's the day on which I was supposed to be born.

Back on March 27, 1972, Mom's doctor told her that she needed to give birth to me *right away* to avert a major health crisis. Mom resisted. She wanted to take me all the way to my due date in two weeks.

Dad did not have any more luck than the doctor. Mom wouldn't listen to him, either. So he made a final, last-ditch effort to convince Mom to heed the doctor's warning and have me earlier than expected.

He bought Mom a life-size Easter Bunny. That Sunday would be Easter.

Mom heard a knock on the front door. When she went to answer it, she saw the Easter Bunny's giant, stuffed face crammed into the window.

"*Now* will you go have the baby?" Dad pleaded when Mom opened the door.

The bunny worked. Against Mom's wishes to carry her firstborn to term, I was born on Tuesday, March 28. I was healthy and home by Good Friday.

This year I got a call on February 29. Mom wanted to know if Valerie, Maddie and I wanted to go out for pizza to celebrate Leap Year. This year, February 29 fell on a Friday, a day on which nine times out of ten the three of us are most likely to go out to dinner with my parents, anyway. So we went. And Mom raised her glass of Coke and toasted Leap Year.

You only get to do that once every four years, you know.

Mom remembers the day when Dad proposed to her in 1971.

She also remembers the day when she walked a mile from her home on Shaw Street to where her father worked at a store near Goodall Hospital. October 22, 1954. She would turn five years old the next day. She embarked on that long trek, without telling her mother, my Memere, who never would have let her go, because Pepere had forgotten to kiss her goodbye that morning and she wanted to collect on that debt.

Every year Mom marks these occasions, sometimes merely mentioning them, other times telling the stories all over again.

I confess: When I was younger, I would roll my eyes. The older I get, though, the more I realize Mom has passed her sharp recall for certain dates and times and her deep appreciation for them on to me.

The knack comes in handy when I write these columns or friends have birthdays right around the corner or people at the newspaper office ask me when such-and-such took place. It doesn't matter if it was 20 minutes ago or 20 years ago. I can almost always pin down the date.

Occasionally, it's a curse. During hard times, such a razor-sharp memory can spring a nostalgic pull that yanks you backward, to periods in your life you believe were simpler, easier, and more secure. Ultimately, though, it is a blessing, for there are the usual holidays we all celebrate, and then there are the ones we make for ourselves.

For Mom, it's April 10. The day Dad popped the big question in 1971. The October morning she walked a mile to get that kiss goodbye from her father. Every year, she pays tribute to these dates.

It's about memory, yes, but it's about memories too. They're two separate things. The former is something you have. The latter are things you make, hold close and treasure.

Mom taught me that.

Americana Under the Stars

My wife and daughter and I caught a movie at the drive-in on Saturday night. If you ask me, there's no better way to kick off the summer.

We saw a new animated feature, the one about the panda bear that becomes a martial arts warrior. We left shortly after the second feature began. Valerie and I had already seen "Indiana Jones and the Kingdom of the Crystal Skull," and we knew better than to stick around and let 5-year-old Maddie see the part when thousands of oversized ants swarm one of the bad guys and haul him away.

Every summer I try to make it to the drive-in. I get disappointed if Labor Day rolls around and I've missed the chance to see a movie under the stars. I've had a poor track record these past few years. When Valerie, Maddie and I took in Saturday's show at the Saco Drive-in, it had been since 2003 that we'd been there. I remember sitting in the driver's seat then and watching one of that summer's endless sequels through the windshield. Valerie sat comfortably next to me in the passenger's seat and Maddie, just a few months old, rested her pudgy baby cheek on my shoulder and slept.

Last weekend we parked in the front row and set up three lawn chairs in front of our car. Before the show started, Maddie got her hula hoop out of the car and gave it a spin on the lawn in front of the screen. Other kids played around her.

Valerie held down the fort while I went to the fast food takeout in the back of the lot. I loaded a cardboard tray with hot dogs, cheeseburgers and fries and picked up one soda for the three of us to share. All of that naughty food is required dining when you go to the drive-in.

By chance, we bumped into my friend Joyce, whom I had not seen in years. She and her husband had decided on Saturday night to make a 50-mile trek from their home in New Hampshire to Saco to catch the show. They arrived in a long, olive-green van plastered with political bumper stickers from yesteryear. Drive-ins recall another era in Americana, so there was something fitting about that "Carter '76" decal plastered beneath the van's rear window.

Joyce and her husband stopped by our car for a visit before "Kung Fu Panda" started.

"We all used to come here in high school," Joyce said.

"It looks like they haven't fixed the screen since then," I joked, looking up at the chips, cracks and lines on the big white wall.

"It's a vintage screen," Joyce remarked, and we both nodded as though agreeing the screen looked as it should.

Yeah, my friends and I caught a handful of flicks at the drive-in back in the late 1980s, right up through that summer of 1990 before we all left for college that fall. Sometimes we'd all pile into one car to keep down the expenses; it could not have cost more than $8 per vehicle back then. Other times, we set up lawn chairs in the back of a friend's truck.

Our nights out at the movies were hardly ever without incident. One time, I parked in the front row, after the movie had started, when I realized the pole there did not have a detachable speaker to hang in our window. I put my car in reverse and tried to back out of the space, but I couldn't budge. I had unwittingly parked on a small mound and stuck my car in place.

So a couple of my friends got out and went to the front of the car and pushed. I stretched my right arm across the top of the front seat, craned my neck around and tried to ease back into the lane behind me.

All of a sudden the lot erupted into an angry chorus of bleating horns.

"What's their problem?" I asked my girlfriend. "We're not making much noise, and I'm trying to move as fast as I can."

"Shawn, turn around," she said and gestured beyond the windshield.

Die Hard 2 had virtually disappeared from the screen. My high-beams were the reason. Apparently, I elbowed the high-beam lever when I turned to look out the rear window.

I kept my high-beams off this past Saturday night. In fact, I didn't turn my headlights on at all as I started up our car, crept out of our space, and turned right in front of the other front-row vehicles and headed toward the exit. I could only imagine the uprising if I had flicked on my lights and Harrison Ford vanished from the screen.

Valerie, Maddie and I never sat in those lawn chairs, by the way. We watched the movie inside our car, so that we could better hear our radio, which was set at 88.1 for the duration of the feature. A few times, though, I sneaked out of the car and sat in one of the chairs, just to remove the filter of our windshield and see the movie in a sharper contrast. More than anything, though, I wanted to see the stars and feel the night's cool breeze.

Drive-ins are a dying breed in America. The ones that remain seem to exist solely for nostalgic purposes, as though their owners are standing up to the proliferation of multiplexes with digital projection on IMAX screens in cinemas with stadium seating. *"No,"* drive-ins seem to say. *"This* is the way it's supposed to be."

Sometimes I drive by a certain development on Main Street and wish the old Sanford Drive-in was still there. I loved movies as a child, and I envied those who lived across the street from that drive-in and could see the big screen from their front porches. They got a free movie, every night, during the summertime. It hardly mattered to me that they probably could not hear the movies over the din of passing cars on Main Street.

Back in the summer of 1975, when I was three, my parents took my newborn sister and me to see "Bambi" at that drive-in. At one point, Dad took me out of the car and propped me up on the hood. To this day, in my mind's eye, I can still see the bright orange flames of the movie's infamous forest fire scene on the screen. I remember Dad standing by, very close to me. Was he making sure I was safe and secure up on the hood? Or had I been scared by that legendary, frightening scene?

That Sanford drive-in is long gone, but, thankfully, the Saco Drive-in seems like it's doing well and will be around for years to come. On Saturday night I took stock of the sights and sounds around me. Some families sat around bright candles that flickered and kept the bugs away. Others sat in folding chairs, wrapped in blankets. A few lounged on the open beds of their pickup trucks.

A bluish beam of light shot across the lot from the projection booth in back to the big screen in front. The noises of the movie, all dialogue and soundtrack, echoed faintly from cars and speakers set up near the takeout joint.

Summer's here. The drive-in's open.

This is the way it's supposed to be.

My Way

"You don't hold your fork the same way as everyone else," Valerie smiled and told me as we ate dinner the other night.

"What do you mean?" I asked and looked down at my fork.

"Most people hold their forks this way," she said, holding her fork with its tines pointing upward. "You hold yours this way," she added, turning her fork upside down.

I just sat there and chewed my food. Shouldn't talk with your mouth full, you know.

"And then you eat this way," she said, poking a piece of meat with her downturned fork and raising it to her mouth a certain way that even I can't describe.

Valerie and I have been married 10 years and this is the first time she has noticed how I apparently tend to eat. Just when I thought she knew me. That's okay. I've been hanging out with myself my whole life and I've never noticed that I use a fork in my own little way.

I guess I'll just have to add my fork technique to the list of quirky things I've done my own way since childhood.

Take my shoes, for example. Well, don't *really* take them. I need them to walk around. Take the way I tie them, is what I mean.

One of the older girls who lived around the corner tried to teach me how to tie my shoes when I was five or six years old. I'm not sure if she taught me the proper way, or the universally practiced way, or if she taught me the way I've been doing it for the past 30 years. All I know is that in a bid to impress her I kept practicing until I got the hang of tying my own Keds. I remember being at the babysitter's house and working doggedly to learn to tie my shoes when I should have been sleeping during nap time.

Here's what I do: I cross the laces once to lock them together. Then I make two loops and tie them together. Done. None of this fancy stuff in which you make one loop, wrap the second lace around it and feed it through to make a second loop. Or whatever it is the rest of you do.

For the record, I tie my ties the right way.

Right way. I just looked at those two words in the sentence above and snorted. Who gets to say what the right way is for tying our shoes or holding a fork?

Or typing? Who decided we have to place the tips of our fingers on the keyboard just so? Let me tell you something. See this column? So far I've typed every single letter using only the pointer fingers on my left and right hands. That's right. I'm a hunt-and-pecker.

No, it hasn't taken me five hours to write everything you've read so far. Instead, I type rather lightning-quick, if you ask me. Here's the reason: I've been typing this way since I was six years old. That's when my Uncle Don and Aunt Noreen gave me their old 1950s typewriter and I started writing stories.

I also hold pens and pencils differently. That too is hard to describe. Let's just say all five of my fingers are on the pen while I write. As a result, I press down harder on the paper and cause the sides of the sheet to curl upward. This too I've done my whole life.

There are other things I do my way. Frank Sinatra would have liked me.

I'm not sure what's behind these three-and-a-half decades of going against the grain when it comes to these small-scale techniques and practices that help keep the world from collapsing into anarchy. It's not stubbornness. It's not rebelliousness. It's not even independence.

It's just . . . who knows. It's just the way I do things, despite the efforts of friends and elders who tried to show me the conventional way to do things when I was a kid. My daughter, Madeline, tends to take after me. Even my mother-in-law thinks so.

"I'm sorry, Valerie," my mother-in-law once told her daughter. "Maddie looks like you, but when it comes to her personality, she's a Sullivan the whole way through."

That may be the case, but I think Maddie's going to skip her old man's tendency to do certain things his own way. Take *her* shoes, for example. These days, Maddie is trying to learn how to tie her sneakers. She gets frustrated as she struggles to get it right. When Maddie, Valerie and I recently visited my parents, Maddie sat on their front steps and fidgeted impatiently with her laces. Looking to turn her day around, I sat down next to her. I reached down to my sneakers and untied my laces.

"All right, Maddie," I said. "Let me help you. Watch me tie my shoes and copy what I do."

"No, Dad," she huffed. "I want to learn how to do it *right*."

'Rocky' Steps

When was the last time you did something crazy? You know, something nutty and offbeat?

For me, it was last Sunday.

I ran up a long flight of steps in just a few seconds. I was winded by the time I got to the top, but make no mistake: I did it. Two steps at a time, no less.

Sounds like no big deal, right? Well, here's the crazy part, then: The steps were the ones that Sylvester Stallone climbed at the Philadelphia Museum of Art in "Rocky," the 1976 Best Picture winner about the southpaw who gets a shot at the heavyweight boxing championship of the world. "Rocky" is my favorite movie.

Crazier still: My friend Richard and I left Sanford at 6:30 on Sunday morning and returned shortly after midnight, roughly 18 hours later.

The craziest part: We took this one-day, 800-mile round trip solely to run up those steps. Richard likes the movie too.

For the record, we did throw in a stop at the Liberty Bell and Independence Hall two miles away from the museum. I had seen both during trips to Philly in 1984 and 2002, but Richard had not.

All in all, we were in Philadelphia for a little more than two hours.

Crazy, right? Yes. But we weren't the only ones.

Richard and I embarked on our mission with no illusions. We knew as we headed down to Philadelphia that chances were strong we'd look like a couple of middle-aged fools as we ran up those steps. We just shrugged and figured we could withstand onlookers' ridicule and contempt because we would be eight hours from home.

As it turns out, we fit right in. As we pulled into a parking space at the museum, we saw a handful of college kids at the top step, laughing and leaping up and down, punching their fists into the air, and pulling off a few boxing moves.

During the next half-hour, as many as 50 people or more would scale that steep flight of steps and do the same thing: Raise their fists triumphantly in the air, throw a few fake-punches, and have their picture taken with the city of Philadelphia sprawled out behind them.

Richard and I were among them. We each took turns, racing up those steps, the famous "Rocky" theme song inevitably in our heads.

Did I mention that Richard and I and everybody else did this while a heavy thunderstorm tapered off and lightning still zapped the Philadelphia skyline?

155

Think about this. "Rocky" played at theaters *32 years ago*. Carter was president. The scars of Vietnam were fresh. The United States celebrated its bicentennial. Now, here it is, more than three decades later, and scores of people were imitating a fictional movie character running up the steps of the Philadelphia Museum of Art on a completely random and rainy Sunday afternoon. *Thirty-two* years later.

I'll be straight with you, and don't feel pressured to keep a straight face. What started as a lark turned out to be an all-American experience, complete with meaning, shared with strangers. All walks of life ran up those steps. Young people. Older folks. Families. Couples. There was even a European guy who gave me his camera and asked me to snap his picture. I told him to raise his fists in the air, just like the guy in the movie who started it all.

I have seen better movies than "Rocky," but it's my favorite. The film pretty much embodies my ideas about everything, particularly when it comes to believing in yourself, facing your fears, doing your best with what God gave you, and pursuing the American Dream. Rocky and his future wife, Adrian, even capture my notion of what makes a relationship successful. I thought about such things as I stood, soaked by the rain, on that top step and enjoyed the view of the city where our nation was born.

But don't let such introspection fool you. Sunday's trip was not about such seriousness. It was about taking off and goofing off, traveling far to do something quick. It was about trying to get home by midnight, lying flat on my back in bed, looking at the ceiling and saying, "I went to Philadelphia today." It was about seizing the joy of life and proving I still have such silliness, even craziness, within me.

Common sense, responsibility, practicality and maturity have nothing to do with it. Sometimes you have to check that stuff at the door. Life's short. We all have something personal and fun and offbeat we'd like to do before our time is up.

I've done my thing.

Now it's your turn.

Free-Wheeling Grampy

Valerie handed me a book the other day and asked me if I wanted to keep it. I looked at the cover and shook my head. I had never seen the book before. I had no idea where it came from or why we even owned it to begin with. It was a guide to being a grandparent.

"Do you want to give it to your parents, then?" Valerie asked me.

"What would *they* do with it?" I asked. "They probably *wrote* the thing."

Grandparents like to say their grandchildren can do no wrong. I'm beginning to think my folks think grandparents can do no wrong, either.

Last week, my parents took my daughter to the beach. "We'll have Maddie home by six," they told Valerie.

Six came and went. So did seven.

Valerie and I wondered if we should just go ahead and have dinner. We had been holding out for Maddie. We decided to wait a little longer.

Seven-thirty rolled around.

"Where *are* they?" I asked Valerie. "They're an hour and a half late."

I figured that Maddie and my parents were fine, but a phone call would have assured me. At this point, Valerie and I imagined that my parents had taken Maddie out to dinner, so we went right ahead and made ourselves a salad.

My parents pulled into our driveway at 7:45. Maddie was damp, tired and sandy from her day at the beach.

"What happened to six o'clock?" I asked Dad.

"Well," Dad said, "we didn't *mean* six o'clock. We just meant that you might want to be home by then because we might be back at that time."

That was not my understanding, but I tried to let it go.

"Why didn't you call to say you were staying out later?" I asked.

Dad said he didn't have his phone with him.

"What about Kelly's phone?" I asked. Mom and Dad and Maddie had spent the day with my sister, Kelly, and my nephew, Rowen.

Dad said he hadn't thought of that.

"Did you at least give Maddie some dinner?" I pressed.

She had an ice cream, Dad replied.

"An ice cream," I repeated. "Really hitting all the food groups there, Dad."

Yeah, but she had lunch at three, Dad answered.

"You mean she hadn't had lunch until then?"

159

And on and on it went. When I was growing up, Dad prided himself on providing structure. "Dinner was always on the table at five, and you kids knew you better be there," Dad likes to say when looking back on those days when he ruled the roost. Now he has now turned into a free-wheeling grampy with no concept of time.

Maddie's most fortunate. She has wonderful grandparents on both sides of our family. I look at my parents and hope to be like them when the next generation of Sullivans comes into the world.

Right now, though, *I'm* the parent and it blows my mind that my mother and father are the same two people who raised my sister and me. I'm most annoyed and perplexed when Dad makes a wounded expression or a subversive comment whenever I have to admonish Maddie for getting fresh or deny her something she wants to do.

"Where do you think I got these rules?" I ask Dad at these moments. *"Do you think I just make them up?"*

They're the same rules imposed on me when *I* was a kid. *There's* your answer.

But Dad has a reply to that one. That guy, the one who sent me to my room when I got mouthy and told me I couldn't go see "National Lampoon's Vacation" with my friends, had it all wrong, he says. He didn't know it then, but he knows it now.

I tried to follow his logic. If I know now what he knows now but did not know then, does that mean I should toss all rules out the window and let Maddie run the house?

I had him cornered. "Yes," he replied.

But he really meant "no." I have to become a grandparent first to see things his way. Fair enough.

Maddie's only five years old, but I think my father's preparation for grandparenthood - - his abdication of parental responsibility and slide toward anarchy - - started 18 years ago during my freshman year of college. Mom and Dad had come up to Orono during homecoming weekend to watch the football game with me.

Dad and I sat high on the bleachers. He finished his Pepsi and threw the empty cup onto the ground several feet below.

"So you're just going to start littering now?" I asked him.

"You're 18," he said. "You're in college. My job of setting an example is done."

Alas, my job's just begun. Maddie starts kindergarten in a few weeks. As she gets older, the need will grow even stronger for Valerie and me to set an example and make some tough decisions.

Someday, though, I'll be able to toss that empty Pepsi cup onto the grass. For all you Defenders of Planet Earth out there, I assure you I just mean that metaphorically. Of course, I can't vouch for my daughter, especially if she grows up taking Grampy's cues over mine.

Five Quick Years

Madeline started kindergarten on Wednesday.

Recently I bumped into a former classmate who knew my daughter would be starting school this week. His son and Maddie went to preschool together. He asked me if I was going to feel sad on Maddie's first day of school.

I told him I'd feel happy and proud, sure, but I'd absolutely feel sad too. After all, my little girl's getting older.

"Aw, come on," he laughed and scoffed. "You don't have to pay child care anymore!"

True. With Maddie in school, Valerie and I will now have hundreds of more dollars in our pockets each month. The thing is, the aspects of the past five years I've enjoyed the most have not cost me a penny.

I went for a walk on Sunday night and thought back on one particular moment when Maddie was five or six weeks old. Maybe even younger.

It was the middle of the night and Valerie and I woke up to Maddie crying in her bassinet next to our bed. I rubbed my eyes, sighed and summoned the energy to get on my feet. It was my turn to rock our newborn back to sleep.

I gently picked Maddie up, shuffled to the rocking chair by our bedroom window, and eased onto it. I held Maddie, rocked back and forth, and hummed. The moonlight spilled through the window and over my shoulder, onto Maddie's round, pudgy face. In the distance I could hear the occasional car passing along our street.

I was exhausted. Dead tired. But I didn't mind. I didn't mind at all. I savored the moment because I knew years down the road I'd do anything to experience it again.

That was five years ago. And already I want to go back to that moment once more.

Maybe you know what I'm talking about. Perhaps you have a child starting kindergarten this week too. Or maybe you have older kids and you remember that first day of school quite well.

Such wistfulness, however, is but one emotion in a whole mixed bag of feelings. I'm proud of my daughter and filled with hopes and happiness for her. The years ahead will be exciting and fun.

On the Labor Day weekend before I entered the first grade, my father took me to the playground at Edison School so I could play on the monkey bars and get used to the area. All these years later, I wanted to do the same for Maddie, but it turns out she already knows her new school pretty well - - it's where Valerie works. The truth is, Maddie's the one who could have given me the tour.

Last Thursday, Maddie and I did attend an open house at her school. Valerie was in her own classroom, welcoming her students that afternoon. Maddie and I met her teacher and found her desk and her locker. We even met one of her classmates.

Times have changed, I tell you. Maddie and her fellow kindergarteners get lockers. My classmates and I had "cubby holes."

It's astonishing to me that I have a daughter who's now at an age that I can recall so vividly from my own childhood. I remember quite a bit from my own days in Mrs. Davies' Purple Room at the old Roosevelt School on River Street. Fun times, those.

And now it's Maddie's turn. This week, the Class of 2021 enters the Sanford School System.

Yeah. You read that right. The Class of 2021. Wrap your head around *that*.

When I brought Maddie to school on Wednesday, I hung around a little bit and waited for a few more of her classmates to show up so she wouldn't be alone. After a good number of them had arrived, I quietly said goodbye. Maddie smiled. Me? I did my best.

As I get older I'm increasingly amazed by one of life's most perplexing paradoxes: It's possible to miss someone even when they're standing right next to you.

I get that feeling sometimes when I'm with my father, who's slipping away to ALS. I felt it on Wednesday morning as I stood with Maddie in front of her school. I looked at the beautiful little girl before me and I wondered what happened to that newborn in the moonlight.

But see, I know exactly what has happened.

Maddie's in school now. She belongs a little less to Valerie and me, and a little more to the world.

Bingo!

Life's filled with lessons that make us wise. I recently learned a valuable one: When playing "Bingo" in a room filled with senior citizens, it is best to let one of them win.

My daughter Madeline and I recently visited my grandmother at one of the local assisted-living facilities. We walked into the dining room, where Grammy and her fellow residents were caught up in suspenseful rounds of Bingo.

The woman who volunteers to run the Bingo games each week welcomed us and handed us cards. Maddie and I took seats next to Grammy at a table filled with Bingo cards, stacks of chips and glasses of water, juice and soda.

I smiled. The setting brought back memories. I had played Bingo with Grammy before, years and years ago, when she and Grampy lived at a retirement resort in Fort Meyers, Florida. I was a sophomore in high school at the time and I flew down to Florida during school vacation in February to spend the week with them. Grammy, Grampy and I went to the resort's recreation center one night and played Bingo.

Each time the host of the game called out a certain number, the crowd erupted with an associated famous expression. Let's say, for example, that the host called out "B-54." Everyone in the room would shout, *"Car 54, where are you?"* And so on.

Car 54, where are you? I asked my grandparents. *What's that all about?* An old TV show, they told me.

There was no such noise during the recent Bingo game that Maddie and I played with Grammy. The seniors and Maddie and I sat quietly at our tables, waiting on the edge of our seats for the next number to be called. I placed chips on my card when the volunteer picked my numbers from the drum. I watched over Maddie's shoulder and welled with pride when she located the right letters and numbers on her own card.

After a few rounds, the host of the game declared the "cover all" phase, in which the first contestant to cover all of his or her spots on their Bingo card would win.

I looked at the cards around me. A lot of them were blotted with chips, with maybe a little more than a handful left of spaces to fill. I looked down at my own card. I was coming along but still had a way to go.

The host continued to draw numbers, and I started to gain momentum. Pretty soon my card was filled with colored chips, with a few number-specked white squares remaining.

I admit I felt a thrill. I like to win as much as anyone, but when it comes to games I tend to take a relaxed approach. I know it's all for fun, so I just pick the card or roll the dice or spin the wheel and go with the flow. Unless it's my family's heated annual Thanksgiving Scrabble match or our croquet tournament on the Fourth of July, I set out with no need, hope or expectation of winning.

If, however, I *do* find myself winning, I get excited - - on the inside, never outwardly - - and set my sights on the finish line. It's not a competitive thing. Instead, it's a boyish amazement in which, in spite of myself, I think, *"Hey, look, I'm actually winning this thing!"*

And that is what happened when I played Bingo with Maddie, Grammy and the other senior citizens. One by one, the host called my numbers until, finally, all the spots on my card were covered.

"Bingo!" I declared.

The room went silent. All eyes turned to me.

The game host shot me a tight smile that masked a set jaw. She shook her head, with her eyes stern yet pleading, and I got the message loud and clear.

I was not there to win.

The idea, I guess, is that the game was not *about me*. I'm a young man with decades ahead of me. Plenty of time there to go out and rack up my own victories.

I nodded to convey I understood. Then I sat there feeling like Larry David in another awkward episode of "Curb Your Enthusiasm."

The host continued to call out numbers. I watched Maddie's card closely and prayed she did not win. She came close, but someone else shouted "Bingo!" and won. I heaved a sigh of relief.

So I learned a valuable lesson. When it comes to Bingo cards, you've gotta know when to hold 'em, know when to fold 'em, know when to walk away, know when to run. It's a good thing I didn't insist that I had won, fair and square. I was seriously outnumbered, and practically everyone else in the room was armed with walkers and canes. If the room had erupted into a rumble, I'm not sure I would've gotten out of there alive.

A few weeks later, Maddie and I returned to visit Grammy again. Once more, we found her playing Bingo with her friends. The same host smiled and greeted Maddie and me. And then she proved that she too had learned a lesson.

She gave Maddie a Bingo card, but not me.

'A Thing of Beauty'

One of my favorite people passed away last week.

After two years of struggling with her health, my grandmother now belongs to the heavens.

Grammy was 86 years old. I always knew her age because she was born in 1922 and I came around in 1972. All I had to do was add 50 years to my age if ever I wanted to know how old she was.

Anita C. Kallis, the woman who gave my sister and me the wonderful gift of our father, was born on February 2, 1922. That's 2-2-22. Every year, I'd call her on her birthday and wish her a Happy Groundhog Day. She'd laugh, and then of course I'd wish her a happy birthday.

The last time I got to enjoy a regular visit with Grammy, my daughter Madeline and I played Bingo with her and her fellow residents at the local assisted-living facility. That night she was the grandmother I always knew - - gentle, smiling, comforting, funny and just plain thrilled to be in the company of her grandson and great granddaughter. In the two months that would follow, she would be in and out of the hospital due to a series of strokes and other setbacks that took her energy, her ability to speak and, eventually, her personality and her life.

Maddie and I sat with Grammy in her room after that Bingo game and talked with her a bit. At one point I picked up the miniature soapstone elephant that she kept on her night stand. I had given her the figurine as a souvenir from a trip I had taken to India. I had bought the little elephant from a peddler on the streets of New Delhi, just outside the park where Gandhi had been cremated 60 years ago. I told Grammy that night that I still couldn't believe I had been to India.

"When I die, you can have that elephant back," Grammy told me.

"Well, I hope you're not planning on going anywhere anytime soon," I responded and smiled, weakly, promptly returning the elephant to her nightstand.

That was three months ago. The elephant now rests on one of my bookcases at home. It will forever remind me of two things - - my trip to India and, most preciously, my Grammy.

She was an extraordinary woman, one of the people in this world I liked and admired most. Dad always called her the matriarch of our family, the unifying force around whom we all gathered as one close family. Grammy earned that distinction not through an iron ruling of family affairs, as some matriarchs do, but through loveliness so pure, quiet and profound that we all wanted nothing more than to shower her with our love, admiration and respect.

And she was *cool* too. That's the word for her. *Cool.* She had energy and a youthfulness that completely erased the years, the *generations*, between her children and grandchildren and her. Up until a couple of years ago, all you had to do was call her and she'd be good to go for dinner, a movie, a play, a concert, a sporting event, a trip overnight, anything. I remember occasionally thinking that she had a livelier social life than I did.

There are little things about her that I'll always remember. She always kept a bowl of M&Ms in her apartment. She made delicious lemon squares, chicken-and-broccoli casseroles and rice-crispy bars topped with chocolate frosting. As children, when we visited her overnight, she'd fold our clothes perfectly and professionally, thanks to her days working downtown at a prominent clothing store.

She had wisdom too. She acquired it through her intelligence and the hard challenges she met in life.

She frequently said, "It all comes out in the wash." That was her way of saying that things tend to work out. We'd take her cue and tell ourselves that whenever life got a little too tricky.

And then there's this little nugget she imparted a couple of years ago: When discussing parenthood, she said, "It's best to stop at *two* kids."

She had been sitting next to Dad when she said it. Dad's her third child.

Shocked, Dad laughed and called Grammy on that one. She laughed too but stuck to her guns. Over the years, Dad had repeatedly and playfully reminded her of her gaffe, and she'd just smile and glow and say, "You're never going to let me live that one down, are you, hon?"

Nope. Even at her funeral last week, we fondly recalled her stop-at-two-kids comment during her eulogy.

I miss Grammy. She figures large in my heart and memory. It was her voice, so soft yet strong and defined, that I heard a few mornings after she died, telling me that it was time to wake up, go to work, get back on track and resume enjoying life as best as I can.

My step-grandfather, a wonderful man I called Grampy, passed away in 1996. He said it best when it came to Grammy.

He called her a "thing of beauty." He'd see her first thing in the morning, after she woke up but before she got ready for the day, and he'd call her a "thing of beauty." She'd burn a pot roast and, because she had made it, Grampy would call the burnt meat a "thing of beauty." She could do no wrong.

She *was* a thing of beauty. Her warmth, grace and humor made her so. It felt *good* to be around Grammy. It felt safe, reassuring, peaceful and fun to be with her.

Even during the past several weeks, as her health declined, as her personality vanished, as her consciousness waned and her breathing grew labored, she found strength enough to smile, to laugh, to ask *us* if *we* were okay, and to reach out and touch our faces.

Until the very end, she remained, as she always will remain to my family and me, as Grampy best described her. She was a "thing of beauty."

Molly

Sometimes I called her my little dog in the park.

According to family lore, that's where my wife's cousins found Molly, our Cairn terrier. She was abandoned in a park in Massachusetts when they discovered her. My understanding has always been that Molly had been in a small cage at the time.

Valerie's cousins kept Molly for a few years and then one day Valerie and I got the call. My mother-in-law wanted to know if we'd like to take Molly into our home. Valerie's cousins were moving to New Hampshire, we were told. To this day, Valerie and I have no idea why Molly did not make the move with them.

Valerie and I had been married for one year when we welcomed Molly into our lives in a shoe box-sized apartment in Massachusetts. Molly made us a family.

Molly immediately hit it off with Valerie and me. We'd go for walks and drives. We'd sit on the couch and watch movies. We'd hide treats around the apartment and Molly would sniff them out and inhale them with one gulp. We'd give her long rawhide sticks and she'd waddle around the apartment with them sticking out of the side of her mouth like big-time cigars.

And she always gave me a hero's welcome when I came home from work. She must have thought I had been out building churches or rescuing orphans or teaching the nation's children how to read in order to greet me with such warmth and enthusiasm. I said nothing to make her think otherwise. I liked how I looked through my little dog's eyes.

I used to call her the "deputy," for reasons I've never known. The name just fit her. Several weeks ago, I even called her the "foreman" as she roamed and inspected the piles of leaves that Valerie and I had raked one Sunday afternoon.

Molly ceded the limelight with enormous grace when Valerie and I welcomed a little eight-pound girl into our home five and a half years ago. Molly was not sure at first what to make of this little bundle that woke up crying in the middle of the night and needed constant feeding and care. In time, though, Molly started to like having someone else in the house who crawled around on all fours and saw her eye to eye.

Inevitably, the little girl got up on her feet one day and started walking around, just like the other two people in the house. She got taller and taller too.

But the little girl remained Molly's good friend, despite the growing height between them. Madeline would drape her little-girl clothes across Molly's back, giving our scruffy little best-in-show a bit of fashion sense as she moseyed throughout the house. Maddie also made sure to give Molly a solid hug and a light pat on the head before she left for preschool or kindergarten in the morning. And when Maddie was sad, she'd sit next to Molly on the floor and stroke her fur.

A couple of weeks ago, I found myself standing in the veterinarian's examination room, holding a pen inches above the dotted line of a form that needed my signature. I've signed my name thousands of times throughout my life but never for something so heartbreaking.

"Authorization to Perform Euthanasia." That's what it said on the top of the form.

I hesitated.

No, I froze.

And then I thawed barely enough to lower the pen and sign my name with a shaky hand.

I bent down and smoothed back Molly's ears. Then I patted her back and told her I loved her. I left the room. I turned around just in time for one final glimpse of Molly before the door closed behind me.

Valerie stayed at Molly's side as she slipped peacefully into her eternal rest. I could not. A week earlier, I had already been at my grandmother's side as she too passed from this life into the next.

Our dear Molly had gotten old. She was 15. She went blind a year or two ago. Valerie and I maintained that Molly would be all set as long as she still seemed content in her golden years. Not that long ago, she no longer seemed content.

She appeared agitated, lost and confused. She paced a lot. She bumped into things. She could not climb steps.

Shortly before she died, I saw the writing on the wall. During my lunch hour, I sat in our living room and watched her for a few minutes. She stood in the center of the room, looking around but seeing nothing, taking a few steps here and a few there but not settling down anywhere.

I knew then the time had come for Valerie and me to make The Decision.

Molly is gone, but our minds and hearts continue to trick us. Valerie, Maddie and I still expect Molly to walk into the room. We hear noises and figure it's Molly until our memories correct us. We see shadows of something in the dark and think it's our dog. We miss the sounds of her feet padding across our hardwood floors. We put up our Christmas tree last weekend, knowing that for the first time in nine years Molly would not spend nights sleeping underneath it.

Last week, I turned off the television and walked through my dark house to my bedroom after deciding to call it a night. "Good night, Molls," I called out, and then I caught myself.

I've even accidentally called Maddie "Molly" a few times.

I'm astonished that absence can have such presence. Molly's absence hovers in our home, turning silence into a force that speaks volumes. Like everyone, I have lost loved ones before. However, this is the first time I've lost a member of my household.

I have spent the past two weeks thinking back on Molly's happiest moment. Seven or eight years ago, before Maddie was born, Valerie and I stayed with friends as they house-sat at a country home in New Hampshire. Our friends had their own dog, a pit bull named Ginger that they had to put to sleep a few years later. As Valerie and our friends and I barbecued and sat outside and laughed and talked, Molly and Ginger ran side by side along the wide-open front lawn.

I can still see the boundless joy in Molly's face as she galloped alongside her newfound friend. She radiated youth, happiness, energy, friendship and adventure.

I like to think that's what Molly is doing now. I'd like to think she has rejoined Ginger at that scene in the afterlife, so that they can run side by side in the country, on a continuous loop that will always ensure the joy they knew that night long ago.

I can think of no greater reward for my little dog in the park.

Sniffles, or the End of the World

I'm convinced I stood at death's door this week, but my wife's insisting all I had was a "common cold."

At least we agreed on some things. We both know I looked and sounded awful. I coughed and sneezed a lot. My joints ached. My head felt disconnected from the rest of my body. I did not have an appetite. All I wanted to do was sleep.

The difference is, Valerie knew I would survive, whereas, to quote her, I was acting as though "it was the end of the world."

"Men are such babies when they get sick," she told me.

As I lay in bed, I asked Valerie to take my temperature. She felt my forehead and told me I didn't feel hot. I insisted that I felt warm, and I asked her to go get the thermometer. She rolled her eyes and complied.

"You're at 99 degrees, Shawn," she told me as she peeled the thermometer-strip from my forehead.

"See? I told you I had a temperature."

"That's just a bit above normal," Valerie replied. "You don't have a fever."

I coughed and sighed. "You know, you're hardly Florence Nightingale here . . ."

"Oh, stop."

"Really," I pressed. "You're not exactly Juliette Binoche from that 'English Patient' movie."

Valerie did not fall for this. She knows I've liked the actress Juliette Binoche ever since I saw her in a naughty Louis Malle movie nearly 20 years ago.

"Shawn, that guy in 'The English Patient' was burnt to a crisp," she countered. "You have a temperature of 99 degrees."

Still. In the two days ahead, my coughing and sneezing continued, my throat went sore, my drowsiness and aches persisted, and I passed from shivering to sweating. Something was up.

"Right," Valerie said. "You have a cold."

Valerie let me sleep off my sickness and she brought me orange juice and soup. However, her notion that I was milking my ailments with great drama is consistent in Sullivan relationships.

There was that time, in the 1970s, when my father felt convinced he was having a heart attack. "The Big One," as he had called it.

At the time, Mom wasn't buying it. She figured Dad was only experiencing indigestion. She told him to call my Uncle Don for a ride to the emergency room because she had to bring my sister and me to school. Uncle Don dropped Dad off at the hospital entrance and then he continued on to work.

As it turned out, Mom was right. Dad had not experienced a heart attack. He simply had had a bad case of indigestion. He was relieved but still shaken.

Dad called Mom at work and asked her to pick him up at the hospital and give him a ride home. She explained that she couldn't because she had already taken her lunch hour.

"No one would come and get me," Dad lamented when retelling the story this week.

He had to walk home from the hospital. It's a mile, with hills. Good for the heart.

This week Mom reveled in the gallows humor of it all.

"Dad was in the hospital, and the rest of us all went about our daily routines," she said, through tears of dark laughter.

There were other times, before his ALS diagnosis, of course, when Dad insisted he felt ill, but we all knew better. He has always said that when he dies, he wants his tombstone to read, "He called our bluff."

I'm the same way. When I returned from a trip to India last year, I thought I had caught a horrible disease for which I had not been vaccinated. Turned out it was just jet lag.

Apparently, though, it's not a Sullivan-thing. It's a man-thing. All of the women with whom I've spoken this week have told me the men in their lives are big wimps when they catch a bug and feel under the weather.

"Men think it's the end of the world when they get sick," Valerie explained to me. "Women are different, especially mothers. They don't have time to be sick, so they soldier through it and then crash at the end of the day."

Fair enough. We all know why women are tougher than men because we've been told a million times. None of us would have ever come into this world if it were not for women and the strength they needed to get us here. We've all heard the line about how the human race would be extinct if men had to have the babies.

So why are we men the way we are? Not sure. My wife and some other women have said we have a low tolerance for pain and even discomfort. Sounds about right. I also think we men just dislike being taken off our game. I think we resent being temporarily sidelined from our big march through life.

I dunno.

It's something I can think about, I guess, when my time comes for that long walk home from the hospital.

He Prefers To Laugh

May, 2009

My father, Gary Sullivan, expects to send his book to the printers this week.

He hopes to have copies of the finished product in his hands soon because May is the right month to get them out there. It's ALS Awareness Month.

The book is called "I Prefer to Laugh," and it's Dad's account of living for the past six years with amyotrophic lateral sclerosis, also known as ALS and Lou Gehrig's disease.

According to the ALS Association's website, ALS is a "progressive, neurodegenerative disease that affects the nerve cells in the brain and the spinal cord. Motor neurons reach from the brain to the spinal cord and from the spinal cord to the muscles throughout the body. The progressive degeneration of the motor neurons in ALS eventually leads to their death. When the motor neurons die, the ability of the brain to initiate and control muscle movement is lost. With voluntary muscle action progressively affected, patients in the later stages of the disease may become totally paralyzed."

It gets worse. While the body is paralyzed, the mind remains intact. An ALS patient keeps his or her memories and thoughts and feelings but loses the ability to express them.

The disease is known to strike and kill quickly. Dad seems to be an exception, though, and not the rule; he recently visited his specialist in Boston, and she told him he will still be on his feet next year at this time. Dad has known more than a few people who were diagnosed with ALS after him and have passed away before him.

Right now Dad still uses his braces, his cane and his walker to get around. He did purchase a motorized wheelchair for a trip we took down south in April - - that proved a smart move because Busch Gardens in Virginia turned out to be one steep concrete hill after another. He has not had to use the wheelchair since.

The accumulation of the disease is starting to show, however. When Dad gets tired, for example, the muscles in his jaw and throat become slack and he slurs his words together. He has a hard time raising his right hand above his shoulder too. He falls a bit more. And despite his braces, he needs to lock his arms with two people on either side of him if he hopes to walk even the shortest distances without his cane.

It's painful to witness. I no longer remember what Dad looked like when he walked with ease or what he sounded like when his voice was full and free. Those days are gone.

There are no two ways about it, though: My family and I are blessed. When Dad was diagnosed with ALS in December of 2004, we thought we had no more than two or three years remaining to be with him. Back then, my sister Kelly even moved her wedding up a few months because she feared Dad would not be able to walk her down the aisle. He was able - - and he danced with her that day too.

That was four years ago.

Dad falls into the 10 percent of ALS patients who are able to live with the disease for five to seven years or longer. He has used this unexpected time afforded to him to raise funds and awareness to fight against ALS and find a cure. He has served on the board of directors of the ALS Association's Northern New England chapter. He has founded the ALS-Maine Collaborative, which connects ALS patients throughout the state with the tools and resources available to them.

And he's written this book, "I Prefer to Laugh."

He started it just weeks after his diagnosis. You can tell. The first chapter chronicles the events that led to his diagnosis and shares the grief and fear that followed it. Dad's anguish and suffering are clear on every page. Many of the chapters, though, explain the title. Dad tells some of his favorite stories from his life and frames them around what he's going through now. A funny anecdote about his ill-fated effort to try on a pair of pants in a changing stall at the mall suggests the guy did not necessarily always have balance before ALS came into his life and took it for sure.

Several weeks ago, Dad and I locked ourselves in a hotel room in Newington, New Hampshire, and went through the book word for word. I read the book aloud and we stopped whenever we thought a word or sentence or paragraph needed a grammatical correction or an artistic tweak. We only stopped to eat twice and catch a few hours of sleep. We never stepped out of the hotel; we didn't take a break to see what was playing on HBO. We took 13 hours to complete our mission.

At the twelve-hour mark, I turned away from the laptop screen and looked at Dad.

"I need to take a break," I told him.

He understood.

I left the hotel room and went outside. I took my first whiff of fresh air in 24 hours. Then I did something curious: I went to the hotel's exercise room and hopped on the treadmill. For three minutes I ran at a rapid clip. Then I went back to our hotel room.

Dad and I spent two more hours editing his book, and then we drove back home to Sanford.

I think I know why I ran on the treadmill. I refuse to run *away* from ALS, so I figured I'd at least run in place.

In the beginning, I coped with Dad's ALS by passing through all the usual stages. At some point, I achieved a healthy holding pattern that continues to this day. I know I will lose Dad, but he's here with me today, and this holding pattern allows me to enjoy the moment and leave the future to the future. My marathon editing session with Dad had created a ripple in that holding pattern, that coping mechanism I have created for myself, because for hours straight we focused on nothing but ALS.

But it was worth it. Helping Dad with his book has helped me know I'm doing all I can to help him and be there for him. He's done so much for me throughout my life.

Since his diagnosis, Dad has attacked ALS on many fronts. He prefers to laugh, yes, but he also prefers to fight.

Dad has always been a good man. His response to ALS has made him a great one.

Cocoa and Tootsie

Our new kittens finally have decided to let us sleep through the night.

Once in a while, they still jolt me awake. One night this week I woke up to the two of them wrapped around something and fighting for it with their claws and teeth. It was my arm.

During those first few nights, though, Valerie and I experienced as much disrupted sleep as we did during those first several weeks after Madeline was born. And even then Maddie never walked on my head as I tried to sleep. Nor did she bite my nose, make loud noises in my ear, attack my hands and feet, lounge on my chest and sit on my neck and stare at me for minutes on end.

In the past month I've had more scratches than an old record and more bites than a finished apple.

All of this has been lots of fun, mind you. These two little furballs have restored much energy and joy to our home. We had been lacking both ever since our dear Cairn terrier Molly had passed away in November.

Their names are Cocoa and Tootsie. Maddie came up with them. They are black-and-gray tiger kittens.

Santa Claus brought Cocoa and Tootsie to our home on Christmas Eve. He had a lot of help from the Safe Haven Humane Society, a nonprofit organization that makes sure pets find the right homes.

Maddie woke up on Christmas morning and opened her presents. During this time, Valerie and I hid the kittens in our home office, so that we could bring them out as the grand finale.

Keeping Maddie clueless proved a challenge because the kittens kept meowing from behind closed doors in the other room. Valerie and I played a little Christmas music in our living room to drown out the squeals. At one point, our neighbor, Bev, stopped by our house to wish us a Merry Christmas and offer us some doughnuts she had gotten at Tim Horton's. I wonder if she saw me sweating a close call as Maddie stood in our kitchen, just feet away from our home office's door, and talked with her. Those kittens were getting louder. Hitchcock could not have crafted tighter suspense.

But all went well. Maddie had no idea she'd be getting two kittens for Christmas, so in a way she had no reason to hear them. If you know what I mean.

Cocoa and Tootsie are brother and sister. Cocoa, the boy, is named after my aunt - - she's a folk singer from Vermont, and that's her stage name, although she spells it without the "a." Tootsie is named after a cat my family owned when I was a teenager. That Tootsie had thumbs, two different colored eyes and a personality that a pediatrician would have called "spirited" if she had been a three-year-old child.

Valerie and I have gotten a lot of advice since welcoming Cocoa and Tootsie into our home.

"You have to get them fixed," the guy at the local video store told me.

"We will," I assured him. "We're supposed to make an appointment later this month."

"You have to do it *soon*," he pressed.

"We're on it. Besides, we have nothing to worry about. They're brother and sister."

"Doesn't matter," he shook his head and said. "I have father-and-son cats I have to separate all the time."

I nodded, as though to say, "I see." Got the message.

We also got some advice on how to rein in these kittens when they're on a tear.

"We need to get one of those water guns," I told a friend after Cocoa knocked over something he should not have.

"Spray bottle," Valerie corrected me. "Bottle. Not *gun*. That's such a guy thing to say."

Sure enough, we got a spray bottle that gently envelopes the cats in a harmless cool mist whenever they get into mischief. Valerie took it upon herself to buy it, evidently figuring that I'd come home with one of those militaristic super-soakers if the chore had been left to me.

They're fun to watch, Cocoa and Tootsie. We love them. The other night, Cocoa got his claws stuck in a lamp shade. He pulled and yanked but could not unhook his claws. He sat for a moment and plotted his next move. You could see the wheels turning behind his eyes. Then he came up with a plan.

He started casually licking his arm. You know, as though he had *meant* to get his claws stuck in the lamp shade so that he could hold up his arm to wash it.

Cocoa's Number One Rule: Stay cool. Even if you have to fake it.

I like that.

'See The Birdie, Daddy?'

Dear Madeline:

Congratulations. You and your classmates officially have finished kindergarten. In just a few short months, you'll be in the first grade. You're in the big leagues now.

It's funny how your last day of school felt so much like your first. On Tuesday morning, I stood at the kindergarten entrance and smiled and waved as you walked down the hall toward your classroom. You turned and waved back. You and I shared this routine all year long whenever I brought you to school in the morning. I thought for sure at one point you'd outgrow me and stop asking me to stay and wave, but much to my gratitude that never happened.

There were a few times when I was sure it would. There were mornings when you'd ask me to stay and wave at the door, and then you'd walk down the hall, chatting and laughing with friends as your little tote bag filled with class work dangled at your side.

And then there was that morning in front of the school when a boy in your class ran up to you and smiled and said hello. The two of you went about your merry way like two peas in a pod and did not look back. I'll never forget that morning - - I thought for sure it was the end of our routine of smiling and waving to each other as you walked down the hall to Mrs. Morrison's room.

As I walked back to my car on Tuesday morning, I thought and felt the same way I did when I dropped you off for your first day of kindergarten back in September. I caught a little lump in my throat, held back a tear or two, and thought, *"Boy, that was quick."* Those first five years of your life, from your cradle to your classroom, passed in the blink of an eye. And, I suspect, the next twelve years of your schooling will pass just as quickly as this single one just did.

That's why Mom and you and I have to make every moment count - - even the ones for which I, as your father, must take the long view in order to appreciate. I'm thinking of a couple of weeks ago, when you stood in our driveway and blasted water from our garden hose through our living room window and soaked the brand new couch Mom and I bought. When I looked at the couch I bit my lip and reminded myself that it was just water. Later that evening I managed to chuckle about the incident with friends. Now, weeks later, I think it's a funny story.

Every moment has to count because each one is fleeting. The newborn went from a baby to a toddler to a little girl in no time. You will always be my little girl, always, but just the other day I referred to you as such and realized it's probably time I stopped saying "little" to describe you. You're a big girl now.

I'm sure every Dad is looking at his kindergartener this week and shaking his head in disbelief and marveling at how much his child has grown in the past year. I know I am.

The biggest change I've seen in you is your ability to communicate, whether through writing or speaking. You now say what you mean and mean what you say. You listen carefully and ask smart questions. The days of trying to interpret you are over. So too, it seems, are the days when you'd get a word mixed up or you'd say something the way you think it's supposed to be said. You know, the kind of chestnuts we adults like to file under "Kids Say the Darnedest Things."

It has been several months, for example, since you told me about the rabbits.

"Dad," you told me one day in the car, "Niagara Falls is dangerous because of all the rabbits."

Rabbits. I had to think about that one for a moment. *Niagara Falls is dangerous because of all the rabbits.*

Ah! I got it! Rapids! Niagara Falls is dangerous because of all the *rapids*!

I will always be thankful to you for inspiring in me the lasting, wonderful, childlike image of hundreds of harmless, fluffy white bunnies swirling around in Niagara Falls. It's a comical sight.

The "rabbits" remark is probably my favorite. A close second would be when you were two years old and you told me that Easter is about celebrating "Jesus Rice."

I enjoyed our trip to Dairy Queen the other night. I got a hot fudge sundae and you tried out the new Blizzard. We sat on the red bench on the side of Dairy Queen that faces Radio Shack. We ate our ice cream and talked about a whole bunch of topics.

"See the birdie, Daddy?" you asked me.

You pointed and I looked. A small, stout bird sat on top of the Radio Shack building and talked up a storm.

"He sure has a lot to say," I noticed.

"You can see his beak open and close every time he chirps," you said. "What do you think he's saying, Daddy?"

I listened to a few chirps. The bird sounded adamant about something. I told you I wasn't sure what he was saying, but it sure sounded important. I asked you what you thought the bird was talking about.

You listened to him a bit more and found your answer.

"I think he's trying to tell the other birds that a storm is coming," you said.

It had just showered an hour before while we were eating supper. Sure enough, later that evening, it rained and rained and rained.

I think you were right. I think the bird was calling out to his friends and letting them know that it was going to rain.

Sunday is Father's Day, Maddie. It's the one day of the year in which we fathers are singled out and celebrated. We are reminded of how fortunate we are. We feel grateful.

Conversations such as the one you and I had about the bird make every day feel like Father's Day, Madeline.

Love,

Dad

Cats on the Counter

How can you keep a couple of kittens off the kitchen counter?

No, seriously. I'm not just throwing that out there as a tongue twister. I wanna know.

I realized a while ago that I'm not in charge of my household. Actually, as the only guy in my house, that truth occurred to me years ago. Our family's two new cats, however, have really driven home that point to me.

Cocoa and Tootsie love to hop onto our kitchen counter and traipse over our stove and the dirty dishes in our sink. Sometimes, if the sun falls just right through our kitchen window, they will sit on the counter with such peace and contentment I want to climb up there and sit next to them. But then I realize I'd become part of the problem if I did that.

I knew things had gone too far when I went home during my lunch hour one day and the two of them were fully sprawled out on the counter and cleaning each other with their tongues. I mean, *come on*. Valerie and I prepare our family dinners up there.

Just the thought of the cats on the counter turns Valerie's stomach. They sit up there after squatting in their kitty litter all day, she says. I can sympathize with Val. I think of that litter box every time Cocoa or Tootsie walks over my face in the morning when I'm in bed. And when Tootsie steps on my nose I think of that time I came home from work and found her with her two front legs dipped in our toilet water.

Someone had forgotten to put the lid down. I won't say who.

We have a little red spray bottle that we use to zap the cats when they're up on the counter. Sometimes it's effective and hits them with a laser-beam-thin stream of water that sends Cocoa flying off the counter and Tootsie running behind our microwave for cover. Then there are those times when the bottle produces no more of a spray than a half-hearted sneeze. When that happens, the cats luxuriate in a cool, soothing mist and look like they want to thank us.

Actually, Cocoa and Tootsie don't *look* like anything when it comes to their reactions and expressions. Cats are a whole different ballgame than dogs. I submit that to you not as a profound discovery but as an observation from someone who owned a dog for ten years. You can look at a dog and pretty much know what it's thinking. Cats, on the other hand, probably have the best poker faces in the entire animal kingdom.

But let's get back to the spray bottle. It's not working anymore. I'm not sure it ever did, especially with Tootsie. Like I said, she darts behind the microwave, which, of course, is on the counter, so that defeats the purpose.

We lost the spray bottle once. I found it days later underneath some furniture. I am convinced the cats knocked it off the counter, batted it across the floor and stuffed it somewhere they thought we'd never look.

Valerie has tried roaring at the cats like a lion to scare them off the counter. I guess the idea is that you're speaking their language. That hasn't worked, either. Makes for a good laugh, though. You should see her do it.

We've also tried rattling a glass jar of loose change at them. That has worked a few times. We keep needing the change, though, so a lot of time we end up grabbing nothing but an empty jar to shake at the cats.

I've asked friends what Valerie and I can do to permanently keep Cocoa and Tootsie off our counter. Much to my dismay, a few of them suggested using a spray bottle. "Works for me," they added. One friend suggested putting a slippery wax on our counter, so that our cats would fall off every time they jumped up there. Another friend recommended scolding our cats in the low, measured voice of a disappointed parent. "That worked for my mother when I was a kid," he said.

I think I like my idea best: Let the cats win. It's one thing when Valerie and Maddie and I are home because then it's three against two. When I'm home alone with Cocoa and Tootsie, though, I'm outgunned. There's two of them and one of me. Odds are against me.

Besides, every time I do manage to get the cats off the counter, they always change their tune once I put the spray bottle away. They get a little cocky. They saunter around with a cool patience and confidence that says, *"That's okay. You can have your fun with your little water gun. Once you're gone, though, we're going to get right back up on that counter. We'll even invite the other cats in the neighborhood to join us. We're going to par-tay!"*

I believe this. Valerie and I came home one evening and saw a strange fat cat fleeing from our front steps as we pulled into our driveway.

Valerie does have one solution that we've yet to try.

"I think we should build a new wall to close off our kitchen to the rest of the house and use a door to get in there," she said.

"A new wall?" I asked. "That's a little extreme, don't you think?"

"But we have to do *something*, Shawn. This is disgusting."

"There's nothing we can do, Val. Nothing. They're smarter than we are."

Perhaps I should not throw in the towel just yet. Another friend did have a terrific idea that would definitely keep Cocoa and Tootsie off our kitchen counter, once and for all.

We could put a dog up there.

Locked Out, and Get This:
We *Had* The Key

Is there anything worse than getting locked out of your house?

How about getting locked out of someone else's house? I thought of that last week when I could not get into my parents' home to feed their cat while they were away on vacation.

I suppose it's technically impossible to get locked out of someone else's house. After all, it's not your house. How can you get locked out of a home that's not your own? You just can't get inside, that's all.

As far as last week went at my parents' house, there's a catch: I had a key and *still* I could not get into their house.

Nobody could. I know because a group of seven of us tried over a 24-hour period. We all tried the key, turning it in the side-door's deadbolt with the same brute force that a schoolyard bully would put into a nipple-twister.

It started simply enough. Our family friend, Louise, came to my office on Wednesday afternoon and told me she could not get into my parents' house to feed their cat, O'Rourke. The deadbolt was just plain stuck, she said.

I gave her my own key to my folks' house, for some reason thinking that'd be the answer to her problem. It wasn't. Louise returned a few moments later to say my key could not get the job done, either.

I went to my parents' house during my lunch hour and tried to open their door. No success. I tried again after work. Ditto. These two efforts involved a lot of grunts and profanities. Given the might and energy expended, they also caused the key's indentations to be branded on that soft spot where my thumb and index finger meet.

Honestly, James Bond could not have gotten into my parents' house that day. The bad guys in "Goldfinger" had an easier time getting into Fort Knox.

I called my parents down in the Amish country. I had to find out if they too had ever had problems with their deadbolt and perhaps knew a trick - - say, the right flick of a wrist or something - - to getting into their fortress.

"You have to pull on the door handle while you're turning the deadbolt," Dad said.

"Yeah, I tried that."

Dad's solution: Call a locksmith.

I had been trying to take care of the problem and avoid taking that step. Or, more specifically, I had been trying to get out of paying for it.

By then, Dad's solution did not matter. An army had already descended upon his house and started developing a strategy to break into it. The army kind of formed by itself. It started with Louise and me, spraying my key with enough WD-40 to blow another hole in the ozone layer. It expanded when three of my parents' neighbors noticed this comedy of errors and joined it. Then it increased by one when one of the neighbors, Betty, called her grandson in Springvale to come to the house to crawl through the one window Mom and Dad left cracked open before they departed.

Betty had called her grandson while I was across the street at her house, fetching one of her ladders. While I was getting that ladder, another one from our team of volunteers was pushing Dad's grill through his flower bed and against the house, in the hopes that I'd climb onto it, grab hold of the open window's ledge on the second floor, and shimmy up the vinyl siding to get inside.

So there I was, carrying an old, frail wooden ladder across the street to my parents' house, where five others were feverishly plotting ways to break and enter.

Did I mention that two police cruisers were in the neighborhood at this time, parked in full view of my parents' home while a couple of officers stood in the street and handled what seemed to be an unrelated domestic matter? That must have been some unrelated domestic matter because the cops showed absolutely no interest in what *we* were up to.

I tried climbing the ladder to my parents' second-story window, but it started to creak and bend when I reached its middle rungs. Louise begged me to get off the ladder before it snapped in half and I fell and broke my arms and legs and died. I told Louise I was fine. She kept getting on my case, though, and I finally relented. Moments later, while I was talking again to my parents on the phone, I overheard Louise tell Betty's grandson that he was needed to climb the ladder because *"Shawn's afraid of heights."*

In the end, I followed Dad's request and went to the local hardware store. The woman at the counter gave me a transmitter and I spoke to a locksmith who was out on the road at the time. I explained to him that I needed to get inside my parents' house to feed their cat. He agreed to meet me at my folks' house the next morning.

"If we were talking about a dog, I would have met you tonight," he told me.

He added that he'd need to see my ID before he let me in the house. The next morning, he showed up and smiled. No need to see your driver's license, he told me. He knew my Dad and said I looked just like him.

In less than two minutes, I found my new best friend - - the locksmith turned the key in the deadbolt and opened the door.

How'd he do it? He detached my key from its ring and attached it to a set of pliers. He stuck the key in the deadbolt and used the pliers' handle as added leverage. Voila. We were in the house in no time.

"The deadbolt's fine," he told me. "It's just that whoever locked it really, *really* cranked it."

Mom, I thought. *I knew it.*

I knew it because Mom and Dad's house got burglarized last September while they stayed at a hotel while their home underwent repairs. The burglar got into the house by using the same key that the construction crew had been using and leaving underneath my Dad's wheelchair ramp after a day's work.

I know my mother. I could see her locking the deadbolt to the side door before she and Dad left for their trip last week. I could picture her grabbing the deadbolt's lever and cranking it to the left with enough savage force to intimidate an undefeated arm-wrestler at a seedy roadhouse.

I could imagine her thinking, as she headed out the door, *Nobody's gonna get in the house* this *time.*

Not even her son.

"I guess I don't know my own strength," Mom told me in that innocent way of hers when I later explained to her that she had been the caper's culprit. "All those chores I'm doing around the house are paying off."

You're probably wondering how the cat fared during those 48 hours between Mom and Dad's departure and my hard-fought entry into their home. Well, don't you worry about him. You know cats. O'Rourke was fine. If anything, he enjoyed the show. He sat on the kitchen floor and watched through the window as the whole neighborhood tried to break inside his house to feed him his Fancy Feast and clean up the stink-bombs in his kitty litter. He had that same calm and unaffected look that all the other cats in the world have. I even detected a touch of amusement.

A whole lotta help *he* turned out to be.

Late Bloomer

One of the greatest joys of parenthood occurs when your child does something sooner and better than you did when you were a kid.

Madeline recently learned how to swim. She's six. I was seven when I learned.

Valerie, Maddie and I spent three days last week at a rental house on Sebago Lake with our friends, Nathan and Pam, and their children, Milla and Andrew. On our second day there, Maddie dunked her head underwater without having to pinch her nose. She did this as all children do in the beginning, with a quick submergence that lasted barely seconds, but this feat represented a culmination of efforts that began earlier this summer with her holding her nose, squeezing her eyes shut tight, and gingerly placing only her face just below the surface of the water.

On our third day on the island, something clicked and Maddie figured out how to slip underwater and swim a bit of the breast stroke for a good 15 or 20 feet.

"Back up, Daddy," Maddie said as we waded inches apart in three-and-a-half feet of water.

I did as I was told. When Maddie and I had several feet between us, she submerged and swam her way toward me, with a pair of goggles helping to show her the way.

"Maddie," I asked. "Did you swim this whole way?"

"Yup."

"Your feet never touched the ground?"

"Nope."

Then I looked to the beach, where Valerie sat in a chair and took it easy. *"Imagine that,"* my expression said. I couldn't believe it.

Maybe six years old is about the right time when kids learn to swim. All I have to go by are my own memories and experiences, and I was a late bloomer when it came to making my way in the water. I was seven. My parents were so thrilled when I finally got the hang of swimming that they took me to Portland to see "The Muppet Movie." I guess they were just relieved to see two summers of swimming lessons finally pay off.

"You weren't necessarily a late bloomer," Nathan told me as we both sat on the beach last week. "You just liked to goof off during swim class, so you did not pay attention and learn as quickly as the others."

Nate may have had a point. In the 1970s, he and I got banned from the local YMCA for two weeks due to our rowdy behavior at swimming lessons.

But I dunno. I was a late bloomer when it came to learning to ride a bike too. My parents took the training wheels off at a reasonable age, but it took me a few months longer before I could ride with confidence and ease. So yeah, when I was a kid, some things took a while.

One time, at a family gathering, I saw some old grainy film footage of me learning to take my first steps when I was a year old or so. In the film, I stood near our dining room table with my left hand wrapped securely around one of its legs. Slowly, but surely, I began to scoot in little sidesteps toward the windowsill just a few feet away. The thing is, I held on to the table leg as I did so; I seemed intent on releasing my grip from the leg only once I had my right hand squarely clamped on the sill.

Alas, my wingspan would not support such a strategy. At one point, I had my left hand on the table leg and the tips of my right fingers just inches shy of the windowsill. When I realized I had been stretched too thin, I listed back toward the table and plopped safely on the floor on my rear-end.

"Ugh!" I blurted and threw popcorn at the television screen, much to my family's laughter. *"I'm the same way today! Nothing's changed!"*

So I'm a late bloomer. Fair enough. But you still have to watch out for me. Once I finally do get started, I get better and better as I go along.

While I view my daughter as her own person and try not to frame her experiences within my own, there are times when I

210

look at her with pride when she gets the hang of something sooner and better than I did as a child.

She must take after her Mom.

But not completely. Maddie came home from school on Tuesday with more good news: she had learned how to tie her shoes.

"But tell Dad how you do it," Val told Maddie.

"Daddy's way," she said.

I tie my shoes differently than everybody else. I simply make two "bunny ears," as kids call them, and tie them together. It's quicker. None of this fancy loop-de-loop stuff that the rest of you do the so-called "right way." Now Maddie does it the same way as me.

She and I smiled at each other when we realized we now have this in common.

Headless Horsemen, Tell-Tale Hearts

Valerie and I woke up at four a few mornings ago to the sounds of our daughter waking from a bad dream. We trudged through the darkness to her bedroom to see what the matter was.

"Is everything all right?" I asked Madeline.

Maddie rubbed her eyes and nodded her head.

"Did something scare you?" Valerie knelt down beside her bed and wondered.

Maddie nodded again.

"What was it?" I asked.

Maddie relaxed a bit. It's always reassuring to wake from an unpleasant dream and realize everything will be fine. She mumbled two words.

"Headless Horseman."

Ah. It all made sense. Valerie looked up at me as though to say, *"Good going, Sullivan."* No Father of the Year Award for you.

I had read Maddie a children's version of Washington Irving's "The Legend of Sleepy Hollow" before she went to bed. We sat together in our living room with just a lamp and the warm orange glow of a jack-o-lantern to help us see the words.

I gave the story everything I had. During tense scenes, such as the one when schoolmaster Ichabod Crane passes through the pitch-dark forest convinced that someone was following him, I lowered my voice to a slow, drawn-out whisper. For scenes of high suspense - - such as moments later, when it's clear Crane *is* being followed, by a ghost with no head - - I picked up the tempo and read with clear and sharp pronunciation.

My father used to read this way to my sister Kelly and me. Kelly and I would giggle and squirm with anticipation in our seats while he read "The Three Little Pigs" and recited with escalating relish the Big Bad Wolf's threat to huff and puff and blow the houses down.

I knew I had Maddie in the palm of my hand because she listened to "Sleepy Hollow" with a quiet stillness and stared at the spooky illustrations on the page with a certain intrigue.

When I finished the story she had a lot of questions. Chief among them: What happened to Ichabod Crane?

"Not sure," I told her. "Nobody knows. He just . . . disappeared."

She had gobbled up the tale. Like her old man, Maddie loves Halloween. She ventures without fear into the haunted houses that local organizations present every October. She likes the scarier episodes of "Scooby Doo."

Maddie asked if I could read "Rip Van Winkle," another Irving tale which followed "Sleepy Hollow" in the book, but it was time for bed.

"Looks like I did too good of a job when I read her that story last night," I told Valerie after we returned to our bedroom.

Yet Maddie loved it. And when she went to bed the next night she expressed no worries that she'd again be haunted in her dreams by the Headless Horseman, that legendary soldier of the American Revolution who had his head knocked clean off by an enemy's cannonball.

It's strange but true: We like to be scared.

Sometimes. Only if we know it's all make-believe.

My friend Cane sent me an email last week alerting me to an old record on sale on eBay that had scary stories on it. I looked at the album cover and knew exactly what it was. When we were kids, Cane and his brother and three sisters had this record and we would play it on autumn afternoons, right when the sunlight would seep into that kind of foreboding dusk in the weeks before Halloween.

The record included a reading of "The Tell-Tale Heart," Edgar Allen Poe's horror story with a narrator who, shall we say, goes to extremes when an old man's milky blue eye gets under his skin. As my friends and I listened to the narrator tell his tale, we were perhaps too young to understand what exactly was taking place, but it did not matter. What scared us was something even more primal on the soundtrack: a rising and quickening heartbeat that grew louder and louder as the narrator started to figure that the best place to hide his problems was under the floorboards.

My friends and I loved this record. We played it over and over. I looked at the eBay advertisement that Cane sent me and smiled. "All we need now is a record player," I wrote back to him and joked.

I also remember attending Edison School on Halloween in the late 1970s. The teachers would host spooky events in their classrooms. Our principal offered the biggest thrills. Throughout the rest of the year, he wore his long hair back, but on Halloween he let it hang loose around his face, which he painted into a menacing and ghoulish pallor. We'd venture into his classroom every October 31, and we'd sit at his feet while he read and acted out frightening tales.

One of my friends fled the room one year and waited in the hall for the terror to finish. Me? I sat with the same rapt attention I saw in Maddie when I read her "The Legend of Sleepy Hollow" last week.

Why do we like to be scared? It's cathartic, we are told. Cathartic for *what* exactly, I have no idea.

Nor do I want to know.

It's scarier that way.

Still On His Feet

December, 2009

Dad said something interesting the other day. It was nice to hear.

"I'm done dying," he declared.

Dad's statement comes nearly five years to the day since his neurologist gave him this death sentence: He had ALS and had between three and five years left to live.

December 8, 2004, that was. Now, five years later, Dad is still on his feet, thanks to two leg braces and the rolling cane and walker he uses. He has a motorized wheelchair he uses to get around whenever he goes someplace that calls for canvassing considerable distances, but complete use of it remains relatively distant in his future.

ALS stands for "amyotrophic lateral sclerosis," a progressive neurodegenerative disease that destroys nerve cells in the brain and spinal cord and paralyzes those who suffer from it. ALS is popularly known as "Lou Gehrig's disease," after the beloved Yankees ballplayer who succumbed to the illness in the early 1940s.

The disease is notorious for striking its victims and killing them with merciless haste. The crawl with which Dad's ALS is advancing is quite rare, statistically placing him as the one person out of ten who lives with the disease as long as he has. Dad has known people who were diagnosed with ALS after him and have died before him - - including, in a cruel twist of fate, his ALS specialist at Massachusetts General Hospital in Boston.

While Dad is still on his feet, the telltale signs are there that the disease is nonetheless taking its toll. His voice slurs when he is overtired and speaks too much. He lists a bit farther to the left or right when his balance gives. Brushing his teeth, using a fork and pulling off a sweater are arduous tasks.

"Lifting a pillow is like lifting a ten-pound bag of potatoes," he told me the other day.

A pillow.

Dad's statement that he is "done dying" might strike some who know him as curious. To them, he has always kept living and fighting. During the first years after his diagnosis, he served as vice president of the ALS Association's Northern New England Chapter, a position that called for him to travel to meetings, hold numerous "phone bridges," and advocate for research and funding in Washington, D.C. In 2008, he founded the ALS-Maine Collaborative, the state's first-ever network to increase the visibility and accessibility of resources available to those who have ALS. And this year he published "I Prefer to Laugh," a memoir in which he chronicles the past five years and offers a few stories from earlier in his life that help suggest how he is coping with his disease.

All of this - - the activism and the book, as well as the friendships he keeps and the trips he and Mom take - - has suggested that Dad has been living it up all along. In several ways, he has. However, his recent declaration that he is "done dying" makes clear that for five years now his demise has figured prominently in his mind, denying him the chance to live in the moment and undercutting all joy.

To be sure, some of that still persists in considerable measure. And Dad's new approach coincides with his elation over recovering from one of his darkest experiences to date; for eight weeks this fall, he suffered a temporary palsy of his left eye that rendered him unable to drive, use his computer, read, watch television with ease, and leave the house alone. For Dad, the whole episode of being homebound with very little he could do provided him with a chilling glimpse of the paralysis that awaits him.

But I know my Dad. He prefers logic and common sense and practicality. When he says he is "done dying," this does not mean he is going to create a new bucket list and start jumping out of planes like Jack Nicholson and Morgan Freeman in that movie. He's not going to drop everything and fulfill his lifelong dreams of traveling to Australia with Mom or running for governor.

No. When Dad says he is "done dying," he means that he is going to stop regarding his life as an hourglass with little sand left to pass through it. He is going to start coexisting with ALS. He is going to proceed with his days living alongside the disease with an understanding of where things stand in the moment - - a peace about what he can and cannot do.

It may have taken five years to find it, but there's a word for that.

Acceptance.

O, Christmas Tree!
You're Going Down

Our cats are determined to take down our Christmas tree. I just know it.

"No, Shawn," Valerie tries to assure me. "They just want to climb it, that's all."

I'm not buyin' it. I see the way Cocoa and Tootsie stare at our tree. I've caught them batting away at the fragile ornaments that dangle from the lower branches.

The other day I walked into our living room to see the tree jiggling as though it had a bad case of the shakes. I approached the tree and peered through its fake branches. My eyes met those of Cocoa, who at one year old is the size of a panther. He was lurking around the pole at the center of the tree, balancing on a few of the back middle branches.

"Get out of that tree," I told him and produced the same spray bottle I've used to shoo him and his sister away from our kitchen counter.

Cocoa looked at the bottle and laughed.

"You know, I wouldn't have to do this if you let me out once in a while to climb that big Oak in the yard," he replied, in

the same kind of little thought-bubble you see above Garfield's head in the comic strips.

I shook my head. "That's not gonna happen."

The other day I woke up and swung my legs out of bed. I stepped on something small and fuzzy on the floor. I looked down and saw a snowman ornament that one of the cats had plucked from the tree overnight and placed on my side of the bed.

"Oh, that's cute," Valerie said. "One of the cats brought you a present."

I saw it another way. I've seen "The Godfather," when the movie mogul woke up one morning to a horse's head at the foot of his bed.

"No, I know what this is," I told Val. "I'm being sent a message. Those cats are determined to take down our tree, one piece at a time."

Elsewhere in the house I found a knitted mouse ornament.

We have anchored the tree to the wall with the use of some thin wire, but does anybody out there know where we can get an invisible shield? You know, something we can set up around the tree that allows us to see it but not approach it? We just need one to get through the holidays.

In previous years, we have put up our tree and then kicked back for the season, relaxing and enjoying the soothing glow of its colored lights. This time around, we are readjusting the tree on a daily basis. We're picking ornaments up off the floor and putting them back on the tree, unless they are broken and need to be thrown away. We're straightening branches that have bent and sagged under the cats' weight. At one point, Valerie took the rows of colored beads from the tree and tossed them out; she had gotten tired of repeatedly threading them around the branches after the cats had clamped down on them with their teeth and unspooled them.

We did not have such problems last year. Santa Claus brought Cocoa and Tootsie as a gift for our five-year-old daughter. They were a couple of cute kittens, two balls of fluff who were too light and small to affect the tree whenever they scaled its seven feet.

It has been a tense few weeks since Valerie, Maddie and I put up the tree while listening to carols. Once our cats showed interest in this new addition to our living room, I knew it was going to be a long Christmas season. As I watch television or read a book, I glance at the tree and see a few things askew - - loose beads; a shattered ornament; several branches all matted down and out of whack - - and it takes everything I have not to succumb to an uptight moment and fix the tree right away. If I'm in another room and I hear a branch rustle, I wait for a loud crash to follow.

I returned home from work the other day with my fears realized. The tree looked the best it had in a while, but only because Valerie had spent her afternoon making it so. The cats had indeed toppled it earlier that day.

I was pleased to see the tree look so well but I was frustrated that the cats had succeeded in their mission.

But I could not afford to be too upset with Cocoa and Tootsie. Here is where I must come clean.

A couple of weeks ago, I turned off the television at midnight and enjoyed a moment of peace in my chair by the tree. I noticed that one of the cats had bent one of the back branches so that it sagged to the floor and risked falling out of its hole in the pole.

I resolved to fix it.

I got down on the floor on my back and eased under the tree like a mechanic slipping underneath a car. I took the damaged branch and gingerly attempted to finagle it back into the pole.

Let's not pretend we don't know where this story is going.

The tree crashed down on top of me. Ornaments that did not smash on impact scattered across the floor.

It took just a quick moment for the tree to fall, but it lasted long enough for me to holler one bad word loud enough to land me on Santa's "naughty list" if he heard me say it. Valerie, who had gone to bed an hour earlier, rushed out of our bedroom. She saw me pinned underneath the tree and asked with tremendous urgency if I was all right.

Moments like these guarantee that I will never run out of ideas for columns.

I chuckled and told Valerie that I was fine. She lifted the tree and helped me up. We swept up the broken ornaments and redecorated the branches as best we could.

"Where are the cats?" I asked Valerie.

"They're sleeping on our bed," she answered.

I nodded. I picked a shard of an ornament out of my elbow. Then I looked at Valerie and made one request.

"Let's not tell them this happened, okay?"

Soap's Soap

"We can't use that!" Valerie blurted. *"That's boy soap!"*

"Boy soap?" I asked. "How can you tell?"

I looked down at the four-pack I had placed on our counter and wondered how someone could possibly tell a soap's gender.

Valerie laughed, but not without exasperation, and explained to me that the soap I had brought home from the supermarket was for men.

"Irish Spring?" I asked. "Really?"

Really. Evidently, I had forgotten about all of those television commercials from 30 years ago that emphasized that Irish Spring was a "manly deodorant soap." I remembered that someone in those ads used to cut a bar in two with a knife and expose the soap's green and white shades, but that was it.

I looked up an old Irish Spring commercial from 1977 on YouTube. Valerie stood over my shoulder and watched with me.

In the ad, two Irishmen are slaving away in a field. One of them, Mike, says to the other, "Howzit goin?" in that inimitable brogue.

Mike's friend walks over to him and says, "You're a strong man, Mike."

Mike agrees, but not in the sense his friend meant. He shakes his collar as though to waft the sweat of his labor and says, "A mite *too* strong."

Mike's friend's ready for him. Out of nowhere he produces a bar of Irish Spring soap and, sure enough, on the box it says, "A Manly Deodorant Soap."

He hands Mike the soap and says, with a wink, "Shower up with this. It really gets a strong man fresh."

I don't know many guys who carry around bars of soap in their pockets, but perhaps it's a good thing for Mike his buddy had one on him. Mike's friend gives him a chummy slap on the shoulder and sends him on his way.

Next we see Mike in the shower. He pauses, sniffs the bar, and declares, "What a fresh scent!"

But then the ad cuts to a beautiful woman - - and *she* says, "That's why I use it too!"

"Well, hey," I said, turning from the computer to Val. "See? Women use it too."

Valerie just rolled her eyes and replied, "You just bought it because it has the word 'Irish' on it."

Okay, that part might be true.

But here's the thing. To me, soap's soap. I've bought soap for my family before, but I'd be hard-pressed to tell you which brand I've bought. I look for the bargain on the shelf and throw it in my cart. I know if I spend too much on anything, I'll hear about it. This time I just happened to buy Irish Spring.

My wife holds her breath every time I go shopping. I rarely bring home what she's hoping I'd get. Most times she makes out an elaborate list of items she wants me to buy, but even then I find a way to put my own twist on it.

There was that time I brought home "senior" cat food for our kittens, for example.

From what I've heard, a lot of husbands screw up the shopping lists their wives hand them. In December I bumped into an old friend at Walmart. His wife had sent him out to buy blue tinsel for their Christmas tree. At the store he clutched a transparent sandwich bag with one small strand of blue tinsel in it.

How bad is that? Blue tinsel is blue tinsel, but his wife gave him two inches of it for reference at the store because she didn't want him to screw up.

I had some fun with this phenomenon several years ago. My sister asked for a Bundt pan for Christmas. I told my parents I'd get that gift for her.

On Christmas Eve, we all gathered around my parents' tree and Kelly unwrapped the gift. The look on her face was priceless.

"A . . . bedpan?"

"Yeah," I told her. "Didn't you say you wanted one for Christmas?"

"A Bundt pan, Shawn. *Bundt.* For *cakes.*"

Ahhhhhhh. That.

All right, back to the Irish Spring. We've just about run through the bars I bought. I do not have a sense of smell - - I was either born without one or fell on my nose as a kid - - so I cannot tell you if my wife and daughter and I smell like a bunch of Irish guys working on a farm.

I do know this: We need to set aside at least one bar because Valerie wants to slice it in half with a knife. She has wanted to do that ever since she saw those commercials as a kid.

Oh, and just so you know: I *did* get my sister a Bundt pan that Christmas. She opened that gift a few minutes after the bedpan, which to me had been too priceless a sight gag to pass up.

Mom's Got Mail

There's something about my mother that I'm trying to understand: Every time "You've Got Mail" airs on television, she has to record it.

My problem is not with the movie, which stars Tom Hanks and Meg Ryan as competing booksellers who dislike each other by day but fall in love by night during anonymous online chats. Valerie and I saw the flick when it played in theaters and enjoyed it.

Nah, see, what's got me scratching my head is that Mom records the movie *every single time* it's on television, even though she owns it on DVD. I bought her the movie so that she would not have to worry about missing it on cable.

"Mom, you *do* know you own this, right?" I check with her every time I visit the house and she's watching the movie on TiVo.

"Don't even get into it, Shawn," Dad calls out from their bedroom, which is where he hides now whenever the movie is once again playing in their house.

I bet Mom has seen the movie at least a couple-dozen times. For that matter, if you were to piece together all the scenes

I've caught while visiting my parents, *I've* probably seen the movie about twenty times myself.

I wouldn't be puzzled if Mom came across this movie while channel-surfing and decided to watch whatever was left of it. I understand that. It's one of the small pleasures in life to unexpectedly happen upon the movies we cherish most.

And I'm definitely not judging Mom for the number of times she watches "You've Got Mail." No way. I'm in no position to do that. As a child, I watched "The Muppet Movie" and "Star Wars" every time they played on HBO. As a teenager, I wore out my videocassettes of "National Lampoon's Vacation" and "Die Hard." These days, Valerie and I watch "Jaws" every Fourth of July. I'm also good for an annual viewing of "Rocky."

Our favorite movies are meant to be watched again and again, so that we can internalize them and come to regard them as old friends. It's the fact that Mom owns the movie but still records it that trips me up. "You've Got Mail" is right there on the shelf with her other favorite movies, "White Christmas," "Desk Set," "Home Alone," "The Birdcage" and "Guess Who's Coming to Dinner?"

I've asked Mom why she has to record "You've Got Mail" every time it airs. Sometimes she just smiles and shrugs her shoulders. Once in a while she'll come up with a doozy of an answer.

"I knew there was going to be a snowstorm, so I recorded it so I could watch it then," she answered one time.

230

I shook my head and told her that she *owns* the movie and can just stick it in the DVD player whenever there's a snowstorm or the mood simply strikes her.

"I know," she conceded. "But it's fun to just sit there on a Sunday afternoon and watch it with a hot cup of tea while the snow's blowing around outside."

If you noticed, Mom *still* didn't answer my question.

There was another time, maybe as recent as a few weeks ago, when Mom called me out of the blue one night.

"I'm watching 'You've Got Mail'," she told me.

I think we were on the phone all of 20 seconds. She called me just to tell me that. In the background I could hear Dad yelling for help, begging to be freed from the continuous loop on which "You've Got Mail" plays at their house.

Sometimes Valerie and I come across the movie while flicking through the channels at home. We debate whether to call Mom and let her know it's on. If I feel like antagonizing my father, like he enjoys doing to me on a regular basis, I'll pick up the phone. Most times, though, we figure Mom already has the movie programmed to record on TiVo whenever the film airs.

"A Christmas Story," the 1983 classic about a boy named Ralphie and his quest to get Santa to bring him a rifle, is the closest I can come to understanding Mom on this issue. Valerie and I own that movie on DVD. Every December, we take it off our shelf and watch it. Every year, though, TBS runs a 24-hour marathon of the movie that starts at eight on Christmas Eve and finishes at eight on Christmas night. Both Valerie and I enjoy tuning in from time to time during that period to see as much of the movie as we can. And sure, come eight on Christmas night, there's a chance we've seen many of the scenes more than once.

Part of me thinks Mom gets a kick out of confounding us with her "You've Got Mail" quirk. She knows *exactly* what she's doing when she does things like call me, tell me she's watching the movie, and hang up. That's fine by me. She's having her fun.

But still I wonder. Can't she at *least* take the cellophane off the DVD I bought her?

Darren

May, 2010.

I see Dad all the time, so it's often challenging to gauge just how far his ALS has progressed. Once in a while, though, I see him out of our usual element and I can glimpse the toll the disease has taken on him.

Valerie and our daughter Madeline and I traveled with my parents to Virginia last month to visit our relatives. We had a terrific time. We relaxed at our relatives' home on the Rappahannock River, toured sites of the Civil War in Fredericksburg, and ate lunch at an Irish pub in Richmond. Valerie and I even got to sneak away to catch a movie one evening.

For me, though, the trip did serve as an alert to the latest details of my father's condition. At one point I needed to take a walk and sort out some of what I was seeing.

There was that moment during the drive south, for example, when Dad and I walked through the parking lot at a rest stop in Connecticut and Dad had to pause to right the angle of his head. Most of us walk around without a thought as to what our heads weigh and what it takes to keep facing forward. Dad,

233

however, is losing muscle strength in his neck and often has to fight his head from pitching forward. He says his head feels like it weighs four times what it once did.

He told me the other day that his doctor is talking to him about wearing a neck brace.

"Permanently?" I asked.

Dad just nodded.

Also during our drive down to Virginia, we stopped at a Burger King in Maryland. Dad stood at the counter and tried to fish a few dollars out of his wallet to pay for a slice of pie. Without the help of his rolling cane, Dad's stood with his knees bent and he wavered back and forth a bit. I feared he would collapse, but he assured me that what I was seeing was normal. I stood behind him, ready to catch him if he fell.

Valerie, Mom and I drove the whole trip. Dad, who had taken the wheel during family vacations for nearly 40 years, no longer drives on the highway.

In the morning, Dad sometimes falls forward as he struggles to brush his teeth or wash his face at the sink.

If he talks too much, his voice slows to a thick slur. Sometimes it is hard for others to understand something he has said. We have a running joke in our family that Dad has several aliases because people often mangle his name after he gives it to them.

Let's say he's at a takeout restaurant, for instance. He'll tell the guy at the counter that his name is Gary. When his order's finished, the employee often will call out "Barry" or "Larry."

At one sandwich shop in town, everyone calls him "Darren."

"Does Darren even *sound* like Gary?" Dad always asks us afterward.

"Say your name," we tell him.

"Gary."

We pause and give it some thought. Sometimes we ask him to repeat his name. Always, we end up answering, "Yeah, actually, coming from you, it does."

So goes life. Where Dad is today is far from where he started out when his neurologist told him, with a cold indifference he will never forget, that he had amyotrophic lateral sclerosis. The fatal illness, also known as Lou Gehrig's disease, destroys a victim's muscles in a brutal march toward complete paralysis. A victim's mind, however, is spared; thoughts, feelings and memories persist but remain unexpressed.

But Dad is still far from where the disease will ultimately lead. His ALS started seven years ago, right around the time when my daughter was born. Now, all this time later, nobody's talking to him about a wheelchair just yet.

"He's still on his feet." That's what I tell people when they ask me how Dad's doing.

It's May. This is ALS Awareness Month. Knowledge is power. That's why Dad spreads awareness about the disease as best as he can, whether it's through the book he published last year, the speeches he gives, or the fundraisers he helps organize.

If you'd like to learn about ALS or consider joining the cause for a cure, please hop online and check out The ALS Association's website, www.alsa.org.

Darren will thank you for it.

Nice Going, Chevy

I plopped down next to my daughter and asked her how her evening went. I had just gotten home from a fundraiser at Goodall Library.

Maddie said she watched a little bit of television and drew a few pictures. I asked her what she drew, but she waved off the question. You know how kids are.

Maddie should have been asleep. While I was at the library, Valerie had gotten Maddie through her nightly routine of putting on her pajamas and brushing her teeth. Valerie then let Maddie fall asleep in our bed. When I got home, though, she was wide-awake. I could sense a goofy energy still coursing through her.

"Guess who I saw today?" I asked Maddie.

"Who?"

"Senator Susan Collins. Do you know who she is?"

Maddie shook her head.

"She's one of our Maine senators," I explained. "She came to Sanford to visit a local business. Do you know what a senator is?"

Maddie said no, despite the fact that my Dad and I had bought her a children's book about how Washington works when he and I attended the National ALS Association's conference in D.C. back in 2007. The story was about a mouse who was elected to the Senate. Something like that.

"A senator is someone we elect to go to Washington, D.C. to represent us and vote on the big issues," I said. "There are only 100 of them. You know how we have a school here in Sanford named after Margaret Chase Smith?"

This Maddie knew. She nodded her head on her pillow.

"Well, Margaret Chase Smith was once a Maine senator, and now Susan Collins has her seat."

I'm not one for name-dropping. I wince when people do it. But yes, I admit I was trying to impress my daughter by telling her I had spoken with a United States senator that day. What Dad does not want to impress his daughter?

Judging from Maddie's reaction to the conversation I've described here, it looks like I need to keep trying. She has seen too much to be impressed by her father or consider him invincible.

For example, Maddie caught me making two blunders the other day as I made a smoothie in the kitchen. I poured a glass of orange juice into the blender without realizing that I had not attached the spigot to the front. As a result, the juice went right through the open spigot-hole and spilled all over the kitchen counter and floor. I used most of a roll of paper towels to sop up the mess.

When I was done I attached the spigot and poured another glass of juice onto the strawberries and bananas and blueberries I had piled into the blender. The problem was, I had not closed the spigot. Again, orange juice flowed out of the spigot and onto the counter and floor in a sticky rush.

This time I blurted out a certain word, twice. It wasn't the worst word I could have said, but it was one of the seven ones George Carlin used to say you can't say on television.

"Bad word!" Maddie scolded me from her view on the couch in our living room.

My friend Nate had a quick quip when he heard about the incident.

"Nice going, Chevy," he said.

I laughed at Nate's remark but realized he spoke the truth. Seven years into fatherhood, I now accept that I am more like Chevy Chase as Clark Griswold in those National Lampoon "Vacation" movies than, say, any of those ideal versions of fathers presented in those old TV shows from the 1950s.

Case in point. Chevy Chase is known for pratfalls. When my conversation with Maddie about her evening and Senator Collins came to an end, I kissed her on the forehead and wished her a good night. I started to get up to leave, and Maddie grabbed my arm and joked that she was not going to let me escape. She dared me to try to surpass her strength and break free from her grasp.

I played along. I attempted a few times to pull my arm from her grasp but had no luck. The kid's getting stronger every day.

Then I had an idea.

"Hey, watch this," I told Maddie. "I don't even need my arm. I can just get up and walk away with you attached to me."

I got up from the side of the bed with Maddie clinging to my forearm, and I started to walk away. I'm not quite sure what happened next. Both Maddie and I were laughing and Maddie kept pulling at my arm to keep me from getting away. She proved strong enough to drag me down a bit. At one point we bumped heads. Maddie got knocked somewhere on the side of her noggin, and I got smacked on my right eyebrow.

"Aw, man," I said, rubbing my eye. "Are you okay?"

Maddie said she was but rubbed where she got conked.

My eye pulsed. For a moment I wasn't sure what shape I was in.

"Let's go get some ice," Maddie said.

We trudged out of the room and saw Valerie as she sat at our computer.

"What did you two do now?" Valerie asked.

One of us - - Maddie, maybe - - told Val that we had knocked heads. Valerie rolled her eyes. She looked like she thought she had two children, not one.

Maddie and I opened the door to our freezer. Maddie grabbed a bag of frozen broccoli. I didn't see which bag I grabbed. String beans, I think.

Maddie applied her bag to her head. I stuck mine over my eye. I went into our bedroom and rested flat on my back on the bed with the bag of string beans over my eye.

Seconds later, I heard Valerie say, *Why is there broccoli all over the floor?"*

Maddie apparently had taken an open bag from the freezer.

Valerie stood in our dining room and listened to Maddie's version of events. Then she came into our bedroom and stood and looked at me collapsed on our bed with a bag of frozen produce over my face.

"Shawn, I had her in bed with lights out and everything," Val said, not with anger but definitely with exasperation.

With my good eye, I could see Valerie looking at the bag of veggies on my face and could hear her thinking, "Look at the two of you. This is pathetic." Then she said something about how Maddie's and my routine of horsing around before bedtime had to stop.

As she walked away, she muttered something about the broccoli.

Maddie felt fine and went to sleep in her own bed. I rested a few minutes and then got up to throw the bag of string beans back in the freezer. I checked my face in the bathroom mirror and expected to see the purplish makings of a bona fide black eye. I had a bit of a bump, but that was it.

My reflection in the mirror stared back at me. I knew what it was thinking.

Nice going, Chevy.

B.P.

Squish.

As I trudged through our dining room I stepped in something cold and wet with my bare feet.

What was it? I had no idea. It was the middle of the night and it was pitch dark and I was half asleep. All I knew was that I had just answered the call of nature and I wanted to go back to bed.

"What did the cats do *now*?" I asked, figuring Cocoa or Tootsie either had forgotten where we keep their litter box or had rejected something they had eaten.

I shuffled over to the light switch and flicked it. What I found surprised me.

A large puddle of black paint had gathered on our floor. And, of course, a trail of black footprints led across a few tiles from the puddle to where I was standing.

"Oh," I said. "Wow."

And yes, I said wow. I have told a few people this story and they could not believe that I did not say something more colorful. But I did say "wow," and I said it because more than anything else I was impressed by the size and implication of the mess.

"What happened?" Valerie called. I told her she had to come see for herself.

Valerie and I painted our living room a couple of weeks ago. No, we did not paint it black. We are not morbid people. Instead, we painted the room "Tempered All Spice." The last I checked, that is not a color, but that's what it said on the little paint card. We painted our front door black.

For the past couple of weeks we've kept the paint cans on our dining room floor, alongside the wall, as we've touched up a few walls and windowsills here and there.

"How did *that* happen?" I stared at the spill and asked.

Val sighed and said she must not have sealed the paint can tight enough.

"Okay. But that doesn't explain how it tipped over."

We checked the cats. Neither had a drop of paint on them. Also, we did not see tiny paw prints anywhere. All the same, we figured they were the culprits. Such mischief seemed right up their alley.

But it was the Christmas tree all over again. Last December I spent most of the holiday season coiled in suspense as Cocoa and Tootsie repeatedly climbed our tree, whacked ornaments off its limbs and threatened to topple the whole thing. As it turned out, though, I ended up knocking down our tree after I had shimmied underneath it to fix an artificial branch that one of the cats had bent.

And this time *I* was the one who knocked over the can of black paint. Hours earlier, I had turned off the light above our kitchen stove and ambled through the dark on my way to bed. I forgot that cans of paint sat in my path and banged my shin into one of them. I didn't realize that I had tipped over the can. It took me until the next day to recall this incident, and even then I swore to myself it had occurred not the night before but earlier in the week. Sometimes one day just runs into the other, you know?

Valerie grabbed a roll of paper towels. I headed into the bathroom and stuck my coated foot under the faucet in the shower. Afterward, Valerie and I tried to clean the mess together.

Misfortunes involving paint are a hassle. As teenagers, my friend and I helped our neighbor paint a house he owned across town. We spent the whole afternoon spraying the exterior of the house with its new color. Then a thunderstorm broke and the rain washed away our efforts in messy streaks. For the record, when this happened, my neighbor said plenty, but he did not say "Wow."

Valerie and I got down on our hands and knees and swabbed up the paint as best we could. We caught some of it but much remained and took on the circular patterns in which we wiped.

"We can use an SOS pad to scrub off the rest tomorrow," Valerie stated when matters looked more under control. It was 1:30 in the morning. We wanted to go back to sleep.

I found our copy of the Sanford News and spread some of its pages over the blotches and streaks and footprints that remained. It's always humbling when I see my hard work put to some other use beyond bringing the good people of Sanford their local news.

"What a mess," I said, standing with my hands on my hips. Referring to the recent oil rig disaster in the Gulf of Mexico, I added, "Now I know how Obama must feel with the oil spill."

Of course, in our house, BP stood for something else.

Black Paint.

Rein's Deli

In the late Eighties, my family and I stopped to eat at Rein's Deli in Vernon, Connecticut. One of Dad's coworkers recommended the place, knowing we'd be in the area during our family vacation that summer.

We gave the place a shot and we must have liked what we ate. We have returned there several times ever since.

It's a tradition. If we're embarking on a trip or heading home from one and we're on Interstate 84, we have to take exit 65 and head over to Rein's at 435 Hartford Turnpike on Route 30. My wife, daughter, parents and I did this when we drove back to Maine from a trip to Virginia a few months ago. We did the same thing on our way home from another trip last year.

The restaurant is a traditional New York-style deli that offers, to quote the menu, "food that feeds the soul and warms the heart." You can get entrées and salad platters, Reubens and Rachaels, cold veggie, specialty and triple-meat sandwiches, soups and burgers off the grill, and desserts. The waitress brings you a bowl of pickles to start you off.

The dining area is divided into sections known well to anyone who either has lived in New York City or has visited

247

there - - Queens, Manhattan and Staten Island, for example. The Statue of Liberty stands at maybe ten or eleven feet tall in the center. There are two bathrooms, one on each side of the deli; a sign directs you in either direction to the "Can Can," or, my favorite, "Flushing."

On our way out, my family and I almost always stop at the bakery counter to pick up a sweet for the ride home.

We eat at Rein's Deli because we love the food and atmosphere, yes, but there's admittedly something else going on when we visit there. It goes relatively unspoken between us, despite the memories we recall while there, but here it is: returning to Rein's Deli brings my parents and me, and my sister when she joins us, full circle to the more innocent time when we were all younger, living under the same roof, and doing everything together.

My wife, Valerie, realizes this, as she sits there and eats her egg salad sandwich. I'm sure she knows the tradition will continue, well after my parents have departed, every time we venture south with Maddie or, some day, our own grandchildren.

Truth be told, these pilgrimages may be as much about the town of Vernon as they are about the restaurant. The funny thing is, I can tell you very little about Vernon. I've never strayed from that one road where the restaurant is found. But in the summer of 1984, a few years before we first ate at Rein's, my family and my grandmother and I stayed at a hotel on that one road as we traveled to Maryland to visit our relatives.

We got into Vernon after dark because we had left Maine late in the afternoon, a bit after my sister and I finished summer camp for the day. We checked into a room at one of the hotels in town. Dad fiddled with the television dial to see which channels we would have during our stay. We were pleased to get the three basic networks. Remember, this was well before we all had hundreds of channels that broadcast around the clock.

At around nine that evening, Mom, Dad, Kelly and I relaxed on a grassy hill behind the hotel. Kelly and I ate M&Ms and drank from Hi-C juice boxes.

Our Memere joined us after a few minutes. She had gone to the hotel lobby to get a complimentary cup of coffee. Memere, who was 65 and widowed for three years then, looked quite content when she emerged with the coffee after a three-hour drive in the back seat with her two grandchildren.

My family took a lot of vacations when I was growing up. We did not have a big yard, two cars or a swimming pool, but there was a reason for that - - what money Mom and Dad did make they put toward family trips. That and Christmas, of course.

In the space of ten years, we went to a number of places. Of all of them, though, you know which moment makes me smile and fills me with the most warmth? That evening on the grassy hill in Vernon, Connecticut.

Valerie and I went to Vernon several years ago, during the carefree summer of 2001 before the September morning that changed everything forever. We went there on a whim. Valerie had to go to southern Massachusetts for an appointment and we figured we'd make a trip out of it and drive out to Rein's Deli. Valerie had never eaten there before.

When we arrived in Vernon, we looked for the hotel where my family and I stayed back in '84. We thought we found it, but when we went inside we learned from the clerk at the desk that we were at a whole other inn. We were told that the hotel where my family and I had stayed had burned to the ground a year or two before. Gone, like so much else.

Rein's was still there, though, and the sandwiches hit the spot.

The Twentieth

My friends and I stood at the top of the hill that leads down to the Sanford Junior High School's parking lot. We had just returned to Sanford from pulling an all-nighter with our fellow graduates during the senior cruise on Lake Winnipesaukee.

It was a quiet morning, maybe just a few minutes past six or seven. We had just grabbed a couple of doughnuts in the cafeteria of the Memorial Gym. We skipped sticking around and chatting with our classmates over cups of juice. For one thing, we were tired. For another, we just . . . well, we knew. We knew that was it. Our time with the Sanford School System had come to an end. Our future stretched out before us like the Great Unknown.

Apparently, I said something profound yet hilarious as we stood atop the hill on our way down to our friend Brian's car in the junior high lot. A few years ago, my friend Nate reminded me of what I said after he stumbled upon an old e-mail that told the tale. When I contacted Nate a few nights ago, though, he could no longer recall it. The remark, like so much we say in life, is lost in time. Its echo across the ages has died.

Nate did say that I said something that put everything - - those first scant 18 years of our lives, our futures before us, and the moment at hand - - into perspective. He also said my comment included a reference to the doughnut I had just eaten.

We exercised a bit of poetic license and figured I had stated that everything in our lives to that moment had come right down to that doughnut. The Sanford School System had given us an education for twelve years; thirteen, if you count kindergarten. The system had handed us our diplomas the night before. It had given us the gift of an all-night cruise that included music and dancing and food. And now, after everything else, the school system had provided us with one more thing.

The doughnut.

My thinking is, I knew that once I ate that doughnut, that was it. The Sanford School System had given me all it could. Once that doughnut was gone, I was on my own. The time had come for my friends and my classmates and I to make our own ways in the world.

That sounds like something I'd say or think. I enjoyed making offbeat but true observations then just as much as I do now.

Twenty years ago, that was. The Summer of 1990.

The father of a future president was president.

"Dick Tracy," "Total Recall" and "Die Hard 2" were big at the movies, and then the sleeper date flick "Ghost" came along and busted them all at the box office.

"Cheers," "Roseanne" and "The Cosby Show" were among the most popular shows on television.

On the radio, Madonna was all the rage with "Vogue" and rapper MC Hammer told us, "U Can't Touch This." Hammer wore those silly parachute pants as he rapped. Not that we knew those pants were silly at the time, of course.

I remember that summer of 1990 well. It had its share of good times and drama, as all summers do when you're a teenager. It ended in late August when a bunch of us reported to Brian's house not long after sunrise one morning. We joked a bit, said we'd all see each other again sometime soon, and promised to write. We didn't trade e-mail addresses, of course, because we had not heard of e-mail yet.

Then Brian got into the car and off he went, the first of the ol' gang to leave for college.

This Saturday, I will join my classmates for our twentieth class reunion here in town. I'm looking forward to it. I attended our tenth with my wife, Valerie, and had a good time. That reunion was true in the sense of the word; it brought my classmates and me together for an evening, a whole decade after we each parted ways and set on our own diverse paths.

This time around, there's something familiar and even comforting about the coming event. I could be wrong, but I think the bond between classmates strengthens, not weakens, as the years pass. You see it with classes that celebrate their fortieth and fiftieth and sixtieth reunions; there's a feeling of shared roots, forged during simpler times.

There's another reason behind such a notion: Facebook.

Thanks to Facebook, most of us are brought up to speed with one another. We know where we're all living now, and what we're doing for work. We know about our children's soccer games, scraped knees and academic achievements. And, given the frivolous nature of this popular social network, we even know when we're all bored, heading out to the movies, taking a trip, feeling exhausted from work, unable to sleep late at night or eating a ham sandwich.

Like the rest of the world, we're all connected, plugged into each other's lives, online all the time.

But here's the thing. The Class of 1990 was one of the last ones to enjoy some semblance of peace and privacy as the world once knew it. Just a few years after my classmates and I graduated, cell phones, the World Wide Web, around-the-clock news channels and other leaps in technology and communication began their conquest of the world.

Our class was one of the last ones to write notes and pass them, not "text" them, when our teachers were not looking. To listen to the hit songs of the day on clunky Walkmans attached to our hips. To get our news at 6:30 in the evening, if we were even interested in what was happening in the world beyond our young lives.

There's something old-fashioned about reunions that's appealing. While Facebook allows you to keep tabs with your classmates, reunions give you the chance to *see* them - - to be with them, laugh with them, and enjoy their company, face to face.

Those of us in the Class of 1990 have been out in the world for twenty years now. We're older, yes, and hopefully wiser, and - - sorry, gang, it's true - - pushing the Big Four-Oh.

But the promise we felt two decades ago, however shaded in uncertainty, is still with us to this day. Now is the future we could not see that morning after we graduated. It keeps unfolding, with these reunions along the way, thankfully, and there's nothing between us and everything we can do to continue to make something of our lives.

Not even a doughnut.

Little Do We Know

Dad ambled from the car onto the lawn and smiled for the camera. Then he turned and faced the ocean. In the distance, several boats idled on the calm, sun-dappled water.

It's a view he once knew well. He had taken his first teaching job there in Stonington, somewhere off the coast a few hours north from home. He and a coworker split the rent on a trailer on this very lawn in the late 1960s. On many mornings he'd wake up and shuffle out the front door to head to class, and this shore and sea would be what he would see.

Valerie and Madeline and I went with Dad and Mom to Stonington a couple of weekends ago. Our idea was to get away from it all and give Dad a chance to retrace steps he took more than 40 years ago.

We found the seaside property on which Dad's trailer once rested. A trailer no longer sits there. In its place is a fresh lawn, thick and green. I asked Dad to stand where he imagined his front steps used to be. I wanted to take a picture of him there, with the ocean sights behind him.

He positioned himself with as much sturdiness as he can muster these days and took care to tuck his rolling cane behind him. Dad is open about the accommodations he needs to compensate for the toll ALS has taken on him, but he's sensitive about appearing in photos with his cane, walker or motorized wheelchair. Moments come and go, but photographs are forever. Keeping his cane out of frame helps him shape how his grandchildren will remember him.

Dad smiled and I snapped the picture. Then Madeline joined him, and I took another.

Little did Dad know. Little did Dad know 42 years ago that one day he'd return to this site, with his seven-year-old granddaughter by his side.

Dad's former home did not quite match how I'd always imagined it. Given his stories over the years, I had always pictured his trailer balanced precariously on a jagged cliff as gray and turbulent waves crashed against rocks during unforgiving storms. But I'm not charging Dad with embellishment here; he lived in Stonington not during its warm and picturesque summers but instead during its cold and deserted winters. Also, he said he was prone to loneliness and homesickness when class was not in session, and he was not surrounded by fellow teachers, students and friends.

Dad also took us to another home where he lived during his time teaching in Stonington. This one was a pale green house, located a stone's throw from an intersection that lends itself to gallows humor - - that of Sunset Avenue and Cemetery Road.

A restaurant is next door to the house. Dad told us of a time his college roommate's in-laws stopped and visited him during a swing through Maine. Dad called the restaurant and ordered them a turkey dinner. The cook promised to lower the shade in the restaurant's window that faced Dad's house as a way to let Dad know the meals were ready to be picked up. His guests, sophisticates of Long Island, laughed and marveled at such low-tech folksiness.

We also visited the school where Dad taught. The building is no longer used for classrooms but for offices. It's a two-story structure, painted white, and has a staircase in front. Facing the building, Dad glanced up at the windows on the left side of the top floor and told us that's where he taught high school history.

The former school's gymnasium can be found in the back lot. It's this facility, even more so than the school, that is the centerpiece of Dad's memories and stories about his time in Stonington. It's here that he coached basketball, even though he knew little about the game at first.

I approached the gym's front door and peered through its opaque windows to the darkened court inside. A few images swam into view. The court itself had a nice sheen. I could see one of the baskets in the distance, suspended in front of a stage.

I tried to make out the sidelines to catch the ghost of my father, kicking a chair or throwing down his clipboard after a bad call from the ref. With affection for his brash, younger self, Dad admits to having had a temper on the court, always toward a ref or a disagreeable parent and never toward the players in his charge.

Again, little did Dad know. Little did Dad know, as he confidently strode into that gymnasium 42 years ago, that he'd return to that site decades later, with his youthful swagger replaced by careful and uncertain steps, with his son's arm locked in his for support.

Do not mistake these reflections of my father's life, both past and present, as somber in tone. We enjoyed our trip and filled it with much laughter and relaxation. The trip even proved triumphant, for my father had not been sure whether he'd ever return to where he started a career in education that lasted more than 40 years.

Twice I've said "little did Dad know" because I continue to be amazed at the way life plays out. We do not know the future, but when it arrives and becomes the present, it is astonishing to circle back and behold everything that has happened in our lives. It is mesmerizing, even comforting, to return to places we once knew, with loved ones whom we did not know at the time - - or had not yet brought into the world.

Something occurred to me as we drove out of Stonington, toward the steep bridge that would return us to the mainland. In August of 1983, Dad brought me to Stonington. We added his old teaching haunts to an overnight camping trip we had taken to

259

Bangor an hour away. I remember very few details about the time we spent in his old stomping ground. I was, after all, only eleven years old at the time.

Dad, on the other hand, was 38.

The age I am now.

All those years ago, as a boy with so much life ahead of me, I never would have figured I'd return to Stonington with Dad at the precise age he was then.

As well, the wife I'd meet in college and the child we'd have nine years later were faceless strangers in 1983. Back then I could not have imagined I'd be accompanied by Valerie and Maddie when I returned to Stonington 27 years later.

Little did I know.

The Saddest Day

Saturday morning was a bright and warm one, just like it was on the same day nine years earlier.

As I walked across Shaw's Field with a bag of soccer balls slung over my shoulder, I realized I had missed the moment. I had let 8:46 come and go without notice.

For eight years I had paused at this very minute to mark the moment when terrorists crashed the first plane into the World Trade Center and set the world on fire. On Saturday, though, 8:46 got lost in the rush of getting my daughter Madeline and me out the door in time for our game at 9:30.

I woke up that morning knowing it was September 11. I thought of the victims who died that day. I wondered how a few first-responders that I know were feeling as they recalled the brothers and sisters they lost in the flames and rubble and that overpowering cloud of dust and smoke that choked Manhattan. I thought of my friend who was there that day and escaped the destruction; I felt glad that he's back in Sanford now, safe at home.

At one point on Saturday morning, though, the here-and-now took over. For the first time since 2001, I missed the

261

collective moment of silence our nation takes just a little after a quarter of nine on September 11.

I looked around the soccer field on Saturday morning - - it is *the* busiest place in town during the weekends of September and October - - and scanned people of all ages, from the little ones scrambling on the Pee Wee turf to the older kids battling for goals during the junior matches to the parents and grandparents and siblings who crowded the sidelines.

Life does go on, I thought. *That doesn't mean that we have forgotten anything, but life does go on.*

All the children at the field made that clear to me. Most of them were not alive on September 11, 2001. The rest were too young to recall what happened.

I looked at Maddie and wondered when she'd learn about September 11. Valerie and I have tried to explain to our daughter the importance of certain occasions of remembrance, such as Memorial Day and Veterans Day, so that she can grow up appreciating their true meaning. On the subject of September 11, though, we've said little to our seven-year-old.

Is it because we think she's unable to appreciate or understand what happened that morning? No.

Is it because we do not want to scare her - - make her afraid of airplanes or prompt her to add terrorists to the list of bogeymen that already live in a child's imagination? That's part of it, sure.

On the whole, though, I look at my daughter and see life as it was on September 10, 2001.

We all know where we were and what we were doing when we heard the news on September 11. We know all that has followed since. But do you remember what you were doing on September 10, 2001? Can you recall how it felt *not* to have the images from the next morning plague your mind? How it felt before our national consciousness became steeped in nine years of threats and close calls and all-out war?

I looked at Maddie on Saturday morning and thought it best to let it be September 10 for her a while longer. The time would come soon enough when she would become aware of that tragic day in history and start asking questions.

Alas, the moment came later on Saturday evening. While Maddie read in her bedroom, Valerie and I watched a documentary on the History Channel about a mother and daughter who fled that nightmarish plume that darkened Manhattan once the towers fell. Maddie came into the room at one point and saw all that smoke and dust on the screen. She started asking questions.

Valerie and I admittedly were not prepared and did our best to answer. We told her the images on the screen happened nine years ago, before she was born.

"It was one of the saddest days in our country's history," I said.

We explained to Maddie that some bad guys had caused two buildings to fall in New York City. We did not tell her how they managed to do this. Maddie pressed a bit further, but Valerie and I offered her a loving smile and told her one day she would be ready to learn more. She accepted our answer and returned to her room.

Valerie and I looked at each other and hoped we handled the issue well. If we had any doubts, we were able to overcome them moments later when we tucked Maddie into bed. That was when we found the right thing to say to our seven-year-old about the awful events of September 11, 2001.

"Here's what you need to know for now about today," I told Maddie in a soft tone. "September 11 is a day when we remember certain people who are no longer with us, and it is a chance to make sure we let the people in our lives know we love them."

Stan

"Maddie, look over there! It's Stan!"

We'd see the chipmunk, sitting in our driveway, or next to our picnic table, or on top of one of the tires of our car, and then he'd dart out of sight. He'd often disappear into our bushes.

Every time I see a chipmunk, I tell Maddie it's Stan. This is a running joke between my daughter and me.

It didn't quite start out that way. At first Maddie rolled her eyes when I pointed Stan out to her. Then she would get frustrated. I think she thought I was trying to pull a fast one on her.

"They're all different chipmunks, Dad," Maddie would say. "They're not all the same one called Stan."

But I persisted. Valerie started thinking that I was just out to pester our daughter - - that I was following in my father's footsteps and antagonizing my child as he did me out of some kind of misguided show of affection. It's true that we Sullivans only tease the ones we love. To tease someone we do not like would not be nice.

But this was not the case. I explained to Maddie that I was not trying to convince her that we were seeing the same chipmunk every time. I told her I was just trying to establish a cute joke between us, a connection that'd make us smile and wink every time we came around to a chipmunk. Of *course* all those chipmunks are not the same one named Stan, I told Maddie. I wanted her to know that it's okay not to be so literal all the time, and that it's rather fun to dabble in the absurd.

Maddie nodded. She didn't seem eager to start getting in on the joke, but I could see that her annoyance had disappeared.

Later we took a trip with my parents to Stonington. After we settled into our hotel room one evening, I sat on the front porch and read for a while. At one point a chipmunk scurried out of some nearby bushes and stood out in the open on its hind legs.

"Maddie, come here," I called out.

Maddie appeared in the doorway, and I pointed to the chipmunk.

"Stan," she said. And she smiled when she said it.

"How about that," I said. "He followed us all the way from Sanford. That's quite a ways from home."

In the weeks ahead, Maddie started pointing out chipmunks and telling me, "Hey, Dad, look. It's Stan."

We went camping in New Hampshire. A chipmunk appeared out of the dark of night and stepped into the flickering light of our campfire. Maddie and I noted that Stan had done it again. He had traveled far and wide from our Sanford home to join us on a trip.

Maddie started asking me questions about Stan. I'd answer them, and soon we had created a biography for the little guy. We had given him a life.

A couple of weeks ago, I went down into our basement to throw a load of clothes into the washer. One of our cats, Cocoa, followed me. After I finished my chore, I wandered into the next room in search of Cocoa, so that I could nab him and bring him back upstairs for the night. I proceeded with caution; the single bulb affixed near the wall was throwing more dark shadows than light.

I turned a corner and walked in relative darkness, my slippers scuffing the concrete floor. I spotted Cocoa and headed over to him.

I heard a crunch. Felt it too.

I sighed and thought, "What did I step in *now*?" I recalled another late night, earlier this year, when I ambled through our dining room and stepped in something thick, cool and wet that turned out to be a small sea of black paint spilled from a can with a loose lid.

I looked down and saw the shadowed outline of something that had been flattened. It was too big to be a mouse. I was hoping it was too small to be a rat. *Please, God,* I thought. *Let it not be a rat.*

I flicked on another bulb, and there it was. There *he* was. Stan.

How he got into our basement, I have no idea. How long he had been there, I also didn't know. Let the record show, though, that he had departed our realm long before I came along and stepped on him.

I looked down at him and felt bad. A little nauseated too.

Whoever invented slippers, I thank you.

Maddie took the news well. She heard Valerie and me discussing What Was Downstairs.

"Was it Stan, Dad?" she asked me.

I stood there for a few seconds and did not say a word. I had worked so hard all summer to get Maddie to lighten up a bit and play along with the whole "Stan" deal. I had gotten her, *us*, to the point where we shared a running gag, one that made us smile and play along. For Maddie and me, every chipmunk we saw was Stan.

It's bad enough the little guy that had sneaked into our basement did not live long enough to sneak back out. Must we lose Stan too?

"No," I finally answered Maddie. "That was Stan's very old Uncle Walter."

575 Cracker Barrels to Go . . .

Dad thinks Mom is the "Sarah Palin of Cracker Barrels."

You can stop scratching your head over that one. I'll explain.

The Cracker Barrel is a chain of quaint and rustic restaurants that offers home-cooked meals and sells retro-goodies in fun gift shops. It's Mom's favorite restaurant. She often eats at the one in New Hampshire - - just did last week, come to think of it - - and she keeps an eye out for other ones whenever she and Dad hit the road on vacations.

She loves that moment when she and Dad are cruising the highway in a faraway state and she spots a Cracker Barrel off the next exit. The two of them always pull over and sit down for a meal.

"It's the thrill of the hunt," Mom said with that trademark smile of hers that says she has left this world behind and is now in her own. Actually, it's not her smile that says that. It's the gleam in her eyes.

So that's why Dad calls Mom the "Sarah Palin of Cracker Barrels." Palin, the 2008 GOP vice presidential nominee from

Alaska, loves to hunt and, well, so does Mom. One hunts deer, moose and Democrats. The other hunts eating establishments.

The image of Mom hunting Cracker Barrels is a priceless one. I can see her in a helicopter, dressed not in fluorescent orange but in her dinner clothes with a napkin tucked into the front of her collar, armed not with a high-powered rifle but instead a fork and knife. She soars through the air, high above the trees and strips of interstate, her binoculars sealed to her vigilant eyes.

"There's one right there!" she yells to Dad and points. *"I can see the sign sticking out of the trees next to Exit 47!"*

But see, the funny thing is, it's never a hunt. Mom always knows where to find a Cracker Barrel. She has a huge map of the United States that pinpoints every Cracker Barrel in the country. There are a lot of them.

Mom recently opened the map and showed it to me.

"See?" she asked. "There it is. Five-hundred-and-ninety-five Cracker Barrels in 42 states."

I think Mom hopes to visit all of them before she leaves this life and heads to the Great Cracker Barrel in the sky. She said she and Dad have been to about 20 of the restaurants so far - - ones in New Mexico, New Jersey, Virginia, South Dakota, you name it. She and Dad also have eaten at the original Cracker Barrel in Spartanburg, South Carolina.

"All I have to do is think of the Saint Ignatius Spartans, and it helps me remember the name of the town," said Mom, a graduate of Saint Ignatius High School's Class of 1968.

Mom first discovered Cracker Barrel when she and Dad drove my sister across the country to her new apartment in San Diego back in September of 1995.

"We stopped in Joplin, Missouri, and there was a Cracker Barrel in the distance, off the highway," she recalled. "I've been in love with it ever since."

I've been in love with it ever since? Wow. That's something. I've never heard Mom sound so smitten and devoted, so swayed by the power of love at first sight. Not even when she talks about Adam Lambert from "American Idol." Not even when she tells me the story of when she first met Dad in line at the movies for a showing of "To Sir, With Love" back in the late sixties.

Mom always gets the same meal at Cracker Barrel: a serving of chicken and dumplings that she shares with Dad. She calls this meal and the others on the menu "home-cooked comfort food."

Mom often orders the same thing at restaurants. If she's not at a Cracker Barrel, she'll almost always get a turkey club sandwich. In 1996, Mom and Dad traveled to Italy. Rather than bask in the succulence of the native cuisine, she ordered nothing but turkey club sandwiches. Dad couldn't believe it.

Mom has learned that a Cracker Barrel is opening in South Portland in November. You'd think she would be thrilled - - well, of course she is - - but she's a bit disappointed that there's not a restaurant opening in Portsmouth instead.

"Portsmouth is one of your Dad's and my favorite spots, ever since we were dating and got married," she explained.

But Mom knows beggars can't be choosers. When Cracker Barrel opens in South Portland, she'll be there, eating those dumplings and relaxing in one of the several rocking chairs the chain always places along the front entrance.

But rest assured: Nothing has changed. The hunt *will* continue.

"I want to cruise along Route 66 on a Harley Davidson and stop at every Cracker Barrel I see on the way," Mom said, getting that look in her eyes again. "Your father can ride along in one of those sidecars."

Why do I have the feeling that my mother has this whole other life that I know nothing about?

B.S.

On Veterans Day, we had a visitor at the Sanford News who said he was going to Applebee's for a special dinner. The restaurant had offered free suppers to veterans that evening.

"This is *my* meal," he said to me, as though I might try to take it from him.

"Right."

"Did you ever serve?"

"No," I told him.

"Well, this is a special menu they're offering, just for people who served."

I nodded.

He shuffled a few dollars around in his wallet and gave me a sidelong glance. "The next time you see me on my day, you stand on your feet."

He looked serious when he said it. I scanned his face for a hint of a smile or a wink in his eye but saw neither. I smiled and rose to my feet, in a slightly hammy way, I grant you, because I did not want to seem so easily pushed.

"All right, then," the veteran said. Then he left to go get that meal.

I drove home that night wondering what was up with *that*.

I've known this guy for years, but I admit I had no idea if he was serious during this exchange or if he was pulling my leg. Either way, I stood by my reaction, including the moment I got up on my feet. It was Veterans Day, the man was a veteran, and I never served in our military. Save for the slight comic exaggeration with which I stood at attention, I erred on the side of playing the situation straight.

I found out the next day that he was kidding. Completely.

"I love it," I laughed and said. On the whole, I'm not the kind of guy who gets flustered or defensive when he has been had.

I'd bet not too many people would say I'm serious, or humorless, but there would be some who'd say I take *others* too seriously.

It's a fair charge. Rather than risk offending someone, I will take a person at face value, even if on the inside I have my doubts. I'm much more inclined to take this approach with elders than I am my contemporaries or those younger than me.

It's not that I'm gullible when someone tries to pull a fast one on me. My inner B.S. detector may not hum like the finest-tuned fork, but it does work serviceably enough. Quite simply, the case is as I've stated it: In a professional capacity, and sometimes in a personal one, I prefer not to roll the dice and react in a way that could hurt someone's feelings or rub them the wrong way.

When this approach makes me seem too literal or serious-minded, as perhaps it did on Veterans Day, there is admittedly some justice in it. After all, I've pulled a few legs myself.

I get some of that from my father, yes, but he's more prone to teasing than making things up to amuse himself. More than anyone, though, I believe such mischief comes from my maternal grandfather.

Pepere passed away in 1981, when I was nine years old. I think about him often. It's hard *not* to think of him; the Sanford News office used to be a funeral home, and my desk sits in the exact same corner where I saw Pepere for the very last time during his wake.

Pepere loved to pull pranks. One time, he and Memere came across an old friend as they were out on a drive together. They stopped and chatted with him a bit.

"How are you doing?" the friend asked Pepere.

"Oh, well, thanks," Pepere said, and then added, "We just got back from California."

The friend smiled and approached Memere's side of the car. He leaned in to her window and asked her how she enjoyed the trip. He looked at Memere and smiled and waited for her to answer.

Memere paused and then nodded. She muttered something about having a fun time.

But here's the thing: Memere and Pepere never *went* to California. Ever. Pepere was just feeling mischievous, and the joke he was playing was not so much on his friend as it was on my poor grandmother.

Memere, a serious-minded woman who could never, ever tell a lie, was furious with Pepere for pulling her into his foolishness and putting her on the spot. *Furious.*

"Well, I suppose I finally forgive your father for what he did that day," Memere once told my mother. Decades after it happened. Long after Pepere had died.

I'm capable of the same shenanigans. The difference with me is, I do *not* expect you to believe me. I relish the playful challenge of trying to make the wildly outrageous seem plausible, but I'd like to think I put just enough of a wink into the task to tip you off. Part of me is hoping you will jump in and play along, so that we can build the foolish tale together and keep a straight face while doing it.

I told a coworker once that Congress had passed a bill to combine Halloween and Christmas into one holiday. I said families would have to dress up in their costumes on Christmas morning before they all gathered around the tree and opened presents. Trick-or-treat bags would replace Christmas stockings over the fireplace. Santa Claus would step aside and some kind of yuletide ghoul would take his place.

Moments later, I felt awful, downright *lousy*, when I found the coworker looking on the Internet for a news story to tell her more about the legislation.

In college, I went out to Wendy's for dinner with my girlfriend and my friend, Valerie, who at the time I had no idea I'd marry three years later.

As we sat and ate our burgers, dark clouds gathered outside and thunder rumbled in the distance.

"I got struck by lightning once," I said.

I then proceeded to spin a crazy tale, one with far-fetched flourishes that I did not expect anyone to believe.

Years later, when we were newlyweds, Valerie asked me about the time I got zapped.

"Are you serious?" I asked. "You *believed* that?"

"You had a straight face when you said it," Val told me.

"Yeah, but . . ." I trailed off. "You've believed that all these years?"

I felt sorry then too. I had not tried to fool Valerie that evening. I just expected her to shake her head and recognize my tale for what it was: bored, restless and misguided creativity, something that should have been written as a quick story rather than inserted into a conversation.

So you can see now that I have it coming to me when someone pulls my leg and I think they're serious. From now on, though, I will resolve not to be so easily duped. In the meantime, so as to not invite such just desserts, I'll hold off on pulling other people's legs.

I welcome the fresh start, now that I'm back from California.

Let There Be Lights

My wife is brilliant.

Every year, Valerie and I debate which lights to hang on our Christmas tree. She favors the clear ones because she likes the soft, simple and uniform glow they cast. I lean toward the colored lights because variety is the spice of life and the reds, blues, golds, greens and oranges throw a certain warmth off the tree that fills the room.

This difference in taste is consistent in our relationship. Valerie likes plain cheese pizza. I like pepperoni and olives and a few other toppings spread on top of mine. Valerie prefers vanilla ice cream. I prefer mint chocolate chip and peppermint stick and often order one scoop of each in a single cup. Valerie's idea of a nice vacation is going somewhere quiet and staying there and making no plans. My idea of one is a whirlwind tour that does include days of rest but features soaking up the sights, attractions and ways of life you cannot find at home.

For the record, I appreciate this dynamic. Because of Valerie, I better appreciate the simple elegance of a spoonful of vanilla ice cream; it's a nice break from my constant quest for a variety of flavors. Because of Valerie, I like those quieter days during the busy trips we take; I use that time to read a book, take a walk and enjoy being around loved ones. I'll stick with my pepperoni and black olives, though; I bite into a slice of cheese pizza and feel the bland disappointment of wanting more.

There are a few other contrasts between my wife and me. She is patient. I am not. She is reserved. I am not. She has a beautiful and full head of hair. I . . . well, that's a different story.

As for Christmas decorations in general, Valerie would prefer to have Martha Stewart decorate our house in quaint, classy and delicate splendor. I'd like to have Clark Griswold, Chevy Chase's hapless father from "National Lampoon's Christmas Vacation," on hand to help.

Rest assured, I am entirely fond of the Norman Rockwell approach that Valerie advocates. But also know this: We have a four-foot Frosty the Snowman on our front steps that my parents bought back in the kitschy year of 1972, and for Valerie his placement there is a major concession.

Valerie has warmed up to Frosty over the years. The large bulb inside his midsection has dimmed a bit and retreated until it's just about hanging out the hole in his back. I've not replaced the bulb or pushed it back inside Frosty's hard-plastic frame. As a result, he is backlit and looks more attractive from the street. Valerie never liked it when Frosty shined much brighter because the increased illumination had a way of exposing the ingrained dirt and dust that Frosty has collected after the decades he spent in my parents' cellar and our garage.

"You *could* clean him, you know," Valerie says to me.

"I have," I assure her.

She then explains to me that patting Frosty down with a damp paper towel is not enough. What Frosty needs is a blast from an industrial-strength hose plugged into the nearest fire hydrant.

On the subject of lights on the Christmas tree, Valerie and I have found a compromise over the years. Our daughter, Maddie, breaks the gridlock in my favor because she too prefers colored lights, but what we have done over the years is alternate. One year we'll hang clear lights on the tree. The next we'll drape colored ones. And so on.

Last year we went with the colored lights. That made this year a clear-light one, fair and square. Valerie, however, made a skillful maneuver that ensures we will have clear lights on our tree for years and years to come.

A couple of weekends ago, we set out to buy a new artificial Christmas tree. Last year, we knew the one we had, a hand-me-down from my folks, needed to go. Its far-reaching branches had seen better holidays, and its wide berth crowded our living room so much we had to put our couch on the front lawn and watch TV through the picture window.

There was also the matter of our two cats, Cocoa and Tootsie, who considered the tree their personal Mount Everest and climbed it often just because it was there. They knocked the tree down once, shattering ornaments of sentimental value. I knocked down the tree down once too, in a failed attempt to fix a sagging branch on which they had sat.

So this year we needed something stronger. We wanted the same height of six-and-a-half feet but desired fuller branches and a more slender gait.

Valerie and I found a tree we liked at one of the local box stores. Maddie was not so sure about it. She wrinkled her nose and stated that it was too small. We told her the tree was the same height as the old one, but she wasn't buying it. We tried to explain that the tree *looked* small because it was sitting high on a table, next to taller trees in a big store large enough to serve as an airplane hangar. In our much smaller living room, it would fill the room just right, we said.

Maddie still disapproved. She wanted the tree that they lit in front of Rockefeller Center last week. I put an end to the debate by doing what all parents do in these circumstances: I moralized. Yes. This means I told her the story of Charlie Brown's decrepit little tree that magically transformed into a rich fir once his friends stopped calling him a blockhead and helped him give it love.

Sure enough, we picked a winner. The tree is up, and Maddie and Valerie and I are enjoying it.

We seemed to have foiled the cats too. The tree is too narrow and the fake branches are too thin and tangled to climb.

They seem to know this as they stand underneath the tree and cast a longing gaze through the branches above them. So far they've had to amuse themselves by smashing a few ornaments hanging from the bottom limbs.

But here is where my wife is brilliant. The tree came *pre-lit* with clear lights. This means we will not have colored lights on our tree for at least the next seven or eight years, or however long artificial trees are meant to last.

It also means we will not have colored lights *anywhere* at our house - - in our bushes, along the garland hung from the ceiling - - because even I have enough of an uptight sense of decor to feel all our lights should be uniform for the best possible visual presentation.

Good grief, as Charlie Brown might say.

"I *told* you the tree was pre-lit when we were looking at it at the store," Val told me. "You nodded your head."

Perhaps I did. But it doesn't take a marital expert to tell you that just because spouses nod their heads, it does not necessarily mean they heard.

I took a simpler approach to the tree. I liked the way it looked, and we could afford it. I follow the same impulse when buying cars and sneakers.

When we got home and I discovered that the tree came in three pieces, with the branches already inserted into the poles, no less, I was thrilled. Gone are the days of sorting out individual color-coded branches and plugging them into a wooden pole.

Ah, but those lights. All of the color has gone out of our Christmas.

"Well played, Val," I told my wife. "Well played."

"But I didn't *play* anything," she insisted.

I smirked as though to say *"Suuuuuuuuuuuuuure."*

But of course those lights are beautiful. They make the ornaments sparkle. They cast the kind of soft and soothing glow that not even the smallest lamp with the darkest shade could provide. They shine with simplicity and class.

Don't tell Valerie I told you this, but here's the truth: I see those lights through my wife's eyes, and I love them.

Catch A Cold In The Rain?

I went for a walk the other day and got caught in the rain.

Like most people, I prefer warm and sunny days and usually choose to stay inside when it's wet outside. On the whole, though, I like rain if it does not last for days or bring a raw snap to the air.

We were told as children to head indoors whenever it started to rain. The reason was a matter of life and death: "You could catch a cold out there!"

I wonder who first used that scare tactic. You just know it had to be some little kid's mother. There's no way a drill sergeant first issued that dire warning, commanding his soldiers to get the bleep out of the rain and into their barracks before they caught the sniffles.

There's just something about that whole catch-a-cold line that has never held any water for me. After all, what's the difference between getting caught outdoors in a summer storm and taking a shower inside your home?

I'll tell you: clothes. In one case, you're wearing 'em, and in the other, you're not. Parents want their children to come in from the rain because they don't want to deal with sopping wet clothes and shoes that track mud on their floors. Also, they don't want their neighbors to see their kids out there and think they have bad parents. Because, after all, they could catch a cold out there.

I remember the first time I got caught in the rain and chose not to head inside. I could not have been more than five or six years old. I was playing with friends in my neighbor's driveway when it first started to sprinkle and then picked up. I may have even heard rumbling in the sky. But I stayed outdoors and played, and after a while I thought, "Why isn't Mom calling me in from the rain?" I had a great time staying outside; I felt like I was getting away with something.

When my friends and I were teenagers, we went to Aquaboggan in Saco for the day. In the afternoon, the sky turned dark and the clouds unleashed torrential rain that lasted a while. But the managers never closed the park. This made perfect sense to me. Why shut the place down due to inclement weather? It was a *water* park. We were in lines to ride flows of chlorinated water down slides that led to pools. The wetter, the better.

I've taken lots of walks in downpours over the years. When I was younger I'd just head outside without an umbrella. Eventually, I did start taking one. Most often, I'd take these walks to sort through something on my mind. I enjoyed these walks, provided I could warm up afterward and take it easy when I got home. I did not like it when my friend Nate and I had to trudge a mile and a half up Main Street to school on rainy mornings. We'd arrive at school, drenched.

As a kid I played a game or two of soccer in the rain. As a father, I've coached games in the rain. It's actually a little exhilarating, that moment when sprinkles and drizzle give way to rain and the soccer association passes that point of no return and decides to let games continue rather than cut them short. It's fun.

These days, while I still enjoy being out in the rain, I am more likely to find some kind of shelter to stay dry. My home does not have a porch, so when it pours during the summertime I'm known to grab a folding chair, head to one of the parks in town, sit underneath a gazebo or covered picnic area and read and drink coffee. I always place my chair just a foot or so out of the rain. It's the best of both worlds: you're out in the rain, yet you're not.

Rain inspires or prompts all sorts of reactions in people, just as snow and sun do. There's a reason why the movies are filled with scenes that take place in the rain. Rain creates an atmosphere in the way it leaves puddles that reflect light and makes sounds as drops ping off sidewalks and roofs. If rain falls a certain way at a specific time of day and is accompanied by particular temperatures, it can bring back all sorts of memories. I have one friend for whom dark and stormy mornings remind him of sitting in his classroom at Edison School in the late 1970s; he used to gaze out the window on such occasions and watch the rain fall in the woods behind the school.

I can relate. I treasure a childhood memory of walking home from Edison through those woods one afternoon during a rainstorm. On most days I walked up Ridgeway Avenue to the babysitter's house after school; on this afternoon, however, my father had the day off and was waiting for me at home on Shaw Street. As I walked through the thick and unruly woods, I heard the rain patter off the leaves around me. I took my time, winding my way through those woods; I felt like an explorer of a new world.

It rained on my and Valerie's wedding day. We're talking about an unrelenting deluge of biblical proportions here. It started in the morning, continued through the day and night - - and lasted for several days more back home while we took our honeymoon in Jamaica. Even though we did not get those nice outdoor wedding pictures we were hoping for, we didn't let the rain damper our big day. On the contrary, it made the occasion seem even more eventful. And all these years later, that memorable October storm has even provided a bit of mystique when we tell our daughter stories of the day her parents got married.

Looking back on these memories, I do see one common factor that runs through all of them like a stream.

Never once did I catch a cold.

The Matinee Kid

I held assorted jobs as I grew up and made a slow but sure transition into a career. I was a paperboy as a kid, a camp counselor as a teenager, and then a supermarket cashier and a retail manager, among a few other things. However, it's my stint at the former Sanford Cinema Center that ranks as my favorite.

The theater in my neighborhood had been called the Sanford Twin Cinema during the first fourteen years of my life. In 1986, the theater closed for renovation and reopened as the Sanford Cinema Center, which had four screens instead of two. A family called the Spinellis owned the place during its final years, before it closed for good and got knocked down in 2009 to make way for the town's new police station.

I worked at the theater during the spring and summer of 1990, when it was the Sanford Cinema Center. That August, I packed my bags and left for college.

I thought of that movie-theater job last week when I read the story in the newspaper about the three University of Southern Maine marketing majors who will be leasing and running the beloved drive-in in Saco this summer. *Good for them*, I thought as I read the story and saw the photo of the three of them, standing arms-crossed and businesslike by the drive-in's big sign on Route One. *They're going to have a blast.* They're sure to experience the usual headaches that come with management, but to work every night under the stars with the summer's biggest blockbusters projected on a screen? Sounds like a dream to me.

I love drive-ins, right down to their last detail. The open summer evenings, sometimes cool, sometimes humid. The beam of light that shoots over the tops of cars and produces images of movie stars caught up in action, adventure, romance and laughs onscreen. The echo of a movie's dialogue and soundtrack - - or, rather, the chorus of car radios all tuned into the same station - - as you sit in your lawn chair and watch or make your way to the concession stand in the back. And yes, there's the greasy food at that takeout joint - - the popcorn and fries, the cheeseburgers and pizza, the candy and soda.

I realize here I'm talking about enjoying a night at the drive-in and not working at one, but still. As a guy who loves movies, I'm content to believe the line is blurred in between the two.

I never did get involved with the nuts and bolts of running the Sanford Cinema Center when I worked there. I regret that. I never loaded the movie onto the projector and stared out the little window to make sure everything looked right on the screens. I never changed the "Now Playing" and "Coming Attractions" posters on Thursday nights, ahead of the opening day on Friday. At eighteen years old, I was one of the guys who worked at the concession stand, scooping hot and buttered popcorn into bags and pouring soft drinks from the tap. I also helped clean the lobby before the seven o'clock shows and after the nines. If I could go back - - say, borrow that time-machine DeLorean from the "Back to the Future" movies - - I would try to learn everything about the place and how it operated.

I remember the manager at that time. Before I started working there, she called me "The Matinee Kid" because every weekend I'd show up and see a movie in the afternoon, regardless of what was playing. I grew up down the street from the theater. I begged my parents to take me there as a child. I started going with classmates and friends from the neighborhood as I made my way through elementary and middle school. In high school I started going there on dates.

That might have been how I got the job that spring of my senior year. At one point, the manager must have looked at me, realized I was always there, and said, "Hey, why don't you just work here?"

So I did. My first day on the job felt like being thrown into the deep end of the pool and being told to swim. I started on a Sunday afternoon during the opening weekend of "Teenage Mutant Ninja Turtles," which, you might find hard to believe all these years later, was actually a huge hit. I hustled behind the counter that day, filling those cups and popcorn bags and retrieving candy bars from underneath the glass. I loved it.

As you might imagine, there was a lot of down-time in between the shows. My coworker and I would clean up the counters, vacuum the stray popcorn kernels off the rug, restock the shelves with more Sno-Caps, Twizzlers and Good 'n Plentys. When those tasks were done, we chatted, played a few video games, or did homework. That spring, for English class, I read Mary Shelley's "Frankenstein" during my breaks.

I used to write movie reviews as a teenager. I had a disparate critical eye, in that I tended to rate movies in an all-or-nothing way, reserving middling judgments for flicks I might not have been able to follow or understand. The manager at the Sanford Cinema Center liked what I wrote; she even let me post one of my reviews at the front counter, come to think of it. A lot of movies played there that summer of 1990. Some were good. Some were bad. Flicks like "Dick Tracy," "Die Hard 2" and "Ghost" and a few others come to mind.

Sometimes I romanticize past jobs, overlooking certain aspects of them in the process. I recall my days as a supermarket cashier quite fondly, for example, but forget that standing in one place for eight hours a day made me restless and full of aches. I look back on one of my jobs in retail management and remember liking my coworkers and bosses and believing we were selling quality products, but I forget wanting, badly, to get a writing career off the ground, perhaps in the newspaper business. There's no flip side to the movie theater job, though; I'm quite confident about that. It was rewarding and fun, through and through.

So I'm sure to think of those three USM guys when my family and I go to the drive-in this summer. I'll wonder if they're having as much fun as I'll imagine them having. The age of home theaters has stolen just a bit of the glow and uniqueness from movie-going. However, for me, much of the magic of cinemas and drive-ins remains.

What ALS Cannot Take Away

May, 2011

I stopped at my parents' house to use their scale this week. I'm six weeks into a health and fitness kick and I wanted to check my progress. I've yet to buy a new scale to replace the one at my house that broke a while ago. No, it didn't break because I stepped on it.

After weighing myself, I stuck around for a few moments and chatted with Dad before heading home to eat. I was on my lunch hour. Mom was in New Hampshire, baby-sitting my nephew.

Dad had just woken up and gotten himself ready for the day. Ever since he retired after his ALS diagnosis six years ago, he has gone to bed well after midnight and has gotten up at noon or later. Some nights he hits the sack as late as four or five in the morning. He even has pulled an all-nighter or two.

"I listen to my body now," is how he puts it. ALS is known to cause insomnia in some.

On this particular day, Dad was up, dressed and ready to go at a little after noon. He was going to meet his brother and sister for lunch. All he needed to do to make himself presentable to the world was comb his hair.

Easier said than done. As he looked in the mirror, he struggled a bit to hang on to his comb and lift his hands high enough to reach his head.

We enjoyed some small talk. He asked me about the weather. I told him it was yet another dreary one out there, drizzly and a bit raw. He grabbed his coat and tried to put it on. He managed to slip his arms into both sleeves but asked me to help him with the rest. I brought the coat over his shoulders and adjusted his collar.

He had been using his walker to get around and said he needed to go find his rolling cane. He asked me if I could stick around long enough to see him outside.

I had an image of him standing out there in the driveway, waiting for my uncle to come get him to go out to eat.

"You're going to wait outside?" I asked him.

"No, I'm going to drive."

Dad wears two solid braces on his legs that make it easy for him to drive without taking any chances. I had not seen him at the wheel in ages, though, so I guess I must have been assuming he no longer drove. I've often seen Mom drive the two of them around, and she's the one who makes quick daily trips to get him a Coke from the tap at McDonald's or the raw sugar from Jerry's Market that he likes for his tea.

Dad found his cane, and we headed out the door. We walked down the wheelchair ramp to the Jeep in his driveway. He opened the car door and put his cane in the back seat. Then he pivoted as carefully as he could and got into the driver's seat.

I said goodbye and headed toward my car. He said goodbye too and started up his Jeep. As I approached my car, I thought I heard him call out to me but then decided it was my imagination. Sure enough, though, he called out again and this time I heard him.

"Yeah?" I asked, walking back to the Jeep.

"You never said how you did on the scale," Dad said.

"Oh. That. I did very well. I've lost about three pounds since the last time."

"Good job."

"Yeah . . . I wanted to tell you, but I didn't know if it would have been inconsiderate, given what's going on with your weight."

The toll that ALS is taking on Dad is finally starting to show. He has lost so much muscle, and efforts to bulk up on a special kind of fattening shake have led to so little, that he's now down to 137 pounds. That's not a lot on his six-foot frame.

Dad smiled and waved his hand. "Oh, don't worry about that stuff, Shawn. You never have to hold things back because of me and what I'm going through. You know me. I'm not sensitive about this stuff. I joke about myself all the time."

It's true. And he lets us kid him too. He knows it's a coping mechanism. My wife and daughter and I had dinner with my folks last week. When Dad told us how much he now weighs, we joked that a kid in Africa was going to see him in a Sally Struthers ad on television and send *him* money. He laughed.

Maybe you don't think that's funny. Perhaps you think that joke is in poor taste. Or maybe, just maybe, you have been where my family is now, and you know that humor, especially the kind that pushes boundaries, is the best survival tool we have.

Dad's response when I said I didn't want to tell him about my recent success with physical fitness is vintage Dad. He has always felt happiness and enthusiasm for the good fortune and accomplishments of others.

I offer this story about Dad as a tribute to the qualities that this fierce disease cannot touch. ALS is a progressive neurological disease for which there is not yet a cure. From its victims it steals their muscles and leaves them paralyzed. The disease often strikes and kills with merciless haste. Curiously, Dad's ALS is progressing at a slow rate; while he was diagnosed in December of 2004, his doctors trace its earliest signs back to the spring of 2003, right at the time when his first grandchild entered this world.

ALS has taken Dad's strength and independence. It's taking away years that he and Mom had once dreamed would be golden.

But then there's his joy for others and his appreciation for his blessings. There's his sense of humor, and his power to work through distressing developments and setbacks and face each day with increasing acceptance.

These are the things ALS cannot take. It robs the body, but leaves the mind, and comes nowhere close to the spirit.

Cincinnatian Hotel Nichols Taupe

Valerie and I painted our dining room over the recent holiday weekend. We disagreed at first about the color.

We stood at the store and checked out the swatches the night before. I could not decide which color I liked. Valerie at least knew which one she preferred but could not quite narrow it down to a particular hue.

"Be a gentleman, Dad," my eight-year-old daughter, Madeline, admonished me when I grimaced or said "eh" to a number of the colors Valerie pitched.

"I'm allowed to have an opinion, Maddie," I responded.

"What about this one?" Valerie asked me.

I paused and studied the swatch. Eventually, I said, "I like it."

Val smiled and gave me an accusing look. "No, you don't."

"I like it because you like it," I replied.

Val rolled her eyes and wandered off to the paintbrush rack.

Part of the problem was that there were so many colors to choose from. And most of them were not even real colors, if you ask me. For example, Valerie held up a swatch for a paint color called "Dust Bunny."

Dust Bunny?

Actually, Valerie just showed that one to me to rile me. She knows I can't stand the very sight of a dust bunny on the floor at home. I'm not a neat freak or a fastidious person - - you should see the back seat of my car, my socks on the floor, or my uncut lawn - - but for some reason I find dust bunnies totally objectionable. How much so? Two friends of mine, who once told me my column needs an occasional "edge," suggested I write about my problem with dust bunnies.

Yeah, they nauseate me. Dust bunnies, that is. Not my friends.

Whatever you think of such floor-bound collections of dust, lint and hair, can we at least agree that "Dust Bunny" is not a color?

I'm trespassing on my father's turf here. For years he has railed against the thousands of colors that jam crayon boxes and the shelves of paint cans at local hardware stores. There are just a handful of real colors in the world and they all have shades, he asserts.

Take "lilac," for example. That's not a color. It's a flower that's a shade of the color purple.

It gets even more ridiculous, of course. For proof, I just need to tell you the color Valerie and I chose for our dining room. Cincinnatian Hotel Nichols Taupe.

299

Now taupe is a color, I grant you, but even then purists like Dad would tell you it's really a shade of brown. But come on: how can a Cincinnatian hotel be a color or even begin to describe one? It's a *hotel*.

What's next? Washington Monument White? Donald Duck Sailor Suit Blue? Is it just a matter of time before we start saying Flamingo Pink instead of Pink Flamingo?

Check it out - - I'm going to make up a color right now. Automobile Windshield Condensation Grey. Can you picture it? Yeah, I can't, either. But that shouldn't stop us from declaring it a color, no?

So Valerie and I went home and started painting our dining room Cincinnatian Hotel Nichols Taupe. We divided this task in a way calculated to avert the complete destruction of our home. In other words, I got to brush the broad sections of the walls with a roller and Valerie got to do the edges and the trim. The reason for this - - Valerie's reason - - is that I lack the steady and deliberate touch needed to paint the edges and avoid smudging parts of the room not intended for that color. Yes, even with the blue tape.

At first I didn't like the Cincinnatian Hotel Nichols Taupe. I thought it too much resembled the color we have in the adjacent living room, which is painted Tempered All-Spice, which sounds like another invented color. It seemed to me that one room just kind of blended into the other with a certain . . . I dunno. Monotone. I appreciated Valerie's desire to have the two main rooms in our home conform, but . . .

Oh, who am I kidding? What am I now, an interior decorator? I know nothing about this stuff. I just knew I looked at our first coat of the new paint and was not sure if I liked the color.

"But it's the same color as my wedding dress!" Valerie said.

I stood there and looked at her. I'm sure I had a blank expression. After a few seconds passed, I did my best to respond.

"What am I supposed to say to that?"

But Valerie was right. The color did resemble the soft tone of the wedding dress she wore almost 13 years ago.

We finished the first coat, not without bickering and getting on each other's nerves because, man, painting is so painstaking and tedious for everyone involved. We made sure to fasten the lids on the cans resting on our dining room floor. We learned our lesson last summer when we painted our front door and left a can on the floor without the lid sealed. I knocked the can over in the dark and left a big black puddle on the floor. I later stepped in this mess in the middle of the night and unwittingly left a trail of black footprints in my wake.

I stood in the corner of our dining room and gave the walls another look. I noticed the way the sunlight came through the window and highlighted our work.

You know, I thought, *this color really brightens up the room*. I liked the previous color, which was blue - - or "Papa Smurf Blue," what with all these made-up hues out there - - but I had not realized how comparatively darker it kept the room.

"You're right, hon," I told Valerie. "This is a nice color. It brightens up the room."

Valerie smiled. And then I added another reason why I liked it.

"It *does* look like your wedding dress."

Pepper

I went home for lunch earlier this week and the place felt deserted. My family's four-legged friends were nowhere in sight.

I called out to them, but wherever they were, they stayed put. I searched every room but had no luck.

I stood baffled in our dining room and started to fear the worst. Either our pets had packed their bags and fled the neighborhood, or I would have to go down into our basement and discover that a Furball Fight Club had gone awry.

The first scenario was possible. One of our cats, Tootsie, is always trying to flee our house for destinations unknown both to us and to her. All we know is that she sits in the window and stares at the birds and squirrels and craves the freedom to chase them.

But the chances of that second scenario? Slim to none. Our basement door was closed. Even if our pets had thumbs to turn doorknobs, they still could not reach them.

At long last, one of them appeared. Cocoa, our other cat, sauntered into the room in that way of his, as though he thinks he's appearing with George Clooney and Brad Pitt on the poster for the latest sequel to "Ocean's Eleven."

"Where are the other two?" I asked him.

I went into the bedroom and peeked into the closet. I saw Tootsie. She was peeking out from behind the baseboard that has shaken loose from the wall between the closet and our bathroom.

Meatloaf may have said in the Seventies that two out of three ain't bad, but for me it wasn't enough. I still needed to find the third musketeer.

I looked underneath my bed and found her.

Pepper, our brand new, two-month-old puppy, lifted her chin off the floor and looked at me with those chocolate-brown eyes that remind me of our late and beloved terrier, Molly, who passed away three years ago. Pepper made a little noise and started scooching toward me on her belly.

I heaved a sigh of relief. All animals were accounted for. Valerie and Madeline and I brought Pepper home on Sunday. On Monday morning, our two cats and Pepper were alone together for the first time. I've gotta tell ya, when I arrived home to silence that afternoon, I had no idea what to expect. All I could think of was Bill Murray's line in "Ghostbusters," in which he rails against "dogs and cats, living together - - mass hysteria!" as he warns the mayor about the end of the world.

Pepper is part schnauzer, part fox terrier. She was born at an alpaca farm and has four brothers, three sisters and parents named Taffy and Banjo. Yes. I know I sound like I'm making up a country song here, but it's all true. But then, so are most country songs, I bet.

Pepper is as cute as cute gets. If you want to picture her, imagine a miniaturized version of the tramp from Walt Disney's animated classic, "Lady and the Tramp." Just put a plate of spaghetti in front of her and ask her to nudge the meatball with her nose, and the image will be complete.

Several months ago, Valerie and I would have told you we were not in the market for a new dog. We still missed Molly too much and, well, we had grown accustomed to our cats' self-sufficiency and laid-back friendship.

Somewhere along the line, though, things changed. Maddie had stopped asking for a pony and had started asking for a dog. Valerie and I never told her no. We just tried to figure out when we'd say yes. We knew "when" in May when we met Pepper, about whom we had heard through a friend at Maddie's birthday party in April.

"This is the best Father's Day ever!" Maddie declared moments after we brought Pepper home on Sunday. She said it in the way you'd expect a kid to say, "This is the best Christmas ever!"

My neighbor picked up on Maddie's remark and joked that I was playing second-fiddle to a dog on the one day of the year that's set aside for celebrating fathers. I laughed and conceded that was true, but I also agreed with my daughter. We Dads love it when we make our children happy.

So we will be house-training Pepper this summer. That's our big assignment. We have not had much sleep this week as

Pepper wakes up in the middle of the night - - first at midnight, then at two, and then at four - - and starts howling and wondering where her parents and the rest of her pack went.

The good news is that the cats are handling this new development in our home very well. Back in 1983, my family and I got a new cat named Lucky and for two weeks she and our collie, Shannon, fought like . . . well, I'll let you finish the sentence. Anyway, that does not seem to be the case with Cocoa, Tootsie and Pepper. To be sure, Tootsie's keeping her distance, not just hiding in the closet but *behind* the baseboard in the closet; I'm sure she looks at Pepper and wonders why *that* pet gets to go outside and she does not.

But Cocoa's the real surprise. He approaches Pepper and tries to figure her out and does not lash out or act as though we have betrayed him. Until Saturday, Valerie and Maddie and I had affectionately regarded Cocoa as a bit of a surfer-dude oaf. Now he downright seems like a polished elder statesman.

You know, Charlie Brown was right when he said that "happiness is a warm puppy." I thought of that famous comic-strip quote the other night as I stood at our kitchen window and watched Maddie carry pint-sized Pepper around our yard.

"We did a good thing, getting Maddie that dog," I told Valerie. "She really loves Pepper."

Valerie agreed. I watched Maddie and Pepper a few moments longer.

"It's going to be tough for Maddie when Pepper's older and bigger and she can't pick her up and hold her like that anymore," I said.

I had spoken those words without a shred of self-consciousness. But as I continued to watch Maddie with Pepper, it was not long before I realized I understood exactly how those words felt.

The Secret to Marital Happiness

My parents celebrated their 40th wedding anniversary on Saturday. I asked them what they considered to be the secret to their success as a married couple.

Mom pondered the question a moment and then gave a single word for her answer.

"Compromise."

"Which means she says something, and I have to agree," Dad added.

"That's not what I mean, Gary," Mom protested. But then she added, "I do think that if the woman is happy in a relationship, then everyone's happy."

"See?" Dad asked me, as though Mom had proved his point.

But Dad had his own answer.

"Your mother likes mornings, fall and winter. I like nights, spring and summer. Between the two of us, someone is always happy," he said.

This is true. Mom rises before dawn. When my sister and I were young, she used to sing as loud as she could while she did odds and ends around the house at six in the morning. We used to beg her to stop, so that we could sleep just a few minutes more in peace. Now, of course, Mom's predawn singing is a pleasant memory I cherish.

And Mom does indeed like the crisp air and brilliant foliage of autumn. There's a quaint and picturesque intersection in Chester, New Hampshire, through which she must pass every fall or she will feel as though she has failed the season. She also appreciates the quietness and seclusion that winter imposes; on a cold and snowy day she enjoys nothing more than to make some tea and watch "You've Got Mail," that movie with Tom Hanks and Meg Ryan, for the umpteenth time on television.

Dad has always stayed up late. Years ago, he'd watch the eleven o'clock news and a bit of Carson and then head to bed. During these years of his retirement, he stays up well past Leno and watches the cable news channels or surfs on his iPad until the wee hours of the morn. Dad has always preferred the spring, when the world comes alive, and he can get out and work in his yard. He loves the summer, when you can plan all sorts of adventures. When my sister and I were kids, we took family vacations to everywhere from Hershey Park to Disney Land and from colonial Williamsburg to the Grand Canyon.

These comparisons between Mom and Dad also point to the way their personalities complement one another. Dad is outgoing and involved in the community. Mom is reserved and shy and holds sacred the tighter circle of family and a few dear friends.

Gary and Lorraine Sullivan met in 1967 while standing in line to see Sidney Poitier's "To Sir, With Love" at one of the old movie theaters on Main Street in Sanford. They met through friends. Two years later, they began dating.

I've always liked the story of their introduction, and the slightly cosmic part of me has always wondered if my own lifelong love of movies has its origins in the way my parents met. On the day before my sister Kelly was born, Mom and Dad took me to the zoo. Kelly grew up wanting to work with animals, perhaps at a zoo or a veterinary clinic. She's now an elementary school teacher in Massachusetts, so in some ways her dream came true.

The parents of one of my friends from the ol' neighborhood celebrated their 41st wedding anniversary earlier this month. Such news, learned as my own folks' landmark anniversary approached, got me thinking about the tricks time plays on us. A child tends to think that their parents' relationship is eternal - - in existence since the beginning of time and ensured forever more. It makes sense, when you think of it, because the parents have been there the child's whole life.

However, as I look back on my early childhood, I am struck by a realization. In the scheme of things, a lot of the parents in my neighborhood were essentially newlyweds. At the time, they were not as far along the road of married life that my own wife Valerie and I are now at thirteen years.

And they were younger too, not in the obvious sense that we're talking about 40 years ago, but in the way that they embarked on family life at an earlier age than a lot of my friends and myself. For example, I'm 39 and my daughter's eight. When I was eight, Mom and Dad were 31 and 35, respectively.

I remember the first time I detected my parents' youthfulness - - that first time I looked at them and could see the two young people they were when they met in their late teens, early twenties. I was at a Halloween party at a friend's house during my senior year of high school, and they showed up to see everyone in their costumes. I looked at them socializing with my friends with ease, regarding us as young adults, and I felt something that I would not have known how to articulate at the time, but do now. It's this: We're all kids inside. We grow up, we add the responsibilities of families or careers or both to our lives, and we all do the best we can and hope we're succeeding. But if we choose, we can remain young at heart. That's how my parents appeared to me that Halloween night 22 years ago.

Do I still look at my parents, who are now in their sixties, and see them the same way? Yes, actually, I do. It's through a more complex lens that I do, but yes, I do.

To me, this is remarkable because right now my parents are experiencing that part of their wedding vows most often associated with older age: the part about sickness and health.

It would be impossible to celebrate my parents' 40th wedding anniversary without acknowledging that it's a triumph, not just of four decades of love and commitment but also of beating the odds. Seven years ago, Dad was diagnosed with amyotrophic lateral sclerosis, also known as ALS. He was given three to five years to live. Since 2004, Mom and Dad have celebrated their anniversaries without once thinking Dad would live for them to see their fortieth.

But he has.

It has not been easy. Anyone who is ill or has an ill spouse knows that better than anyone. But Mom and Dad have faced this challenge together and have continued to experience joys - - of grandparenthood, of travel, of the little pleasures in life, and of their relationship.

That's the true secret of their success as husband and wife: they're best friends.

'Rocky Steps II'

You know how Sylvester Stallone made all those "Rocky" sequels, right? He made five of 'em over 30 years, and most of them were pretty good, if you ask me.

Well, seeing all that, I feel I have grounds here to write a sequel of my own - - to a column I wrote about a trip to Philadelphia that my friend Richard and I took during the summer of 2008.

Stallone often began his "Rocky" sequels by showing flashbacks of the big boxing match that wrapped up his previous flick. I'll do the same thing here.

Three years ago, Richard and I hopped into his car on a Sunday morning, drove 400 miles from Sanford to Philadelphia, ran up the 75 steps in front of the Philadelphia Museum of Art, just like Rocky famously first did in the 1976 movie, and then drove back home. We were gone from Maine all of 18 hours. If we had not gotten stuck in late-night traffic in Connecticut, then we would have made it home before midnight and would have left and returned on the same day.

Oh, yeah. We also scooted a couple of miles from the museum over to the Liberty Bell and Independence Hall. I had visited both historic sites before, but Richard had never been there. I can still see Richard standing there in the middle of the street and looking at the hall.

"Wanna go in, see the room where they signed the Declaration of Independence?" I asked him.

"Nah," he said, with an easy wave of his hand. "I've seen the building. That's enough for me."

You have to know Richard.

We were not alone that afternoon when we ran up the museum's steps, by the way. Much to our surprise, as many as 75 other people - - of all ages, of all walks of life and from all over the place - - ran up the steps as well and jumped up and down and triumphantly threw their fists in the air when they reached the top. You know, like in the movie. It was quite an experience.

All right. Fade out. Flash forward to the here-and-now. Let's call this column "Rocky Steps II."

Recently, I called my eight-year-old daughter, Madeline, into our living room and fired up the DVD player. She had known this moment was coming, ever since I told her we'd be running up the "Rocky steps" during our trip to see friends in Philadelphia that week.

I played for Maddie the part in the original film in which Rocky wakes up at four on a dark and cold November morning, drinks four or five raw eggs and hits the streets for a jog. This sequence captures the loneliness that comes with starting a personal challenge and ends with our favorite southpaw laboring up the steps of the museum at dawn and wheezing and holding his sides when he reaches the top. Kinda like Richard and I did three years ago.

"All right, Maddie, now check this out," I said and hit the fast-forward button.

I stopped at the film's second montage. In that one, Rocky, now in better shape, races with fierce pride and determination through the streets of the City of Brotherly Love and bounds up the steps of the museum. He reaches the top and throws his hands in the air and shouts with joy. If this happened in real life, of course, we'd look at this guy and say, "Whoa, buddy, calm down. It's a bunch of steps." As it happens in the movie, however, it's one of the high points in cinematic history.

"You know, this would be a better movie if there was no sound," Maddie told me after I turned off the TV.

"What do you mean?"

"Well, everybody just mumbles. You can barely understand what everyone's saying," she explained.

She then did an impersonation of Sylvester Stallone that I had to admit was right on the money.

I chuckled but realized something. All these years I have chosen a big lug from which to draw inspiration. When I sat down with Maddie that morning, I did not show her Gregory Peck standing up for justice as Atticus Finch in "To Kill a Mockingbird" or Jimmy Stewart filibustering his way to what's right in "Mr. Smith Goes to Washington." I showed her a guy who had a limited grasp of the English language and earned his living through taking repeated blows to his head. Maddie has always known that Rocky Balboa is my favorite movie character, but this is the first time I managed to see him - - or, in some ways, *me* - - through my daughter's eyes.

"Rocky's kinda dumb," Maddie said, meaning the character, not the movie.

"Um, well . . . yeah, he's not the brightest guy out there," I conceded. "He's just smart enough, I guess. But I'll tell you what. He knows how to live life, and that's what's important."

And that's true. Rocky loves and respects his wife and child. He's a loyal friend. He loves his country. He makes mistakes but learns from them and stands up for what he thinks is right. He hardly ever complains. When life knocks him down, he gets right back up. He faces his fears, does his best with what God gave him and pursues his dreams.

What's so dumb about that?

So Valerie and Maddie and I sprinted up those steps of the Philadelphia Museum of Art earlier this month. I scaled 'em three times, come to think of it, and even took 'em two steps at a time. I felt good when I reached the top, especially when I spun around and saw the city of Philadelphia sprawled out in the shimmering heat before me. I felt so good that I wanted to stay there, right at the exact spot where real life and cinema intersect.

I also felt a certain pride and satisfaction in leading my daughter up those steps. Maddie probably will not end up watching "Rocky" at any point in her life. She does not like movies that have fighting in them, and that's a good thing.

But I'll be one pleased papa if it turns out she listened to her old man's jabbering at the top of those steps that morning and discovered a few good pointers for living life.

I'm sure to return to those steps of the Philadelphia Museum of Art someday. I find it energizing and inspiring to be there.

And who knows? Maybe someday I'll even check out what's inside the place.

My First Digs

I arrived at my parents' house the other day and looked up at what used to be my bedroom window on the second floor. I felt a backward pull toward a simpler time, but I also wondered how it ever was that I could fit myself and everything I owned into so small a bedroom.

These days I need a full house, a garage, a shed and a yard to feel like I have my own space in this world to stretch my arms and legs and keep everything that my wife and daughter and I have amassed over the years. Furniture in each room. Dishes in the cabinets. Cars in the driveway. Christmas decorations in the shed. Boxes of who-knows-what that have sat in our basement and have not been opened since we moved to town six years ago. Stuff like that.

I liked my bedroom when I was a kid. I never yearned for more space, and it seemed not to bother me that the dim bulb encased on the ceiling, the gray wood paneling and the matted blue carpet all conspired with my bed, desk, bookshelf, radiator and bureau to make the room seem dark and cramped. Over the years I just put a globe of the world on my bureau, stuck a typewriter on my desk and threw a few posters on the walls and called the place my own.

I started out sleeping in another room on the second floor. I have vague images - - I would hardly call them memories, as there are no feelings attached - - of resting in my crib at night and seeing the dark outlines of a rubber Tomahawk hatchet that Mom or Dad had hung on the wall.

When I was three, Dad went to work on transforming the little room down the hall, stripping its walls of its sixties' pastel color and making way for that wood paneling. This was going to be my new room. We were all expecting my little sister and were getting ready to hand my current room over to her once she was born.

There's an old picture of me standing in my new future bedroom during its renovation. I'm wearing a bathrobe - - a plaid one, of course, because it was the 1970s - - and I'm smiling from one big ear to the other, like I was the general contractor of the project and pleased with how things were moving along.

The room proved an ideal space. My window provided a view of the neighborhood that allowed me to watch assorted developments and spot friends I'd want to join outside. When I was four or five I'd look out at night and see the broad white siding of the back of the First Baptist Church on Main Street and my overactive imagination would mistake it for a drive-in screen. When I was older I'd sit on the sill after bedtime and write or draw or read by the gathering dusk. I have one nice memory of sitting there late one summer evening and seeing my Uncle Alan and Aunt Jo-Ann from Harrison pull up in their car for a visit. At eighteen, I pushed my bed next to the window, plopped my pillow down on the sill and spent my last nights at home before college falling asleep with the nights' cool air on my face.

I never needed a flashlight to read in the dark after I had been sent to bed as a child. If I left my door open, the light in the hallway threw just enough of a glow into my room to see the words.

Many a night I fell asleep hearing the theme songs of the television shows Mom and Dad watched downstairs. "Dallas." "Dynasty." "Sanford & Son." "Taxi." "Murder, She Wrote." Dad used to watch a Phillip Marlowe series on HBO, and I tried to listen and follow the plots a few times. Nothing depressed me more than the somber theme of "The Waltons."

And my room must have been well insulated, and my door thick enough, because I'm not sure I ever recall my parents asking me to turn down the music I blared as a teenager. Trust me. Dad would have told me to dial it down a notch if Guns n Roses, Aerosmith and Van Halen were grating on his ears while he tried to watch the evening news.

As cramped as I may be making my old bedroom sound, I managed to create a bit of a clearing. I had an overstuffed "bean bag" where I could sit and spread out my legs before me and read comics or movie reviews in the Boston paper I'd buy on

Fridays in the summertime. On the night before a final exam in high school during my freshman year, I even fell asleep in that bean bag and woke up the next morning with my textbook open in my lap and my notes scattered by the fan I had trained on me.

You know, it's a good thing I liked that room because I repeatedly set and broke records for the number of times Mom and Dad sent me there for mouthing off as a kid. I never liked being sent to my room, of course, but I suppose it never felt like confinement once I was there. It made no difference to Mom and Dad.

"When we sent you to your room it wasn't always to punish you," Dad once told me, perhaps after I had become a parent myself. "We just wanted you out of our hair. We wanted peace and quiet."

My neighbor, Glenna, who lived on the second floor of a duplex behind my house, once told me that she was sitting on her porch one afternoon and saw me sticking my head out my bedroom window. I must have been five or six at the time.

"What are you up to?" she called over to me.

"Mom and Dad sent me to my room," I reportedly called back. "I'm being bad, and I love it!"

These days I visit Mom and Dad a few times each week, but I tend not to go upstairs and see my old room. When I do stick my head in there, though, it occurs to me that life's quite a journey, one we take from place to place for years and years. *This is where it all began for me*, I think as I look around my old bedroom. *I've lived in quite a few places since I was here in this little room.*

My ol' bedroom is now a spare bedroom that doubles for storage. The bed in there is still the one in which I slept and the bureau's the same too. But the wood paneling is gone, and the walls are painted cream. The lighting from the ceiling is brighter. The blue rug has been replaced by a brighter cranberry one.

I'll say this. It looks a lot nicer than it did when I was in charge of the place.

One Last Game of Croquet

August, 2011

Dad used to be quite a terror when it came to croquet.

Every summer we used to break out our croquet set and play the game in our yard or bring it to a friend's house to enjoy after a barbecue. I'm not sure Dad ever played to win. He was more interested in sowing discord among all of us and hoping we'd all spiral down into viciousness and betrayal and lose our souls.

Dad delighted in that moment when his ball rolled across the grass and clicked against someone else's. He would never use the occasion to take an extra shot at the wicket. Instead he would "send" our ball into the bushiest and thorniest corner of the yard. He'd laugh as he did it.

In return, the rest of us - - Valerie, for example, and my sister, Kelly, and I - - thought nothing of sending Dad's ball into the street or through his garden whenever we hit it. When it came to each other, though, we stood united, even as we each hoped we would win the game; if I clicked my croquet ball against my sister's, for example, I would take the extra shot

323

rather than send her. Dad would hoot and holler and call us soft for not sending the other person.

Mom did not like Dad's style and refused to play croquet with him. She'd either sit on the sidelines or head into the house.

Dad used to be the same way at Monopoly too. He'd buy Park Place, load it up with hotels, and then when you landed on it with your miniature race car he'd stick his hand, palm up, near your face and goad you into forking over the cash you owed him. He'd wiggle his fingers to hurry you along.

Mom never played Monopoly with Dad, either.

When it came to chess, though, Dad had an entirely different demeanor. He'd sit opposite me across the board and not talk much as we each took our turns. He was graceful when he won. When I won, he commended me on a game well played. Croquet requires skill but welcomes silliness. Monopoly calls for shrewdness but depends too much on rolls of the dice. Chess demands concentration and careful plotting, so I gather that whenever I won a game against Dad he felt more pride in me than the sting of defeat.

But oh, croquet. That was another story.

I won the big croquet game at my sister's barbecue a couple of weekends ago, but the better story is that Dad played too.

We had not played the game in years. Kelly got out the mallets, wickets and balls after we all finished a delicious lunch of burgers, hot dogs, salmon, scallops and salad. As she and my brother-in-law, Jay, started building a course in their yard, I figured Dad would be sitting out the match. You don't see a lot of people approaching the advanced stages of ALS playing croquet.

But then Dad surprised me, as he often does, much to my pride, when it comes to casting aside his increasing disabilities and rising to an occasion. Dad announced he'd be playing croquet too. He was going to take on me, Valerie, Kelly, Jay and Jay's father, Dave.

He played well too, hitting his ball with more force than I thought he still had in him. He made his way along the wickets, slowly but surely, even keeping pace ahead of Valerie, who would rally only at the end for an impressive second-place finish. He rested in between shots.

Dad sent Valerie's ball once and gave the rest of us his usual rough time. My sister retaliated by sending Dad's ball, and he found comic gold in playing up the sympathy card as he hobbled across the uneven lawn and pushed his walker toward his wayward ball. He'd further "harass" Kelly whenever she unwittingly started her turn before he slowly finished his. Kelly, who's always been adept at dishing it back, would tell Dad she got tired of waiting for him to take his shot.

Jay was the first player to "poison" his ball, and he used his newfound power to try to knock his wife out of the game. I was the second player to get a "poisoned" ball. Soon enough, Kelly and Dave became "poisoned" as well. Kelly knocked out Jay, and I knocked out Kelly. Dave knocked himself out when he passed through a wicket, which is a no-no for a "poisoned" player.

That left Dad and Valerie and me. I ended the game by taking out Val, whose ball had come to a rest mere inches from mine after she had taken a shot. Moments earlier, though, Dad got knocked out of the game on account of my "poisoned" ball. He hit his ball through one of the wickets in the middle of the course, and it bumped up against mine. He was out.

In previous years, I savored the victory of knocking Dad's ball out of the game. I even cheered when someone else did the deed, even if it meant he or she was going to be coming for me next. Dad would play up his role of the foiled villain and accuse his vanquisher of cheating. He'd remain on the scene and try to influence the game's outcome from the sidelines.

With this game, though, things were different. Dad hit my poisoned ball, rather than the other way around. He accidentally knocked himself out.

I'm glad it happened that way. I knew this was Dad's last croquet game, and I did not want to be the one to take him out of it.

On The Soundtrack of Life

Do you have a song that has followed you around your whole life?

This song doesn't necessarily have to be one you like, although it's better if it is. I'm just talking about one particular song that has had a way of popping up now and then at either random or key moments in your life. You do not choose such a song; for better or for worse, it chooses you.

For me, that song is UB40's "Red Red Wine." The band covered the song on an album in the early 1980s. Like a lot of reggae, the song has an easy charm. I'm not sure I'd rank it anywhere among my favorite tunes, but I recognize with affection that it has found its way onto the recurring soundtrack of my life.

I'm not certain when I first heard the song, but that's not important. What interests me is that I can recall the first and subsequent times during the past 23 years when the song has marked particular moments.

The first marker dates back to a sweltering August afternoon during the summer of 1988. My friend Nate and I were helping our neighbor paint a home he owned on North Avenue.

We spent most of the afternoon outdoors, painting the bottom half of the house white and then climbing ladders and standing on the porch roof to get the top parts done. I spent some time inside the vacant house, though, attending to other tasks. In these moments I had my father's old transistor radio playing nearby.

I remember a few details from that afternoon. A drunken man approached us and asked if Ronald Reagan was in the house. We told him no. A thunderstorm broke and washed the fresh paint clean off the house; the neighbor we were helping had a few choice words about that. My parents went to see "Die Hard," my favorite movie that summer, and I looked forward to asking them what they thought of it when I got home.

And "Red Red Wine" played on that transistor radio.

Valerie and I spent our honeymoon in Jamaica in October of 1998. The hotel made an error with our reservation and relocated us to an even better room, one with a balcony facing the Caribbean. We ate well that week and lounged in the pools and snorkeled and saw exotic fish. After dinner one night, we went to a concert in the resort's recreation hall and one of the entertainers led the crowd through singing, you guessed it, "Red Red Wine."

A couple of years later, I sat in my living room one night and watched Martin Scorsese's 1999 film, "Bringing Out the Dead," which starred Nicolas Cage as a burnt-out ambulance driver in the roughest section of New York City. Scorsese, who always knows the right songs to pick for his films, chose "Red

Red Wine" for one mesmerizing sequence in a dangerous apartment house.

Is my viewing of this movie a key moment in my life? Of course not. But ever since, when I have heard "Red Red Wine," I think of the movie and it reminds me of the time in my life when I saw it. Valerie and I lived in a shoebox-sized apartment outside Boston and wondered if we'd ever own a house. I was a reporter at the time, but not too long before I had worked in retail management and dreamed I'd one day have a career as a writer. Our daughter, Madeline, had not yet come into the world.

There have been other times over the years when I've heard "Red Red Wine" and have smiled and marked the moment. The most recent one occurred this summer when I traveled to Ecuador with the pastor and a couple of members of my wife's church. While we were down there, we visited villages in the northern mountains to see if we could find a community with which the church could later join forces on a project.

During this trip, we visited the city of Otavalo, which is known worldwide for the impressive market it hosts every Saturday. Our group broke up into pairs to go looking for souvenirs for loved ones back home. I bought earrings for Valerie, a blanket for Maddie, a sculpture of a turtle for my sister, and a noisemaker for my nephew. I also picked up a coffee mug for myself.

At the end of the evening, we all walked a few blocks back to our car. As I trudged up the middle of one bustling street, tired and sore from a busy day that started with riding a horse up a mountain, I passed a group of young people socializing in and around a car parked at the curb. They had their radio playing nice and loud - - the way music should be played on fun summer evenings - - and by now I'm sure you know which song bellowed from the speakers.

I smiled, of course, and marked the moment. There it was again, "Red Red Wine," all the way down there in South America, still following me around throughout my life, wherever I go.

Happy Trails
(On the Way Up, Anyway)

Maddie and I climbed more than 4,000 feet up a mountain during one cool Saturday morning in Ecuador.

You might be thinking that I'm talking about my daughter, Madeline, but you'd be incorrect. In this case, I'm talking about a horse.

"Maddie" is the name I gave the horse I rode up the mountain. The experience proved a thrilling adventure. At the start of the journey I had felt apprehensive, however, so I named the horse after my daughter to soothe my nerves. Maddie loves horses.

"You do know your horse is a male, right?" one of the others asked me when I told her my horse's name.

"Is it?"

"Yes. Very much so."

I hadn't felt the need to check before I climbed onto the saddle. All the same, I kept the name.

I was in Ecuador with my wife's pastor, Frank, and two members of their church, Tara and Aliyah. We were in Ecuador on a scouting mission, searching for a humanitarian project to propose back home. On the day we rode horses up the mountain, we were joined by three others, Joel and Henry, our hosts who live in the capital city of Quito, and Cesar, a deacon in La Magdalena, the village where the mountain was located.

We all had our own horses. Frank named his "Burrito," and with good reason. We had no idea what his horse ate for breakfast, but whatever it was, the horse ate way too much of it. On the ride up the mountain we'd all stop and bask in a breathtaking view, and Frank's horse would break the silence with an onslaught of loud and fetid gusts. I laughed every time, as I find such noises as funny now as I did when I was twelve, but I avoided the line of fire by making sure I never rode behind Frank.

Cesar greeted us at his church that morning and led us to the stable. He chose a shortcut through a thick patch of woods down a steep, uneven and narrow path. As we made our way through the trees, I wondered, not without concern, if we'd be retracing our steps on horseback on the way back. *There's gotta be a road we can take instead*, I hoped.

At the stable, Cesar asked me in the Quechua language if I had any experience with horses. Joel translated for me.

"Well, I saw 'The Black Stallion' at the movies when I was eight," I replied.

I had been on a horse before, but it was not worth mentioning. I sat on one when I attended a Cub Scout camp in New Hampshire when I was ten, and it ambled along and took me in slow circles. Several years later, I also climbed onto my friend's horse and unintentionally prompted it to break into a gallop when my tense legs clamped its sides.

So I had been on a horse before. But had I ever ridden one to the top of a mountain? That I hadn't done.

I wish I could tell you I just jumped onto my horse and charged right up that mountain like Teddy Roosevelt. What a story that'd be! Unfortunately, it also would be untrue. Here's what I thought moments before I saddled up: *Valerie and I sent Maddie to camp for a whole week one summer so she could learn how to ride a horse the right way, and I'm going to climb to the top of a mountain on one without even a single lesson?*

Made no sense to me.

I know what you might be thinking here: Where's my sense of adventure?

It's a fair question. Here's my answer. I suspect fatherhood has made me too cautious. I showed more abandon as a child and teenager and younger man. Now, though, I'm a Dad who can imagine all the things that can go wrong and takes steps to prevent them from happening. I've got quite the imagination. I looked at my horse, regarded as one of the slower ones in the group, and imagined getting thrown off it and sent tumbling down the mountain. I pictured falling off the horse and being dragged for miles before it raced off a cliff with my feet still jammed into the stirrups. I imagined getting kicked in the head.

I took Maddie to see a horse when she was two. It bit her finger and I had to pry it free from its teeth. She cried and cried. One the way home I sang "Old MacDonald Had a Farm" to try to calm her down. I sang that Old MacDonald had a cow and a pig and a goat, E-I-E-I-O, but I did not sing that he had a horse.

So fine. I wanted to be Indiana Jones when I was a kid. Turns out I've grown up to be one of the adults in "A Christmas Story" who told little Ralphie that Santa wouldn't bring him a Red Ryder rifle because he'd shoot his eye out with that thing.

But I'll tell you what: I know how to set aside my worries and concerns and seize the moment. I know that the alternative to saying "yes" to the opportunities in life is saying "no," and I consider that unacceptable. I like that about myself.

At the stable I hopped onto my horse with surprising athleticism - - stuck my left foot in the stirrup, hefted up and swung my right leg over. You would've thought I had been riding horses my whole life. I felt in great shape as we all rode *up* the mountain. I thought I was John Wayne or Clint Eastwood. Of course, by the end of the morning, after a punishing ride *down* the mountain, I felt like the old woman in those commercials who used to say, *"Help! I've fallen and I can't get up!"*

On the way up the mountain I felt plugged into the splendor of all creation. A cool mist fell on us and dampened our ponchos but cooled our skin. The volcano adjacent to our mountain sat high and still with awesome power. The green hills and pastures extending all around us were specked with thin dirt roads and farms. Our horses labored up the mountain, heaving and grunting as they conquered steep inclines, sometimes wandering off our path of packed earth onto the soft fields of tall grass.

Near the top, Joel's horse just quit on him. The rest of us were a few hundred feet up the mountain and could see Joel and his horse, appearing as miniatures in the distance. Over and over Joel told his horse in Spanish to move. He sounded patient, but there's a chance the breeze in our direction was not carrying his frustration. Joel was too far away for us to discern anything but his horse's frozen form and his faint voice.

For some reason, the rest of us thought all of this was hilarious. I'm telling you, Joel's horse would *not* budge. Joel was repeating "Vamos!" but the horse was the one calling the shots. I laughed more in this moment than I did during the whole nine days we were in Ecuador. I'm sure the thin air swirling around me - - we were already 9,000 feet above sea level before we even started up the mountain - - had something to do with it. I was getting punchy.

If the ride up the mountain was glorious, then the ride down it was something else. I had no idea about the proper way to guide a horse down grassy slopes and steep dips and through jagged patches of hard rocks. As a result I was the textbook case of what *not* to do under those circumstances. I got my feet jammed in the stirrups, which seared into my ankles. I kept the reins too tight because every time the horse - - by now I had stopped calling him Maddie - - broke into a gallop, I could not take the brutal pounding of my tail bone against the hard wooden saddle. On the way up the mountain I uttered words of wonder and praise toward the gorgeous nature all around me; on the way down I grunted all sorts of words you're probably not supposed to say when you're with a church group.

I brought home a souvenir from most of the places we visited in Ecuador. From our trip up the mountain, I brought home bruises and scrapes and a chafed rear-end. For hours afterward, I walked like John Wayne but without his rugged authority - - an eighteen-wheeler could have passed between my bowed legs. On the long plane ride home, I shifted with such care and discomfort in my seat that I'm surprised no one mistook my problem and handed me a tube of Preparation H.

But make no mistake. It was all worth it. As we all sat on our horses at the top of the mountain, I marveled at my situation. In my life I never imagined I'd one day ride a horse to the top of a mountain in such a faraway land as Ecuador. But there I was, and that's what I had done.

The First Time Ever She Saw His Face

My neighbor, John, had a beard for more than 40 years. Last week he shaved it off and left a mustache. His wife, Karen, didn't even notice.

I noticed. John walked my daughter home one evening last week after she visited him and Karen.

"Hey, you shaved your beard," I said right off the bat. "Looks good."

"Karen didn't even notice," he said, with a twinkle in his eye. He knew he had a column idea in the works for me.

"Are you serious?" I asked.

"Oh, yeah."

"You don't think she noticed and is just holding off on saying anything?"

"No, no. Trust me, if she has something to say, she says it."

"Ah."

John, who is in his late sixties, said he got rid of the beard after all these years because one recent morning he discovered a spot of gray in it that had spread across his cheeks and chin. He does look younger without the beard, but then I've always thought of John as young because he has an upbeat attitude and an offbeat sense of humor.

A couple of days later, I visited John and Karen and asked John if Karen had finally noticed.

"No," John said. "I had to tell her."

"You had to *tell* her? When?"

"After a couple of days," John said. "I actually had to take her hand and put it on my face for her to notice."

"Really?"

Karen just smiled. She was standing two or three feet away during this exchange.

"I think it looks great," she said.

So we've all seen John now without his beard, Karen included, and I remain perplexed as to how Karen went more than two days without noticing. She and John met and got married in the early 1980s. She has never seen him without a beard during that time. He had it for about 40 years, he told me.

I know this happens. It's a cliché in sitcoms. The wife comes home from the salon with a new look, the husband doesn't notice, and she gangs up on him for not paying attention to her anymore.

That's most often the way it works, right? It's the female in the relationship who changes and feels hurt when her loved one is oblivious. There's a reason it's rare that the shoe's ever on the other foot, and that's because men hardly ever change their appearance.

Think about it. If you're a woman, look at the picture you have of you and your husband that's been hanging on your living room wall since the Carter or Reagan administration. He still wears his hair the same way, right? There may be *less* of it today, but it's still the same, right? And that shirt he's wearing - - it's still somewhere in his closet, right? Of course it is. Only his belt-size has changed.

Are men, or males in general, reluctant to change their appearance? Maybe. I shaved for the first time when I was 15 or 16 - - and not because there was nothing on my face to shave until then, mind you. No, in my case, I didn't want to get rid of the peach fuzz that had turned up a couple of years earlier because I didn't want to alter my appearance and risk calling attention to myself. My parents were not subtle in their suggestion that the time had come for me to shave; they gave me an electric razor for my birthday. They probably didn't figure that twelve years later I'd go off and shave my whole head too, in a bid to push back on a rapidly receding hairline.

"My Dad used to have hair," my daughter once told someone, "but then he got married."

So I guess all that blows my theory out of the water that men do not care to alter their appearance. Because remember, John changed his appearance too.

Will John grow back his beard? Who knows. This coming winter will be the test. We'll see what happens when he feels the cold slap of Old Man Winter on his bare cheeks for the first time since those groovy Seventies.

I liked the way John handled the whole situation with Karen. He kind of made a fun contest out of it. I think he wanted to see how long Karen would go before she noticed he had shaved off his beard. It was only when the answer seemed to be "forever" that he took her hand and placed it on his cheek.

Both John and Karen laughed about the whole situation; all great couples know to laugh at these things. I found the whole episode hilarious too. But I saw sweetness there as well. And that's what matters. Spouses see each other every day, so much so they may not actually *see* one another. That explains why one guy can shave off his beard and everyone else will notice but his wife won't. Call me a romantic, but I think I know the reason why Karen didn't notice.

She still sees the guy she married 30 years ago.

At The Movies with Dad

December, 2011

My father and I went to the movies in Saco a couple of weeks ago. We saw Clint Eastwood's biopic about legendary FBI Director J. Edgar Hoover.

We walked out of the cinema and gave the movie identical reviews - - it started slow but picked up, and Leonardo DiCaprio deserves an Academy Award nomination for his portrayal of Hoover.

As we headed home, Dad had a great idea: Stop for burgers and fries at Rapid Ray's on Main Street in downtown Saco.

Stop we did. The takeout joint has been a favorite pit stop for us Sullivans over the years. Back in the winter of 1992, for instance, my family picked me up at the Portland Jetport after I completed a fall semester at Florida State University. We stopped at Rapid Ray's on the way home.

Dad stayed in the car while I ordered our food across the street: a burger for him, a cheeseburger and hot dog for me, and fries drenched in vinegar for both of us. As the cooks prepared our order, I looked out the window and up the street. I tried to pinpoint the general area where the old Saco movie theater once existed. Back in the summer of 1978, Dad took me there to see "Star Wars."

I had wanted to see "Star Wars" when it first came out in 1977. I remember playing in our yard one evening as my folks left home to walk up the street to the Sanford Twin Cinema to see the movie. I was just five years old at the time, so I stayed home with the babysitter. My parents were hesitant to take me to a movie that had the word "wars" in its title.

A year later, though, at the ripe old age of six, I peered over Dad's shoulder as he read the newspaper in his favorite chair. I pointed to an ad for "Star Wars" and asked him once more to take me to see it. *Sure,* he finally figured. *He's already got the "Star Wars" bed sheets, curtains and action figures, so why not?*

On a warm afternoon in early August, Dad and I went to see "Star Wars" in Saco. My Aunt Shirley babysat my sister while we went. My mother was working at the bank up the street that afternoon.

Believe it or not, there is little I can remember of the two of us sitting in the cinema and enjoying the movie. Had Dad gotten popcorn for us? Most likely. I think I can picture that famous upward scrawl of yellow words at the start of the film. I trust I was amused by the odd creatures in the cantina scene. I'm also sure my boyhood crush on Princess Leia started that afternoon. On the way home, before we picked up my sister, Dad and I stopped at Rosa's on Pioneer Avenue when we got back into

Sanford. We ate sandwiches, and I drank Pepsi from a plastic "Star Wars" cup.

Dad, a high school guidance counselor, had taken that summer off from work. He was 33 years old then. All these years later, he still names that summer of 1978 as one of his favorites. While Mom worked at the bank, Dad stayed home with Kelly and me. He went a little stir crazy at times, as he wiped the grime off my sister's face after she played outside, picked up what our collie put down in the back yard, and sent me to my room more than once for failing to think before I spoke. All the same, he loved that time at home and says he would not have changed a thing.

Dad took me to see other movies when I was young. He brought me to the 1976 remake of "King Kong," which I watched through my hands over my eyes. We saw one of the "Herbie" movies - - you know, about the lovable white Volkswagen with the red and blue stripes. He took me to a few other Disney movies too. "The Rescuers" comes to mind.

We kept going to the movies as I got older. We often saw action flicks.

Whenever we went on family vacations, Dad and I often took one evening to sneak off to the theaters. During the summer of 1987, when I was fifteen, we saw "The Living Daylights," a James Bond movie, at a multiplex in Secaucus, New Jersey. Two years later, during a trip to California, we saw the next 007 actioner, "License to Kill."

343

When Dad and I saw the J. Edgar Hoover film a couple of weeks ago, it was our first time heading out to the movies together in maybe five years. I'm not sure how we let so much time pass, but you know how life gets.

Dad no longer drives, so I took the wheel that night. We talked just a bit on the way to Saco because Dad brought some dinner with him to eat along the way. His ALS has progressed to the point where it is too risky for him to carry on a conversation while eating.

When we arrived at the theater, I popped the trunk of the car and took out Dad's walker. Next week makes seven years since Dad was diagnosed with ALS, or amyotrophic lateral sclerosis, a neurological disease that destroys muscles and leads to paralysis. He is in the final stage of his illness but remains on his feet, thanks to two leg braces, the walker and a fighting spirit.

Inside the cinema, I set Dad's walker against the wall, out of the way of anyone who would enter after us. Then Dad gripped a railing with his left hand and locked his right arm in mine. We climbed a few broad steps to the third row in the stadium seating. This took all of Dad's strength and will.

I let go of Dad with my usual caution, and he plopped down into his seat. "Plopped" is the correct word, for once he was in the right position, he let himself go, and the full force of his remaining 112 pounds dropped into the seat. At this moment my heart went out to Dad, whom I've loved and admired my whole life, but I soldiered through my emotions and stayed true to our mission: to have a fun time at the movies. It's a mission we accomplished, as easily as old times; on the way home, we discussed the movie and politics and other things and, as you know, we stopped at Rapid Ray's.

Dad and I went to the movies together that evening. However, as I waited for our food afterward, I realized it also could be said I took Dad to the movies. That's when I looked down the street to where the old Saco movie theater used to be.

I took Dad to the movies tonight, I thought and smiled.

Just like he used to take me.

Dad, Remembered

January, 2012

For the past seven years, friends and strangers alike would ask me how Dad is doing. The friends may have been his, mine or ours, and the strangers tended to be nice people who felt they had gotten to know Dad through my column in the Sanford News.

They all wanted to know how Dad was faring in his battle against amyotrophic lateral sclerosis. I always appreciated the chance to answer the question because for me it meant one thing: Dad was here.

I'm going to miss answering that question. My father, Gary Sullivan, passed away at home on Sunday, January 8. He was 66.

He was my hero. He always will be.

These days I am now getting asked another question: How is Mom doing? I appreciate this question as well because it too means one thing: Mom is here.

Mom is doing as well as can be expected under these circumstances. She is sad but strong. She had a daunting, exhausting and heartbreaking task in caring for my father, but she fulfilled it with bravery, devotion and love. She too is my hero. She too always will be.

I went to visit her on Sunday but she was not home, which seemed strange to me because lights were on in the house and her car was in the driveway. I called two of her friends who were most likely to stop by the house and take her out for an evening, but they both told me Mom was not with them. I decided I needed to relax and trust that Mom was *somewhere*. Sure enough, my aunt and uncle had called Mom earlier in the afternoon and invited her to dinner.

"I hope I didn't worry you," Mom told me on the phone a few hours later.

"No, Mom, I knew you were okay," I told her. "I just wanted to check in on you. I'm just getting used to you being on your own, that's all."

While I have lost loved ones before, I have never quite encountered the concept of forever as intensely as I am faced with it now. Dad is gone. I miss him. I feel for others who have lost one or both of their parents too.

As sad as I am, however, I know how to move forward, largely because of the lessons about life that Dad and Mom have taught me.

I learned from my parents that family comes first. When I was young, Mom and Dad were busy with their jobs, and Dad also was very much involved with volunteering in the community, but I cannot think of a single baseball or soccer game or school event that they missed.

Here's what else I learned from Dad: Be loyal to your friends. Treat others as you would like to be treated. Be proud of where you come from. Act on your ideas for a better world and find joy in forming lasting partnerships when making them happen. Unleash your creativity. Laugh - - at yourself and at life, even when life insists it is not funny.

And this brings me to the most significant lesson Dad taught me: When life slams you against the wall, push back. Push back with grace, compassion, determination, humor and a love for life that cannot be extinguished. Push back with *character*.

Dad was diagnosed with ALS seven years ago. His doctors traced the origin of his disease back to the spring of 2003. Those first several months were a nightmare. We were told Dad had only two to five years left to live. Dad felt as though his life was finished, snuffed out by a cruel twist of fate.

Little did we know, his new life was just getting started. In the years that would follow, as ALS destroyed his muscles, took away his abilities and pushed him toward paralysis, Dad managed to do more with less than most do with all.

He learned everything he could about ALS. He served as vice president of the northern New England Chapter of the ALS Association. He wrote a book, "I Prefer to Laugh," about his experiences with the disease. He visited local service clubs and gave speeches to raise awareness about ALS and the need for a cure. He traveled to Washington, DC, and lobbied for more ALS research and other initiatives. He cofounded the ALS-Maine Collaborative, a network that provides a variety of services to ALS patients. And he worked with Massachusetts General Hospital to establish a telecare network that allows ALS patients all throughout Maine to "meet" with specialists in Boston through videoconferencing.

Whenever Dad heard about someone newly diagnosed with ALS, he would call them, even if he didn't know them, and he'd tell them how they could get help. He'd listen to their worries and relate to them so they knew they were not alone. He even made them laugh.

Dad guided his family and friends through his experiences with ALS. We attended fundraisers and took turns accompanying him to doctor's visits. We rolled up our sleeves and helped build a handicapped accessible bathroom in his and Mom's home.

I called myself Dad's right-hand man. When he gave a speech, I stood behind him, ready to catch him if he fell. I edited his book. I traveled to Washington with him and urged our Congresspeople to support ALS-related initiatives.

I wrestled with my role as Dad's right-hand man, always wondering if I was doing enough to help. Dad always assured me I was, but I could never quite convince myself. I now realize my feelings were understandable and were based in the painful realization that there is no cure for ALS.

In the beginning, when people asked me how Dad was doing, I'd smile and say he was fine and that his situation was progressing slower than usual. After a couple of years passed, I'd tell people that Dad was "hanging in there." Even more years later I'd acknowledge Dad was "slowing down." During the final stages of his disease, I offered the truth and told people, "He's not doing well."

Around the holidays, Dad told Mom, "I know you will be sad when I am gone, but please take a moment to be happy for me."

Never again will I be asked how Dad is doing, but this does not mean I do not know the answer. He is free from all struggles and is now at peace.

It is comforting to know that answer will never change.

The Snowman

Madeline and I made our annual snowman on Sunday. We had to be a little more creative this time around.

We had no problem last year, as the conditions in our yard were perfect for packing and building a snowman the size of my daughter. Last weekend was different - - the snow was nothing but fluff.

For a moment I wanted to ask Maddie if we could wait for a storm after which we would have stickier and heavier ingredients for a snowman. But you know how it is with kids. They ask you if you want to do something fun with them and you want to say "yes," no matter what, because you know tomorrow they'll be teenagers, and then the day after that they'll be going off to college and getting a job, and then the day after they they'll be getting married and starting their own families. And so on.

Maddie climbed into her snow pants, slipped into her jacket and pulled a hat over her head. I grabbed my coat and gloves and bundled up too. As we stepped out of the house, my father-in-law, Russ, and his fiancée, Susan, pulled into our driveway. Russ had made Valerie and me a nice, solid bench to put near our front door so we could have a place to sit while we put on and take off our boots during the winter.

Valerie was at a meeting, so Russ, Susan, Maddie and I relaxed in the living room and chatted. When Val returned, she marveled at the bench; she said from here on in she wants her dad to make all of our furniture. It's a beautiful piece of woodworking. Russ told us it was sturdy too and invited Maddie to hop around on top of it. This she did.

Valerie, Russ and I went downstairs to look at our basement and two vacant rooms that we want to convert into an office and family space. Russ spent his career as the head of a maintenance department at a school in Massachusetts, so he's our go-to guy when it comes to advice on various repairs and home improvements. He's good with cars too.

Russ broke out a level and started examining a door we were thinking of replacing and assured us we could fix it just fine and make it all new again. He checked out our water pipes and suggested ways we could conserve heat. He saw lots of potential for that family room and office too. He assured us we could definitely work with what we have.

After Russ and Susan headed home to Massachusetts, Maddie visited our neighbors across the street. She returned at around four, with just enough light left in the afternoon to help us build our snowman.

I packed a snowball and tried rolling it across the yard to make it bigger, which I knew would be a fool's errand before I even started. No snow gathered.

Maddie and I decided to grab shovels, build a large pile in our front yard, and then sculpt a snowman. But this too proved a challenge; the snowman - - er, the pile, anyway - - got wider and wider but not taller and taller.

"I think this is as good as it gets," I told Maddie.

If Maddie felt disappointed, she didn't show it. She said she wanted to dress up what we had made, so she went indoors for a moment. I knelt down in the snow and tried to make the pile rounder along its sides, all the way thinking the mound would end up looking more like Jabba the Hutt from the "Star Wars" movies than Frosty the Snowman.

I stood up, looked at our dog, Pepper, as she watched me from our living room window, and I sighed.

Maddie came out with a small plastic bag and her black hat with a purple ribbon. I grinned when I saw her. She reached into the bag and took out a handful of cherry tomatoes. She etched them into the top of the mound to make a smile. Then she took out three baby carrots and made a nose. At last she withdrew two Life Savers and used them for eyes. She stuck her hat on top of the pile, which now, I admit, started looking less like a pile and more like a snowman.

We searched our yard for sticks that could be used for arms. When we found a couple, we twisted them into the snowman's sides to look like he was raising them into the air.

"I'm going to go get some clothes," Maddie told me.

I stood on the front lawn while she went back inside. I looked at Pepper in the window. She looked back. I glanced at the sun setting in the west and thought of my late father.

Maddie came back outside and once more I smiled at the sight of her. She had an armful of winter clothes. We draped a thin but long scarf around the squat snowman's fat neck. We dangled gloves at the ends of the snowman's stick-arms. We rested a belt across its ample waist.

Then we had a brilliant idea. We took the pair of rubber boots that Maddie had outgrown and pushed them into the front of the pile-turned-snowman. Toes-up.

Get it? Instead of making a snowman that stood tall, we made one that was sitting down. Those boots solved all of our problems. We lacked the hard-packed snow with which to make a tall snowman with a bottom, a middle and a head, so we worked with what we had.

Maddie was thrilled. I was too. A project that had seemed hopeless at first proved fun and resourceful, thanks to my daughter's creativity, persistence and optimism.

We went and got Valerie and she took a picture of Maddie, Pepper and me next to our new wintry friend. And it's a good thing too. Monday's drizzle and Tuesday's spring-like warmth caused our sitting snowman to shrink. He looked as though Mother Nature had squashed him with her thumb.

No problem. It's the memory of Maddie and I making him that will last.

Would I Have Met Her If I Had Excelled At Math?

Twenty years ago I hopped on a plane and headed to Florida in search of palm trees and sun.

I was a sophomore in college seeking to escape the freezing climate of the University of Maine at Orono, which is where I spent my freshman year. I was determined to pursue my passion, movies, and focus on filmmaking at Florida State University.

I was 19 at the time. I want to tell you what a big deal that was for me, to get on that plane in the predawn hours of New Year's Day and leave my family and friends behind. The truth is that I know others my age had left home under even more dramatic and significant circumstances. A year earlier, for example, thousands of guys my age boarded planes for the Middle East to lead the fight to push Saddam Hussein back into Iraq. So yeah, what's the big deal about a kid from Maine heading down to the Sunshine State?

But it was a big move for me, bold even, as I was the first in my family to go so far away for so long. Dad sent me a postcard later that week telling me how proud he was and confiding that the willingness I had to pull up my stakes and leave home is not something he had at my age. I read that post card and basked in the glow of Dad's compliment and confidence in me.

My first few hours in Tallahassee were challenging. I took a cab from the airport to a motel, and the driver pointed to the McDonald's across the street.

"See that McDonald's over there?" he asked me.

It was hard not to, what with those famous yellow arches and all.

"Yeah," I told him.

"Well, stay away from there and the neighborhood behind it. Lots of gangs back there," he said.

Then he drove off and I stood in the parking lot with my suitcases.

I checked into my room and watched a movie on television, something from the Seventies with Richard Pryor. At one point I called a friend back home. Eventually I decided to check out FSU.

The campus felt like a ghost town. It was New Year's Day, and everyone was home watching football. Classes would not begin for a few days, so the dorms and streets were vacant. The dining commons were not open, either. I was on my own.

I felt skittish, like a stranger in a strange land, even though I had been to Florida a few times before. My family and I had visited FSU nine months earlier, so that I could follow up my application with a meeting with an admissions officer in the hopes of making a good impression.

I encountered just two people on campus that afternoon. They approached me at a crosswalk and started talking to me about volleyball. *Volleyball?* I thought. *Why are they talking to me about volleyball?* I told them I liked the game and they gave me two business cards. They were missionaries seeking to recruit me to their church.

That evening I stayed in my motel room. I have no recollection of what I watched on television or ate for dinner. I do know I skipped going to McDonald's. I sat on my bed and realized that four months seemed like an awfully long time. I'd be heading back to Maine for the summer at the end of the semester in April.

I enjoyed my time at FSU. I never quite found my footing - - as a late bloomer, that would only happen during my junior or senior year of college - - but thanks to friends and that warm Florida sun I had no real idea of how lonesome or displaced I felt.

I spent two semesters at FSU. One of my roommates joined the circus on campus. A few of the guys in my dorm actually thought I was a Kennedy at first because of my New England accent. I took classes that had between 300 and 900 students in them. I worked out at the campus gymnasium and filled out my scrawny frame. I landed a job with a catering firm and got to watch the FSU football games from the skyboxes. My friend

Dave and I took trips to Panama City and Alabama. My family visited and we headed over to New Orleans for Thanksgiving. I acted in a student film and it premiered on a silver screen on campus and the director misspelled my name as "Sean" in the opening credits.

Every day I checked my mailbox for letters or post cards or special packages. Email was not yet commonplace back then.

Yup. Just two semesters. During the fall of 1992, I met with my academic adviser to discuss declaring my major. I had my eye on Communications, with that emphasis on film. To keep things interesting, I also considered political science as a minor.

There was a problem. During the Spring 1992 semester, you needed a 2.8 grade-point average to major in Communications. This was not an issue, as I had a 2.8. For the fall of 1992, however, the requirement was increased to a 3.0 GPA. In other words, when I left FSU that spring I was eligible, but when I returned that fall I was not.

My adviser had three suggestions, all of which he offered with the detachment you'd expect from an administrator who had to deal with thousands of students. I could take a few basic courses in the hopes of shoring up my GPA. I could major in a subject for which all you needed was a 2.8 GPA. Or I could transfer to another school.

Courses cost money, so I didn't like the idea of taking so-called "easy" classes for the sake of bolstering my average. And

I didn't want to transfer because I liked FSU and, well, I had already transferred once to get there.

I got out the school's course catalog and flipped through it. Wouldn't you know it? The one subject in which I could major with a 2.8 GPA was the one subject that had dragged down my average to begin with.

Math.

On the whole, I had achieved 3.0s, 3.5s and 4.0s in my other classes, save for a few here and there in the middling range of 2.5 or thereabouts. My math scores, however, were in the basement. I got a 1.67 in freshman statistics up at Orono, for example.

I slammed the catalog shut. I was *not* going to major in math.

That left one option. I picked up the phone and called Dad. At the time he was the director of the guidance department at Biddeford High School. I told him about my situation, and he offered to help me find other schools that might interest me.

It came down to the University of Central Florida in Orlando and Fitchburg State College, now Fitchburg State University, in Massachusetts. I liked the idea of heading to Orlando . . . but even more I loved the idea of returning to New England. I missed being near family and old friends and seeing the change in the seasons. I picked Fitchburg.

Smart move.

I met a girl there named Valerie.

At the Wheel

I've owned three cars since college, which perhaps suggests to you just how long I hang on to them before getting a new one. I felt no sense of loss when I got rid of the first two, a Ford and a Dodge, because I was too excited about the new ride.

Well, Valerie and I got a new car over the Presidents Day weekend and I admit I'll observe a moment of silence when we sell our old one, another Ford. We didn't even bother to try to trade in this Ford, as we doubted it would even make the trip to Saco, which is where we purchased the new car, a Hyundai.

At first I was all set to cast aside the old Ford with an indifferent good riddance. Then Valerie reminded me it was the car in which we first brought home our daughter, Madeline, almost nine years ago.

On a warm day during the first week of May in 2003, Valerie and I exited the hospital in Melrose, Massachusetts, and walked to our Ford Focus parked on a side street. Our newborn eight-pound girl dangled at my side as I carried her in her car seat.

A nurse joined us. I opened the back door on the passenger's side, and she showed us the correct way to install a car seat. She may have been required to do this as part of her job. The nurse set the car seat with Maddie facing the rearview window, made a few adjustments and then felt satisfied after we heard all the right clicks. It was all a far cry from one of my first memories, dating back to the summer of 1975, when I looked out the window and saw my parents arrive home from the hospital, with Mom in the front seat of the car, holding my newborn sister in her arms.

Valerie and I lived in New Hampshire at the time Maddie was born, and I remember well the 35-mile trip home from Melrose. This was our first time as just the three of us. Oh, Valerie and Maddie and I had been alone together in our hospital room, to be sure, but the nurses checked on us often and were always just a ring-of-the-buzzer away from us. This ride home was our first time being out in the world together. It was an exhilarating feeling, filled with hope and excitement for the life as a family that awaited us . . . but yes, we tried not to think too much about the awesome responsibility of having a new life placed squarely on our shoulders.

Given our precious cargo, I drove so slowly and cautiously going north on Route One that I got passed by grannies who could barely see over their steering wheels. Valerie and I pointed out various sites to Maddie that caught our eyes. That's where we go to the Topsfield Fair, we told Maddie, for example. We were introducing our daughter to the world.

During those first several months, I drove Maddie to her babysitter's house as part of my long commute to work in the morning. We chatted about various topics; I spoke in my usual enthusiastic rush of words and she responded with occasional giggles, blurts and sounds I knew at the time were gas. We listened to Don Imus on the radio.

Valerie and I bought this Ford back in the summer of 2002, just a few days before we left on a trip to visit our friends in Virginia. We tossed our suitcases into the trunk and hit the road, each taking turns driving. As we inched along during a traffic jam over the bridge in Delaware, I leaned back in the passenger's seat, propped my bare right foot out the window, and relaxed.

I'll think of these memories when I see this car for the last time.

On to the new car. Given our history of keeping cars a long time, it occurred to me on the night we bought this new one that it's very likely the vehicle in which Maddie will learn how to drive. When I was 15 years old, Dad drove me to the parking lot at St. Thomas School on North Avenue and offered to switch places with me. He got out of the car and slipped back into it on the passenger's side as I edged across the seat to get behind the wheel. For about an hour on that summer evening, he introduced me to the basics of driving a car. He held on for dear life as I peeled off the lot and cut sharp cookies and kicked up large clouds of dust in the adjacent field.

All right, you got me. That never happened. Instead, I practiced turning left and right, reversing and parking, all at a speed no greater than a mile or two an hour. Several months later, during the spring of 1988, I enrolled in one of the local driving schools.

As I drove our new Hyundai home the other night, I thought of Dad teaching me to drive in the school's lot that summer night long ago, and I smiled. That's just one of hundreds, perhaps thousands, of memories I have of him sharing his time with me for my own enjoyment and growth. I looked six or seven years down the road, and imagined taking Maddie to an open lot for a similar lesson on the basics of driving.

New car, new memories.

Waves

March, 2012

Madeline and I caught a recent Red Claws game at the Expo in Portland.

I had been wanting to take Maddie to a basketball game for quite some time. She started playing the sport with the Sanford-Springvale Youth Athletic Association a couple of years ago, and I figured she'd like to see the game played at a professional level.

Imagine my good fortune. In January I attended Literacy Volunteers of Greater Sanford's annual Trivia Night fundraiser at the Town Club. I joined the team assembled by the good folks at Shaw's Hardware, and even though we didn't win the trivia contest we went home smarter. Thanks to one of the trivia questions, I now know snails can sleep for three years. Whether that's for three years in a row, I'm not sure. Either way, that's not too impressive, as I know people who slept as long through college. Nonetheless, the key words of "snails," "sleep" and "three years" will always be linked in my mind as a bit of trivia I may never need again.

But I'm getting off track. At this fundraiser, I entered a raffle to win two tickets to a Red Claws game and won. When I got the tickets at the end of the evening, I saw that they were for the game on Friday, March 2, which would be celebrated as "Irish Night."

Perfect, I smiled and thought. Maddie and I will feel right at home.

On the night of the big game, Maddie and I kissed Valerie goodbye and left her to enjoy what all elementary school teachers crave: a quiet night at home. Maddie and I headed to Portland and grabbed dinner at Johnny Rockets at the Maine Mall. Afterward, we made it to the Expo just in time.

The Red Claws meant it when they said the theme for that game would be "Irish Night." On the way into the arena, we saw Boston Celtics paraphernalia and a booth promoting The Irish Heritage Center. During the game, fans were treated to bagpipers and Irish dancers. I pointed out Ireland's national flag to Maddie and told her the meaning behind its three colors of green, orange and white. Early in the game, the announcer directed everyone's attention to the scoreboard, on which there was an Irish-related trivia question in which former Celtic Kevin McHale was the answer.

We were having a great time, Maddie and me. She could not believe the game's breakneck speed and the players' smooth moves.

At one point I noticed a gentleman sitting courtside on the Red Claws' end. He was in a wheelchair and could not move. Judging from the expression on his face - - a mix of enjoyment and relaxation - - he seemed to be having a fun time.

I wondered if he had ALS, and I thought of my late father.

It never occurred to me that the gentleman might be the evening's special guest. I had figured that his courtside seat was simply a handicapped-accessible location. A few minutes before half-time, though, the man's wife and family began escorting him onto the basketball court. I watched them with great interest.

In no time, the man and his family were at center court. The announcer asked for the crowd's attention and introduced the man as Dr. Bruce Churchill, who indeed has amyotrophic lateral sclerosis.

Perhaps Dr. Churchill's name rings a bell for you. The Portland Press-Herald wrote a heartwarming and inspiring feature story about him a while ago. He's a Cumberland doctor, an assistant volleyball coach at Greely High School, and an advocate for ALS research and fundraising. The Bruce Churchill Classic, an annual state volleyball tournament and ALS fundraiser, is named after him. His wife, Cindy, is one of the key organizers of the ALS Association's annual Walk to Defeat ALS in Portland.

I sat up in my bleacher seat and watched Dr. Churchill smile at the crowd as the announcer described his accomplishments.

This guy's just like Dad, I thought with a son's boyish wonder.

Everyone in the crowd rose to their feet and applauded as Dr. Churchill and his family exited the court. Composer John Williams's soaring and triumphant theme from the 1978 "Superman" movie boomed over the arena's sound system. I clapped harder. The choice of music was appropriate. We had a true superhero in our midst.

Maddie looked up at me and noticed I was visibly moved, perhaps even a little shaken. We had known the game would be an "Irish Night," perfect for a couple of Sullivans like us. We had no idea, however, that the night also would include a tribute to a beloved man fighting the same battle Dad had fought.

Maddie wrapped her arms around me and gave me a hug.

Others have suggested to me that Maddie and I were fated to be at this game - - that my winning of the Red Claws tickets back in January, just five days after my father passed away, was no coincidence. I'm not sure what to think, as I'm inclined to question the likelihood of both Fate and coincidence. I did, however, take away something meaningful from the whole episode, and it is this: Even though Dad is gone, the fight against ALS continues.

"I'd like to go meet him," I told Maddie after everyone sat down and Dr. Churchill and his family returned to their choice spot behind the Red Claws' net.

We got up, walked down the bleachers and approached Dr. Churchill and his wife. I introduced myself and Maddie. Dr. Churchill smiled.

"My father had ALS," I told them.

Mrs. Churchill surprised me with her response: "Was your father Gary Sullivan?"

I broke out into a smile and told her, yes, he was. She said she had gotten to know Dad through the annual ALS walks in Portland in September.

"He was a wonderful man," she told me.

I smiled some more and nodded. I told Dr. Churchill that he was an inspiration and shyly fumbled a bit through an attempt to tell him the announcer's choice of the "Superman" theme was appropriate. I told the Churchills it was a pleasure to meet them, and then Maddie and I returned to our seats.

When we were ready to leave at some point late in the third quarter - - it was close to nine o'clock and Maddie had grown tired - - I made sure to approach the Churchills once more to quickly wish them a nice evening.

Last week I got some mail from a friend. She sent me a piece someone had written about grief, and she said it had helped her through the loss of her mother. I gave it a read. The writer compared grief to the game we all played at the beach as children. You stand there in water up to your waist and wait for each approaching wave. When the wave arrives, it picks you up a bit and in a matter of seconds pushes you back and sets you back down on your feet. Sometimes the wave sets you back a foot or two; other times, farther. And once in a while, there's a big wave that you do not see coming and it does more than set you back. It topples you and wipes you right out. Your only choice is to flail with it and wait for it to pass so you can regain your footing.

The writer is correct. Grief is exactly like those waves. In these two months since my father died, I have found that grief is not a constant state but a complex and recurring force that hits you in waves big and small, in ways expected and unexpected.

Maddie and I had not known that the basketball game would include a tribute to a wonderful person in so many ways similar to my father, from the specific challenge he faces to the grace, positivity and activism with which he is meeting it. The occasion was like one of those waves: not at all sad, mind you, but filled with poignancy and remembrance.

"I miss Grampy," Maddie told me later that evening.

I put my arm around her and kissed the top of her head.

"I know, sweetheart," I told her. "I do too."

Postscript, 2017. *Dr. Churchill passed away after his own valiant battle against ALS in July of 2012, four months after the basketball game at which he was so memorably honored.*

A Good Dog

Our dog Pepper turns one this week. Or is it seven?

Either way, she was born a year ago Wednesday. Last spring, Valerie, Madeline, and I were thinking about getting a new dog. Through the ol' grapevine we heard about a new litter of puppies, all part mini schnauzer, part wire fox terrier, out on a farm on Sunset Road in Springvale. We got in touch with the owner and arranged to visit her home.

We spotted Pepper right away. In a tangle of black and gray newborns, she stood out with her sable coat. I pointed to this puppy and asked the owner if I could hold "that one," not knowing at the time if the dog was a male or a female.

I held the puppy and noticed right away that she had the same round brown eyes as Molly, our Cairn terrier who passed away at the ripe old age of eighteen or nineteen on the day before Thanksgiving back in 2008. That was it. I felt the connection.

"I like that one," I whispered to Val and gestured to the puppy as Maddie took her turn cradling her.

Both Valerie and I agreed that Maddie would get to pick the puppy she liked. Fortunately, she liked this little sable one too. Less than a month later, we brought Pepper home. On Father's Day, to be exact.

We thought of calling her Sophie at first. Then Lily. Then Rose. Valerie suggested Piper. Maddie countered with Pepper. We all smiled and knew we had a winner.

She's turned out to be a little firecracker, this Pepper. Valerie and I did not have to baby-proof our home half as fanatically as we've had to "puppy-proof" it during the past year. I always knew dogs were famous for eating things that no one else would dare touch, but in the past year Pepper has repeatedly astonished me with the range of garbage she's willing to chew with relish and swallow. Of course, by "relish," I mean "enthusiasm," lest you think our dog favors condiments with her ghastly choices of food.

"Unbelievable," I tell Pepper as I pry one of our cats' yakked-up hairballs with a paper towel from Pepper's ironclad jaws. "Unbelievable. Are you telling me you don't know better than to eat something like that?"

Pepper, who is selective in the words she understands, just looks at me at these moments and shifts on her hind legs a bit and grunts as though to say, "Give that back."

"Shawn, she's a dog," Valerie or Maddie then reminds me. I'm not sure if they say this to remind me that it's useless for me to expect Pepper to answer my question or to explain that of course Pepper's going to try to scarf down this, that or the other thing. Both, probably.

This is my first time raising a puppy. My family had a collie named Shannon when I was a kid, but I was not responsible for housebreaking him as I was just a newborn as well. Valerie and I got Molly when she was nine or ten years old, a gentle veteran set in her charming little ways.

Pepper's new thing is that she has found her voice. Oh, she has been barking and growling and snorting all along, sure, but it seems lately she has learned to unleash the full power of her signature sound. I went for a walk the other night and heard a faint barking in the distance behind me. I knew it was Pepper.

"Really?" I asked myself in that rhetorical way that's cool these days. "I'm, like, a third of a mile away."

In the morning, Pepper sits in the window and barks at even the slightest developments. Sometimes it's when one of our neighbors jogs by our house in the morning with his two Labradors. Other times it's when a single snow flake drifts by the window or a lonesome leaf rustles on our front lawn. One time, Pepper barked at nothing my eye could see, so perhaps she was railing against a microscopic particle in the air or something.

In our home, we call these barking fits "The Pepper Report."

Speaking of that picture window in our living room, Pepper also likes to breathe on it and run her front paws on it and - - I'm convinced of this, even though I've never seen it - - lick it. Valerie or I can wash that window clean with a paper towel and a shot of Windex and an hour later it will look like the Pinto's windshield in the movie "Cujo."

Then there are those odd hours of the day and night when Pepper needs to "conduct her business." Valerie, Maddie or I wander aimlessly around our front yard in a series of sharp twists and turns and tight circles while Pepper sniffs out the right spot to leave her mark on the world. It's a good thing we're holding a leash with a dog at the end of it because if anyone ever saw us walking this way without either they'd throw us in a padded room.

"Look at that guy and the way he's walking," they'd say. "He has no idea if he's coming or going. We've gotta get him some help."

Of course, all of this - - the barking, the tug of war over something foul in her mouth, the smeared window, the nonsensical "walks" around our yard - - is part of raising a puppy. The rewards . . . ah, yes, the rewards of welcoming a dog into our family have no number. They are infinite.

Pepper greets us at the door when we get home from work and school. Sometimes, before we even get the key in the lock, she jumps so high against the door we can see her head pop up and down in the window.

When life deals its fair share of challenges, Pepper sits still in our laps and lets us rub her ears and stroke the curly fur along her back.

Even though we never feed her scraps from the dinner table, she never loses hope and faith that one day we will.

When she barks, she's protecting our home.

Pepper revives us with games of fetch and playful roughhousing when we're tired after a long day.

She brings boundless joy to our neighbors, John and Karen, who watch after her while we're at work or school. Karen calls her time with Pepper "Doggy Day Care."

Pepper is a good dog.

That's all you need to say about certain dogs to know everything about them.

Imagine how many of the world's problems would just fall away if we treated each other the way our dogs treat us.

Shriek of Terror

Something in the woods near my home let out a horrid screech just as I was about to fall asleep the other night.

My eyes snapped wide open.

"*What* was that?" I more or less asked Valerie. I may have thrown a couple extra words in there.

Valerie had heard it too but had no idea what it was.

I turned my head and looked at the clock. It was a few minutes before one. Valerie and I had called it a night about half an hour earlier after staying up late to watch "Saving Private Ryan" in honor of Memorial Day Weekend.

The thing screeched again.

At first we thought it was someone howling in unbelievable pain. The next morning, my neighbor, John, would tell me he heard the screaming too and almost called the police because he thought someone was getting attacked.

But I knew what it was. A year ago, my friend told me he had heard such a noise and also thought someone - - a baby or a child, God forbid - - was suffering and crying desperately for help. He ventured outside and into the darkness to investigate.

He followed the sound to a tree and looked up. He saw an odd creature perched on a branch looking down at him.

"I know what it is," I told Valerie, recalling my friend's story. "It's a fisher cat."

I got out of bed and went into our living room. I opened the window facing our next-door neighbor's house and the wooded area beyond it. I sat at the end of our couch and listened. One of our cats, Cocoa, joined me and sat on the sill.

The fisher cat let out more cries. *Good Lord*, I thought as I stared out into the blackness. *What's its problem? Is it lost? Sad? In heat?* I put my money on "ticked off." *Really* ticked off.

I kept staring in the general direction of its cries, unable to see the woods but expecting this creature to materialize on our lawn. I imagined it advancing toward our house and shuddered.

Yet I kept listening for its next outburst. There were a few more, and then there were no more.

I got up and went back to bed. But first I shut the living room window, even though it was warm outside. Did I think this thing would sprint across our lawn, leap through the air, crash through our screen and go on a rampage through our home? Well, hey. You know how the mind works in the dark of night.

"It's cute," my daughter, Maddie, said the next morning when I showed her a photo of a fisher cat online.

Easy for her to say. She slept through that lunatic rant in the woods the night before. Maddie changed her mind when I played an audio clip of the diminutive beast screaming on YouTube.

According to my neighbor, Glenn, we have New Hampshire to thank for fisher cats. Someone brought them over from Europe in the 1800s to address a porcupine problem. Apparently, these fisher cats would charge porcupines, knock them over and attack them through their bellies. I never knew porcupines were a problem. It would seem to me that the fisher cats would be the problem. But then I've never been pierced by a porcupine quill.

I had never heard a fisher cat before and I prefer not to hear one again. If I was camping in the woods, I'd rather experience a real-life "Blair Witch Project" than hear a fisher cat screeching somewhere in the night.

But then I should not be out camping, anyway. I grew up in downtown Sanford, with the lights of Main Street and the two baseball parks a couple of blocks over shining on my home and yard. I used to visit my friend, Joyce, out in Shapleigh, and she'd always tease me about being ill-at-ease when we'd take walks in the pitch darkness on her road. We'd take these walks, and I wouldn't even be able to see her next to me. According to Joyce, I always used to ask her where the streetlights were.

Valerie and I went camping at her father's site in New Hampshire a year or two after we were married. I was miserable the whole time. I couldn't wait for the morning to come. I used to love camping with my parents and sister as a child, but I apparently had become spoiled as an adult. Sleeping on the ground in utter silence with no air-conditioning during a heat wave was not my thing.

At one point that night, I heard a big and lumbering creature approach us. It stopped right outside our tent.

"I swear it was a bear," I told Valerie the next morning.

"That was not a bear," she said. "It was probably a deer. Not even that. A fox, maybe."

"No. This thing had very heavy footsteps."

"Maybe it was Bigfoot."

"It walked right up to our tent and stopped. It never left."

"Of course it left."

"Val, I kept listening for it to walk away, but it never did."

"Of course it did. You just fell asleep and didn't hear it go, that's all."

I disputed this claim and maintained I never dozed off at any point throughout the long night.

Sometimes it's great to have a colorful imagination, as I do, and other times, not so much.

Who knows? Maybe it was a fisher cat outside our tent that night. Looking for porcupines, or something. If it *was* a fisher, then it's a good thing it didn't scream.

Because I'm sure I would've screamed louder.

A Squeak in the Night

There may be people who dislike that it gets colder and darker earlier during this time of the year, but I bet most of them still cherish that extra hour of sleep we all get when we turn the clocks back an hour during the first weekend of November. I certainly like those extra sixty minutes of sleep, but this time around I was denied them.

My wife Valerie and I spent a good chunk of time in the middle of Saturday night chasing a mouse in our house.

I went to bed at eleven on Saturday night, winking to myself that it was "really ten" because I would be gaining an hour overnight. At around one in the morning, though, one of our cats - - Tootsie, I think - - started meowing. Loudly. She definitely had a hot news flash to broadcast to the world. She followed all this meowing by scurrying across our dining-room floor and repeatedly whacking the metal panels of our baseboard heating.

I knew this ruckus could have been one of two things. Tootsie likes to hop onto our bathroom sink, pry open one of the top drawers, fish out one of the small, colored elastics that my daughter uses to make ponytails, and start batting it around the house like a hockey puck. So I knew all the noise on Saturday night could have been that.

Or it could have been a mouse.

When I heard a series of panicked squeaks, I knew that's what it was.

"Did you hear that?" I asked Valerie.

"No," she replied, because she had been sleeping before I spoke.

More squeaks.

"That."

"I don't hear it, Shawn."

Well, I did. I got up out of bed and looked for something to swat with, in case it was not a mouse, but a bat. Valerie marveled that I could hear a small animal squeak but that I need to put the TV's volume on high so I can hear it clearly while watching my shows at night.

I ventured out of our bedroom, turned on a few lights and started looking for the critter. Tootsie and her brother, Cocoa, both looked up at me with expressions that said, "Go back to bed. We've got this." Nonetheless, I pressed forward.

Valerie went into our bathroom and spotted a tiny mouse as it ducked behind one of those metal panels along our floor.

"You were right," Valerie said. "It's a mouse."

I picked up both cats and put them in our bedroom with the door closed. The next day, when I told this story about catching a mouse, a friend asked, "Isn't that what your cats are for?" True.

Catching mice is a cat's bailiwick. But I knew that if I had continued to sleep and let the cats solve the problem, there'd be a chance that one of them would jump onto our bed and plop the dead mouse on my pillow as some kind of bid to make me proud. That would have hardly been a scene out of "The Godfather," when that movie mogul woke up to his horse's head in his sheets, but still. It was a moment we wanted to avoid.

I grabbed a broom, and Valerie and I locked ourselves in the bathroom. I ran the broom's bristles along the baseboard-heating panel, in an attempt to "smoke out" the mouse, as our forty-third president might have phrased it. The mouse did pop out a couple of times and scurried across the bathroom floor. Val jumped and shrieked, but I'll give her credit. She didn't jump back and sit on the sink to get her feet off the floor. Instead, I did.

I couldn't really see the mouse, to be honest with you. I was not wearing my contacts, so I couldn't discern between the mouse when it was still and a dust bunny that I had unearthed with the broom.

We knew we needed something to scoop up the mouse, so Valerie retrieved an empty Dunkin' Donuts cup and the lid of a salsa jar from our recycling bin. After a few more minutes of shrieking and laughing - - Valerie shrieked and I laughed, for the record - - we used the broom to usher the mouse into the cup, which we quickly covered.

I had been wearing shoes this whole time. I made putting them on my first priority when I got out of bed. I remembered the time, years ago, when I stepped on a dead chipmunk in our basement and had occasion to thank the inventor of slippers. This time around, I waited at the door while Val went and put on her sneakers, and I held up the plastic cup and studied the mouse inside. Cute little thing, now that he was trapped.

Valerie and I went outside - - the late-night weather was breezy and a little balmy - - and walked to the small patch of woods across the street. We set the mouse free. We have no idea where he went from there. Maybe back to Disney World. Hopefully, not back to our house. In any event, Valerie and I went back to bed. I fell back to sleep. Eventually.

What is it about the middle of the night that amplifies everything? Years and years ago, my parents were shocked awake when their cat, an old Calico named Lucky, started zipping around the house and hissing and growling and making those awful noises that only felines can make.

Lucky stormed into my parents' bedroom and plunged both of them into terror. Dad stood up in their bed and stepped onto the nearby hope chest, all in an effort to avoid putting his bare feet on the floor and having Lucky, who was surely rabid, sink her teeth into his ankles. He grabbed the nearby phone - - it was a rotary one, that's how long ago this happened - - and yanked the cord out of the jack. He held the phone over his head like Early Man clutching a rock and waited for that awful moment when Lucky attacked and he'd have to do what was necessary to save his life and Mom's. It was all happening too fast; there was not a single moment to wonder how Lucky, an indoor cat who could only sit in windows and dream of the outdoors, could have caught rabies.

"Don't touch her!" Dad yelled to Mom. *"Don't touch her!"*

Finally, after all of Lucky's panicking and thrashing and growling, Dad caught a good look at their cat and found the problem. Wouldn't you know it? Lucky did not have rabies. She just had Scotch tape stuck to the end of her tail and she couldn't get it off, that's all. She was pretty mad about it.

And Dad?

"He was really terrified," Mom told me and laughed as we recounted the story this week. "We were so relieved to see the Scotch tape."

Dad went to work the next morning and told his coworkers about the cat. They laughed. They couldn't believe the part about the phone. Later that day, they drew a picture of Dad chasing a little cat with a phone raised above his head; in a thought-bubble over Dad's head, they drew a big roaring lion, as though in his mind that's what Dad was chasing. They drew a little clock with a late-night hour on it. Nice touch. They hung the picture in Dad's office. He kept it there, right until he retired.

I thought of Dad as Val and I hunted down the mouse on Saturday night. I'm glad we could resolve the situation

384

peacefully. For starters, Val and I did not have a rotary phone handy. Somehow I think I would have been less of a force to be reckoned with if I had been wielding my palm-sized cell phone.

Father's Day

Father's Day is going to be tough this Sunday. For me it's the first one since Dad passed away earlier this year.

We will have a nice time, my family and me. On Saturday, Valerie and Madeline and I will keep with tradition and bring Mom to Kennebunkport to have lunch at The Clam Shack with my sister and her family. We have a few nice and fun ideas for Sunday too.

We are sure to have a wonderful time, but yes, it will be quite different. The man whom I had always celebrated on this special day is gone. Ever since Dad died at the turn of the year, I have found comfort in little details and moments that suggests he continues to exist in spirit.

For example, I sat deep in thought in my car at a stop light a few weeks ago. I can't remember what I was preoccupied with, but I do know I was looking forward to getting home and relaxing for the evening. At one point I looked down at my hands and found both thumbs tucked into my curled fingers. I smiled. Dad used to do that. He once told me he would do it whenever he felt nervous or unsure.

And there I was, five months after Dad died, doing the same thing. Have I also been tucking my thumbs my whole life? Did I pick it up from Dad in later years? Or did I start after Dad departed? I never really noticed until that evening at the traffic light.

I drive by the Midtown Mall a couple of times a week and chart the progress of the construction of the town's new walkway there - - the Gary D. Sullivan Walkway, as it will be known. The town dedicated the site to Dad back in December, a few days before Christmas, when he had less than three weeks left to live. The community wanted to honor Dad for his decades of service to the community.

Earlier this spring, I read Aldous Huxley's controversial classic, "A Brave New World." Dad taught that book to his students when he was a history teacher in the early 1970s. He was intrigued by such novels as that one and "1984," which satirized government and society with their dystopian plots. His decision to include "World" in his curriculum raised the eyebrows of more than a few parents, who wrote letters to the editor and appeared before the school committee to argue that the book's subject matter was inappropriate for teenagers.

Dad handed his copy of the book down to me years ago. Reading it for the first time this year, I admit I understand where those parents were coming from . . . but I admire Dad's boldness and his faith in his students to be able to handle mature themes and develop their thinking.

In the book, Dad had written notes in the margins. As I read I often ran the tip of my finger over the red ink of his distinct handwriting and marveled at his insights and interpretations of the novel. Part of me chuckled and wondered if he used Cliff Notes.

Once in a while, someone will call me Gary instead of Shawn. Or they'll get my name right and tell me I look more and more like my father as I get older. In either instance, I take the gaffe and the comparison as a compliment.

Details and moments such as these prove that our loved ones survive in so many ways even after they are gone. They provide peace and reassurance as we continue our lives in the hope that one day we will be reunited with them.

I think about Dad a lot. All the time, actually. Naturally, I reflect on the last seven years of his life as he struggled against ALS. Once in a while, I will remember him as he was in his forties and fifties in the Eighties and Nineties.

Interestingly, though, I think most about him when he was in his late twenties, early thirties in the 1970s. This requires some imagination, as I was a child then and now have just snapshots for memories. Whenever I go for a walk in my neighborhood, I pass by the small ranch house where Dad and my grandparents lived while and after he was in college. I stare at the driveway and imagine him getting into his car to take his girlfriend, Lorraine, my future mother, out on a date. If I try hard enough, I can see him. He was tall, dark-haired and lanky back then.

I imagine him in his prime. Marrying Mom. Buying a home on Shaw Street. Teaching high school students and becoming a guidance counselor. Raising my sister and me with Mom. Heading out to various meetings in town a few nights a week.

I think about that man from so long ago, and I wonder what happened to him. But the truth is that I already know. He became me. I became him. I'm now the young husband and father, with a home here in town and a job and meetings to attend in the evenings.

Yes, Father's Day will be challenging and different on Sunday. I will honor Dad by remembering him. Best of all, I will focus on my daughter and will celebrate what in later years Dad and I both shared in common.

Fatherhood.

The World Is Her Shoe Box

"Give a girl the right shoes, and she can conquer the world."

Marilyn Monroe said that. I should print out that quote and frame it and give it to my daughter, Madeline, to hang on her bedroom wall. She loves shoes.

My wife, Valerie, and Maddie and I took a whirlwind trip earlier this summer and visited friends and family in Philadelphia, Virginia and North Carolina. On the way home, we threw in an afternoon in New York City.

We had included the NYC stop during the first stages of planning for this trip this past spring but cut it from our agenda after looking for ways to save money. Valerie and I decided we'd instead take Maddie to the Big Apple next summer to see a Broadway musical and enjoy other attractions. When we informed Maddie about our decision, she asked if we could at least visit the city, even if we would not be able to see a show or do anything too extravagant.

"What is it you'd like to do?" I asked Maddie. "Climb to the top of the Empire State Building? Walk through Central Park? Have lunch at Carnegie Deli?"

"I want to buy shoes."

I paused for a moment. "Buy shoes?" I asked her, just to make sure I heard her correctly. "Of all there is to see and do in New York City, that's what you want to do?"

She smiled and nodded. I looked at Val. She shrugged and said sure.

"Okay," I told Maddie. "We'll still go into New York City for an afternoon. So you can buy your shoes."

Maddie has loved shoes for as long as I can remember. She may have even been born wearing them, but I'm not sure. I'd have to track down the doctor who delivered her and ask him.

You know who else loves shoes? Our dog, Pepper. She has chewed on a lot of Maddie's shoes and has even mauled my slippers. I guess it's better than eating our couch.

A few weeks ago, Maddie and I ran errands at the Center for Shopping in South Sanford. I dragged her into Bull Moose Music so that I could buy a DVD, and she asked if we could visit the pet store. After we looked at the ferrets, fish, mice and birds, Maddie asked if we could go to Marshalls too, so that she could try on shoes.

I stood there, restless but smiling, as Maddie kicked off her sandals in the store and tried on a few pairs with girlish enthusiasm. She'd slip into a pair and walk up and down the aisle, checking out her feet in the little mirrors sitting on the floor. She'd look down at one foot and twist it this way and that to see how the shoe looked from various angles. Afterward, she'd dutifully and neatly put the shoes back in their boxes and return them to their shelves.

I watched this little performance with a blend of mystery and bafflement. I don't get the whole shoes thing. It's amazing how foreign, how *alien*, the specific interests of others seem to us when we do not share the same enthusiasm or understanding. The only way I can begin to grasp this phenomenon is to consider my lifelong love of movies and realize that lots of people may have no use for them.

I own two pairs of work shoes. One's brown. The other's black. Don't ask me what brands. I have no idea. Each morning, I pick which pair to wear based on the color of my pants. Then I put them on my feet and forget about them for the rest of the day.

As for sneakers, I've probably owned all of five or six pairs over the last twenty years. I'll get a new pair and then wear them forever. Valerie's usually the one who notices I've literally run my current sneakers into the ground and goes out and gets me a new pair. I got my current pair as a gift for Father's Day last summer.

So let's get back to New York City. Valerie, Maddie and I took a shuttle to the port authority in Manhattan and began our day in the city. I've been to NYC several times, but to see it anew through my daughter's eyes was a thrill. We walked through Times Square and spotted the famous ball that drops every New Year's Eve. We took a picture with actor Morgan

Freeman - - a wax statue of him, if I must be accurate, as we were in front of the Madame Tussauds museum at the time. We browsed at a handful of stores, including Toys 'R Us, which had a Ferris wheel inside. We ate lunch at Carnegie Deli. We took the obligatory walks by Radio City Music Hall, Rockefeller Center and other famous spots.

All of this and more took us to about three in the afternoon. Valerie and I wanted to make sure to return to our hotel in Secaucus, New Jersey, in time for dinner, so we knew it was time to start winding down. It was time to buy Maddie's shoes.

We took a long subway ride north, got off at Penn Station and walked a few blocks to Macy's on . . . well, you've seen the Christmas movie. You know which street. Once there, we rode escalators for seven flights and found the shoe section.

I plopped down onto a bench with such soreness that you would have thought we *walked* up the seven flights. In truth, we had done so much more. Who knows how many blocks we had walked that day. Valerie and I only knew this for certain: we have to have specific plans, definite destinations, the next time we go to New York City. I'm all for spontaneity and for going where the day takes you - - Ferris Bueller is one of my favorite movie characters - - but aimlessly wandering around New York City, block after block, for hours, is exhausting.

Maddie was just as beat as Val and me when we arrived at Macy's. Once we got to the shoe department, though, she sprang to life. She could have run a marathon with this newfound burst

393

of vigor. She was certainly in the right place to get sneakers for one.

I took off my baseball cap, rubbed my eyes and rested. I watched a couple of employees unpack a large shipment and stock shelves and exchange playful banter.

After a few minutes, Maddie reappeared with her shoes of choice: a pair of pink and laceless Converse sneakers for $20. Both she and Valerie raved about them. I smiled, pleased that Maddie had accomplished her dream of buying shoes in New York City.

I suspect Maddie could have bought these sneakers at any store in any town, even right at home in Sanford, but it's not the brand or style or price tag that makes them precious. It's the fact that she bought them in New York City. For her, that makes them special.

Even Pepper seems to know that. She hasn't tried to eat them.

At the Movies with Mom

I took Mom to the movies a couple of weekends ago. What a disaster.

She wanted to see "Hope Springs," the new film starring Meryl Streep and Tommy Lee Jones as a wife and husband who have grown apart over the years. They both travel from Nebraska to Maine to spend a week with a special counselor who helps get marriages back on track. Yes, they eat lobsters while they're here in Vacationland.

I wanted to see the movie too. I've enjoyed some of the noisier blockbusters that Hollywood has served up this summer, but "Hope Springs" seemed like a nice detour into pleasant grown-up fare. I like explosions and car chases and superheroes and teddy bears that say shocking things as much as the next guy, but sometimes it's good to dial it down a few notches, you know?

I picked up Mom after dinner on a Friday night and we headed to the little cinema out there on Route One in Wells. Valerie was supposed to join us, but she bowed out when we couldn't find a sitter for our daughter, Madeline.

Mom and I bought refreshments - - popcorn for her, nachos for me - - and we took our seats in a full house.

I should have known before the lights went down that I'd be in for a long night. For starters, everyone in the audience was on a date with their spouse or significant other. I was the only guy there with his mother. Second of all, I was the youngest one in the room; I'm sure my 40 years did nothing to drop the median age in the room by even a day. To be sure, these two factors alone do not explain why an awkward evening would lie ahead. Rather, they just underscored my squirming discomfort throughout "Hope Springs." This is not a movie that you take your mother to see.

If you've already seen this movie, then you know exactly what I mean. For three hours, Streep and Jones do nothing but attempt mighty strides to get their sex life humming again. Mercifully, one scene involving a banana ended before it started.

Oh, what's that you say? The movie is actually well under two hours? Well, ya coulda fooled me. It felt like it lasted forever.

There is one endless stretch in the film in which the therapist, played by Steve Carell, grills the couple about their bedroom routines and unfulfilled fantasies. The dialogue in this sequence is so blunt and unflinching it even made the Jones character uncomfortable and he's *in the movie*. I finally understand why Man invented profanities and childish euphemisms to deal with the birds and the bees; such words and phrases help us dance around the real words they replace.

Oh, go ahead. Remind me that I'm a grown man who should be able to handle these topics in a mature fashion. Say it all you want. I hear you. But you're forgetting something: I was watching this movie *with my mother*.

Mom laughed throughout the movie - - I see I forgot to mention it's a comedy - - and often jabbed me in the ribs with her elbow and said, "Oh, isn't that awful, Shawn! But I'm not embarrassed! Are you? This is all a part of life!" And then she'd add, "But it's probably not the kind of movie you're supposed to see with your mother."

She said these things to me at least five times throughout the movie. I shushed her each time, lest someone sitting around us would glare at me and ask themselves, *"Who takes their mother to a movie like this???"*

I was trying to be a good guy - - or, more than that, a good son. Mom had not been to the movies since Dad passed away earlier this year. Last November, the two of them went to see "The Ides of March," with George Clooney. Well, George Clooney was not *with* them at the movie theater, sitting there with a tub of popcorn on his lap. But I wouldn't blame you for thinking such a thing, given how I wrote the sentence. I just meant that Clooney starred in the movie and even directed it.

I'm not sure Mom and Dad knew it at the time, but that trip to the cinema would be their last as a couple. The movie provided a bittersweet bookend to the dates they shared during their relationship of more than 40 years. They met each other while standing in line with friends to see "To Sir, With Love" at the former Capitol movie theater in Sanford in the late 1960s. So when Mom told me earlier this summer that she wanted to see "the new movie with Meryl Streep," I smiled, pointed at her with a jaunty finger and told her Val and I would take her. "Mark your calendar," I added.

Dad used to take his mother to the movies all the time, especially after my Grampy died. He even took her to see "Dr. Zhivago" at the old Sanford drive-in in the 1960s; after the movie, he started his car, went into reverse and jumped at the sound of shattering glass. He had forgotten to take the speaker out of his window.

So you can see why I felt good about following in my late father's footsteps and taking my mother to the movies. But how were Mom and I to know that the movie would only have one thing on its mind?

All the same, I'll take Mom to the movies again some time.

Such trips to the movies are part of a larger picture that's coming into focus as we all adjust to life without Dad. Valerie and Maddie and I take Mom out to dinner once in a while and include her in some of our plans; a couple of weekends ago, for example, the four of us went to Meredith, New Hampshire, and I got the sense Mom had one of the nicest times she has had in months. And what is happening during all of this is nice: Mom, who will always be my mother, is nonetheless making the jump from being my parent to being my friend.

I should tell you that I *did* like "Hope Springs." Quite a bit, actually. It's funny. The film is a heartwarming tribute to marriage. I recommend that you see it.

Just not with your mother.

Ol' Jack

You've heard the expression "passing the torch," right? Well, in my family, I "passed the pumpkin" on Monday.

Every year, Valerie leaves the Halloween decorating to our daughter, Madeline, and me. Of the three of us, Valerie's the least enthusiastic about Halloween, so she graciously cedes her "Martha Stewart" approach to decorating to the more ghoulish one shared between Maddie and me. Perhaps one day our home will have cornstalks, uncarved pumpkins and other quaint fare, but until Maddie and I both outgrow Halloween, our home is likely to feature things that go bump in the night.

On Sunday, we went to McDougal's Orchard on Hanson's Ridge Road and picked the perfect pumpkin, big, round and orange, out of the wagon parked on the front lawn. On Monday, Maddie and I sat at the dining room table and prepared to carve this gourd into something with a face.

We divided the chores. With a knife, I turned the top of the pumpkin, stem and all, into a lid. Then I reached inside the pumpkin and scooped out all the goop onto a few layers of paper towels. Maddie waded through these innards, picked out the seeds and dropped them into a bowl for roasting. After I hollowed out the pumpkin, I grabbed the knife and stuck it where I wanted one of the eyes to go.

"Can I carve the face?" Maddie asked me.

For years, I had carved our annual jack-o-lantern. One of the reasons - - the one I told Maddie - - was that I felt Maddie was too young to handle a big, sharp knife. Sure enough, she was. But another reason? The one that I kept to myself, if I am to be honest with you? I love Halloween, and I had grand visions of what a proper jack-o-lantern should look like.

I'm just this way with jack-o-lanterns, mind you. When Maddie and I make a snowman each winter, I help with the hard stuff, such as pushing large and heavy boulders of snow across the yard and setting them on top of each other, but I step back when it comes to bringing the ol' Frosty to life. Maddie takes good charge of the project and finds creative ways to give our snowmen personalities with the smiles and winter gear they wear.

But jack-o-lanterns? They're another story. I take an old-school approach: triangular eyes and a nose and a slightly off-kilter smile that sports three or four uneven teeth. I try to create an expression that blends friendliness and spookiness.

This year, though, when Maddie asked to do the honors, I knew it was time to pass the torch. Or, more accurately, the knife. So I did.

Maddie sat next to me and stuck the knife where she wanted one of the eyes to be. She tried to carve and then wriggle the knife free, but the task proved challenging for her small hand. She gripped the handle and yanked the knife free. She missed bonking me on the nose by a few inches - - with the blade pointed away from me, I should add.

"Whoa, hey, easy!" I said, perhaps too dramatically.

Maddie rolled her eyes and sighed, as kids do when they're doing the best they can and parents interject.

Eventually, Maddie got the hang of it, and I felt I could step away from the table and get out of my daughter's way so she could grow. I checked in on her from time to time, as two large triangular eyes, a pentagonal nose, a large, gaping mouth and jaunty eyebrows came into focus.

When Maddie finished, she stepped back and regarded her creation. I checked it out too and smiled and told her she had done a great job. Looking back now, I wish I had declared, *"It's alive . . . alive!"* Quoting the mad scientist from the movie "Frankenstein" is always a fun Halloween thing to do.

I went to Walmart and bought a few miniature, battery-powered candles, as well as a string of orange lights to drape in our living room window. Before dusk that evening, I placed two of those candles inside the jack-o-lantern, and then Maddie and I carried it outdoors. We placed it on our picnic table, facing the street, so that it could smile at motorists who pass by our home.

Every October, I treasure the sight of a jack-o-lantern on that corner-spot of our picnic table. I go for walks in my neighborhood, and when I return I feel the thrill of autumn when

I see that orange and flickering face. At night I look out the window and see ol' Jack grinning in the night, keeping watch over our home.

We had put our jack-o-lantern on our front steps one year, and someone stole it. Naturally, I was upset that someone had wandered onto my property and did such a lousy thing, but what really bothered me was the thief's indifference to the likelihood that the jack-o-lantern had been giving a child - - in this case, my daughter - - such joy.

Maddie and I had had such a fun time carving that pumpkin that got stolen. She was asleep when Valerie and I discovered the theft, so I went to the store, bought another pumpkin, and tried to carve it as best as I could in the same exact way as the previous one. I wanted my daughter to enjoy that jack-o-lantern. She was all of five or six years old at the time; she had then, as she has now, all the time in the world to learn that there are creeps out there who'll steal the pumpkins right off your steps.

I went for a walk on Monday evening. When I returned home, I saw Maddie's jack-o-lantern smiling back at me. The moment felt even more special than in previous years because this time around my daughter was the one who had brought it to life.

'The Toe'

December, 2012.

Look out, world. There's another Sullivan out there.

Half-Sullivan, that is. After all, he goes by the name of Shafer.

My sister, Kelly, and my brother-in-law, Jay, had a baby boy, my second nephew, on November 29. Finn Garrison Shafer - - his middle name is in honor of my late father, Gary - - came into the world with a full head of spiky brown hair. I am sure you can only imagine why his follicle-challenged Uncle Shawn is impressed enough to mention that feature, as opposed to pointing out the usual statistics, such as what he weighed or how long he was from head to toe.

But while we're on the subject of toes . . .

Finn looks like David, his paternal grandfather. I also think he has the same chin as his Uncle Matt on his father's side. However, and this is no small thing, Finn has my famous toe. Well, okay, it's a toe, so, yes, it *is* a small thing, but only literally. Figuratively, this is a big deal.

This is not the "Sullivan toe," mind you, but the "Bourre toe," as my mother believes that my Memere passed it down to me. In turn, I passed to down to my daughter, Madeline. Kelly does not have the "Bourre toe," so it's a bit of a neat trick that she has nonetheless passed it on to Finn and her oldest son, Rowen.

The toe of which I speak is the second one in from the pinky. It starts out straight enough but explodes into a thumb-like protrusion and curves inward. It hides a bit beneath the middle toe but never makes you feel like you're stepping on it. It's pretty distinct, and you'll have to take my word for it. I will not take my shoe and sock off to show you.

He's a good boy, Finn. He keeps Kelly and Jay up all night, but that's what babies are supposed to do. Kelly says she just likes to sit there and hold him. Rowen, who had the run of the household for nearly six years, has made the transition to big brotherhood like the fine young man he is.

Mom and I drove to the hospital in Exeter, New Hampshire, to be there to welcome Finn an hour after he was born. Auntie Val and Cousin Maddie joined us after school that afternoon. We were joined by Finn's paternal grandparents, David and Doreen, and his Uncle Matt and Aunt Grace.

Finn was asleep, of course, when we first saw him. We gazed at his soft, pudgy face, counted his long fingers and toes and peeked underneath his little cap to check out that healthy shock of hair. The nurse came into the room a few times and gently placed Finn underneath a warmer, and he stretched out on his back and slept soundly under the bulb.

"He's at the beach," we all joked.

I was one of the last ones in the room to hold Finn. After Kelly and Jay, Finn's grandmothers were the first to take him into their arms. From there, his grandfather held him, and, after that, Rowen did.

I eased into a chair with armrests, so that I could have safety buffers on each side as I held my nephew. Yes, I'm that kind of guy - - nervous about holding other people's babies, even ones from my own extended family. There is no more precious a bundle as a baby, and I'm acutely aware of that as I hold one. I always held Maddie with comfort and ease, though; such is the connection between a parent and child.

I hummed and chit-chatted with the little guy, filling his ears with words, words he will use himself one day. Someone in the room told a joke, and I laughed freely.

"That's called laughter," I whispered into Finn's ear.

I looked at Finn and studied his face and marveled at the miracle of birth and the profound wonder of being there to see a person during the very first moments of his or her life. *What are you going to be when you grow up?* I asked Finn, not whispering the words to him, but thinking them. *What are going to be your gifts to the world around you? What will you consider fun, fascinating, worthwhile?*

I often look at Maddie and Rowen and think of these questions, but as they get older - - Maddie's nine, and Rowen will be six in January - - it's becoming possible to imagine their answers. They already have begun making their little marks on the world around them. With a newborn, though, the answers are anybody's guess.

There we were, Finn's parents and grandparents and aunts and uncles and cousin, in one little hospital room, celebrating his arrival.

We felt someone else in the room with us, as well. We knew, in ways hard to describe and comprehend, but made possible through faith, that Dad was with us in spirit.

A complex year, 2012. It began with the death of my father. It ended with the birth of his third grandchild.

"Focus on the grandchildren," Dad told Mom before he passed away. He wanted to give her advice for working through the grief that he knew awaited her.

Welcome to the world, Finn. You may be only weeks old, but, like your brother and cousin, you have already made a strong, life-affirming difference for those of us who this year waited long for your arrival.

No Time for Pit Stops

I can see it now. Decades from now, when my daughter, Madeline, looks back on the trip to Virginia that she took with me, her mother and grandmother in April of 2013, she'll say to me, "Remember that time, Dad, when you got all annoyed because I asked you to get off the highway so I could use the bathroom?"

By then, it might not matter that we had spent three days with dear relatives in a beautiful state that had become like a second home to us. It'll not matter that Maddie had climbed trees, taken daily bike rides, enjoyed the view of the Rappahannock River, played with her younger cousin and the puppy next door and stood in the *very* spot where George Washington was born.

Nay, the story she will tell her kids, *my* grandchildren, will be about the time their Grampy tried to thwart her simple and God-given right to answer nature's call.

"Dad, I've gotta go to the bathroom," Maddie told me from the back seat. "Can we stop?"

"Really?" I replied, my annoyance immediate and clear.

"Yes, Dad. I've got to go."

"We were just at the rest stop ten minutes ago. Why didn't you go then?"

"I didn't have to."

And then I said, "Of course."

I could see Valerie giving me a look that said, "Just get off the next ramp. What's the big deal?" My mother remained expressionless. She stays out of these things.

Deep down, I knew I was making a fuss. We had left Sanford at a little after six that morning, it was now the early afternoon, and we still had a relatively full day stretched ahead of us to get to Virginia in good time.

But here's the thing: We were close to the George Washington Bridge in New York City, right where traffic starts getting really congested and hectic. I've driven this route a few times over the years, and I prefer to just get through it without taking detours and repeating a wrong turn I once took. Once I cross the bridge and pass the border into New Jersey and resume cruising on an open highway, I'm all set. We could pull over at every rest stop named after a president, a sports legend or a famous inventor, and I wouldn't mind.

Valerie pointed out a billboard for McDonald's on our left. The sign said "easy on, easy off," or something like that to imply simple access - - clear proof that even Ronald McDonald knows that motorists who see that advertisement likely will not be inclined to just peel off a major road to get a Big Mac.

So I took the exit. As it turned out, getting to the McDonald's was *not* easy. It was on the other side of a busy route, and I had to first turn right and drive a bit before I could turn around and head left to get there. Then I missed the entrance to the restaurant because it blended in with a side street and the ways to get to neighboring businesses. Eventually, I skipped McDonald's and just pulled into a service station, exasperated.

By now, Mom was laughing pretty hard, in a gallows kind of way, which I admit I appreciated. I knew I was being an impatient grump. By then I had been driving for about seven straight hours, with five or six more still ahead of us. I tried to moderate my mood with edgy but comical remarks.

After everyone had visited the restroom - - yes, as galling as it was, I went too - - I apologized for my impatience and initial reluctance to pull off the highway. Maddie, who in several ways is her father's daughter, teased me about my crankiness. She can do a pretty spot-on impression of me, and it cracks everyone up, myself included.

We pointed the car toward the GW Bridge and continued our journey. We listened to the Eighties station on satellite radio - - it was playing the top 40 hits of that weekend in 1985 - - and I knew I had sealed my Fate. From there, I would be known as The Dad Who Did Not Want To Stop Driving So His Child Could Go To The Bathroom.

"Uh-oh," Maddie would say in the days ahead, before we'd get into the car. "Dad's driving. If you've gotta go, you better go now 'cause we're not pulling over!"

And, of course, as Valerie settled behind the wheel at the start of her driving shifts, she'd say, "If any of you have to use the restroom along the way, let me know. *I'll* stop." What a saint.

Ah, serves me right. What comes around, goes around. I've become my father, you see. However, before you start singing "The Circle of Life," that song from "The Lion King," let me tell you what I mean.

Dad planned these sweeping, elaborate trips when my sister and I were kids. He and Mom worked extra hard and saved money all year long to make these vacations happen. In the summer of 1989, we took our biggest trip of all: we spent three weeks out west, traveling through Nevada, Arizona and California and even spending an afternoon across the border in Mexico.

One morning, we set out to drive along Big Sur. We had skipped breakfast at the hotel to hit the road early. Dad had us on a schedule.

"All right now," Dad told us. "This Big Sur's a long drive. If anyone's hungry, we better stop now because there won't be any places to get food for a while."

None of us were hungry at the time, so we passed.

"Are you sure?" Dad asked.

411

My sister Kelly and I nodded. We were sure. We didn't know at the time we'd be going another 12 hours without a bite to eat, but still. We were sure.

We drove along Big Sur, and it was beautiful, and when we finished the route, we continued north. The more we drove, the louder Kelly's and my bellies started to grumble. We were hungry. Did we beg Dad to pull over to a burger joint somewhere? I can't remember. I was probably too lightheaded at the time. Kelly and I might have sung "We Are the World" at one point. All I can tell you is that when Dad finally did stop at a restaurant that evening, we had not eaten since dinner the night before.

Which restaurant did we choose? A Kentucky Fried Chicken, I think. Maybe a Carl's, Jr. It didn't matter. Whatever I ordered, it tasted like filet mignon.

Kelly and I teased Dad about this. He became known as The Dad Who Went A Full Day Without Stopping The Car So His Children Could Eat. For years, Kelly and I gave him a rough time. We made sport of his Type-A vacation-planning and the busy, time-specific itineraries he set. We never let him forget that 24-hour fast he put us through.

It drove him *crazy*.

"We spent three weeks out there," he'd grouse. "We went to Las Vegas and the Grand Canyon. We went to Disney Land, Knott's Berry Farm, and Hollywood. We took the NBC tour and saw where Johnny Carson parked his car and ate dessert on

Rodeo Drive. We went to San Francisco. And all you guys remember is that 24-hour stretch when we didn't eat."

"We skipped lunch, Dad."

"But I asked you in the morning if you wanted something to eat before we drove the Big Sur."

Of *course* Kelly and I remember everything about that trip. It was the ultimate getaway for our family. We had a great time and will remember it forever. But it was always a gas to remind Dad about those food-free 24 hours.

So now you see why there's a certain justice in my being labeled as the father who doesn't like to stop for bathroom breaks while on long trips. Twenty years from now, Maddie will cherish her memories of Virginia, but the story she'll tell will be the one I told at the top.

"George Washington's *birthplace*?" she'll say to others. "Never mind that. Let me tell you about the George Washington *Bridge*."

Somewhere, up in the heavens, Dad will smile and say, "That's my girl."

The Jetty

Madeline and I walked along the jetty at Wells Beach on Sunday afternoon, stepping and sometimes leaping a bit from rock to rock as we made our way. The Atlantic was calm to our left but energetic to our right as we headed toward the tower at the end of the reach.

Maddie led the way. As I kept a few paces behind her, I watched her every step, keeping my eyes on her flip-flopped feet as she navigated each stone and avoided the gaps and crevices. If she were a few years younger, I would have held her hand, so that we could have walked side by side to our destination. I would have lifted her over those spaces between the rocks, where the salt water of the crashing waves seep.

But Maddie is ten years old now. We celebrated her birthday on Tuesday. A decade ago, the doctor delivered her, held her up to the clock on the wall, and told me to snap a quick photo to mark the time of her birth. I snapped away, clicking my camera repeatedly, getting as many shots as I could. Problem was, I had forgotten to remove the lens cap. My mind was too much of a hurricane of excitement to focus, you see. Valerie,

414

bless her, called out to me from the operating table to take off the lens cap, but to no avail.

Where have all these years gone? I do not know. I asked the same question five years ago when my daughter made the jump from the crib to the classroom and started kindergarten.

Maddie and I reached the end of the jetty, and she gave that tower out there a quick tap to show she made it. On our way back to the beach, as we again plotted our steps on the rocks, we heard a fierce and unnerving wave roll forward behind us. It crashed violently against the jetty and soaked the rocks on our left. Maddie noted she was glad she had stepped to the right in time.

When we got back to the shore, we kicked off our shoes and stood up to our shins in ice water as the tide ebbed and flowed.

"Time to head back," I eventually told Maddie. "Mom must be wondering where we are."

Valerie had stayed in the car to rest her eyes.

I sat on a rock and dusted beach sand off my feet with one of my socks. I put on my sneakers and watched Maddie brush off her toes and slip back into her flip-flops. I absorbed the warm breeze and regarded my daughter. I thought about how she had two days left before she turned double-digits and marveled at how she has grown. She's a tall girl - - she comes right up to my shoulders.

Will I remember this moment? I thought. *Or will it fade into the past like so many other moments?*

I bet every parent asks that question. There's just no way to remember it all. I cradled Maddie in my arms thousands of times when she was a baby, yet these days I specifically recall doing so only once or twice. There was that night, when she was six weeks old, when she woke up crying. I picked her up from her bassinet and sat in the rocking chair next to Valerie's and my bedroom window. It was two in the morning. Moonlight spilled through the window and cast shadows on my daughter's face.

I was exhausted. I had to go to work in the morning. I wanted to sleep. Yet as I watched Maddie's face, I knew there was nothing else in the world I wanted to be doing. I savored the moment because I knew once I returned Maddie to her bassinet she'd wake up in the morning and start walking, talking, going to school and doing all of those other things that await a life.

Years from now, will I remember our walk on the jetty, or will it blend in with all the other trips our family has taken to the beach? Will it fade further into the quick blur that is proving to be my daughter's childhood?

All we have is the moment. Now is what matters most. You can treasure the past you've committed to memory. You can hope and plan for the future. But to enjoy life you have to appreciate moments as they happen. These are not new sentiments, of course. I am not the first to express them. They are clichés. But some clichés are simply lasting truths and have their places in our lives.

I enjoyed walking on the jetty with Maddie. I'm glad I hung back a bit as she forged ahead, making smart choices about where to plant each step and doing her best to avoid the wet spots, the gaps between the rocks and other pitfalls. As a child, she would have needed my hand. A few years ago, she might have needed my direction. On Sunday, she did well on her own.

All the same, I followed her with pride and joy and a quiet eye on her safety. Only occasionally did I speak up and point out a rough spot along the way. I would have been right there for her if she slipped or had a question about which way to go.

How like life, that jetty. How like parenthood.

Cue the Bagpipes

My father always liked bagpipes.

Me? Growing up, I was never too keen on them. I didn't find the sound of bagpipes shrill and grating, as some folks do, but I did consider the music they make to be a little too mournful for my tastes. Now, of course, I fully appreciate bagpipes, and the distinguished, mysterious and beautiful notes they strike; they remind me of Dad, who passed away more than 20 months ago.

Dad had wanted a bagpiper to perform an Irish ballad at his funeral, but we weren't able to have one. I cannot remember the reason why. Maybe church rules did not allow it. Perhaps it was the heavy snowstorm that January morning. Most likely, my family and I did all we could but were too stunned and saddened by our loss to make everything happen as we wished.

We did have a bagpiper perform at Dad's burial, several months later, during the springtime. My mother and my sister and I gathered with family and friends at the cemetery that warm April morning and said our final farewell to Dad. A short distance away, a bagpiper stood solemn and straight and performed my father's favorite Irish song, "When Irish Eyes Are Smiling."

Afterward, Mom and my sister and I thanked the musician for his memorable performance, telling him that Dad surely would have approved.

The other day, Mom decided to visit the Gary D. Sullivan Walkway at the Midtown Mall. At the top of those steps, which now have an elevated view of the waterfall across the way at Number One Pond, there is a plaque that honors my father and his contributions to the community throughout his life. The city dedicated the steps to Dad during a nice ceremony on a crisp October afternoon last fall.

Occasionally, I'll visit the plaque and, if I think no one's looking, I'll run the tips of my fingers over Dad's name. A couple of weeks ago, when the city celebrated the renovation and grand opening of the Sanford Mill on Washington Street, I exited the building after the festivities and could see Dad's pillar at the top of the walkway in the distance; I smiled, a bit wistfully, for I knew Dad would have loved to see inside the newly reinvented mill.

Something odd, but nice, happened when Mom recently visited Dad's plaque for the first time in a while. As she approached the top of the walkway, she heard an unmistakable sound. She discovered its source when she approached the plaque. She saw a man standing near the bottom of the steps, playing a bagpipe.

419

The incident impressed Mom enough that she shared this story with my family and me when we went to Ted's Fried Clams for dinner in Shapleigh on Sunday night. We all agreed that, given the involved factors, quite a few key details had come together for such a thing to happen.

Think about it. You have the steps, named after my father. My father loved bagpipes. A man was playing the bagpipe not anywhere else in Sanford at that moment, but at the foot of the steps. Mom, who had not seen the plaque at the walkway in a short while, chose that exact moment to visit. As a result, she got to hear the bagpipe.

I shared the story of Mom's encounter with friends. All agreed her experience was nice and intriguing. Some believed that Dad's spirit arranged the whole thing, perhaps as a way to say hello or assure us that he's still with us and always will be. Others felt it was a wonderful and random moment, not one orchestrated by any forces. As for me . . . well, I'm never quite sure what to believe at such moments.

But such moments are nonetheless a marvel to behold. This past summer, a friend told me he went jogging one evening and experienced sagging energy as he made his way along Riverside Avenue. He glanced at the mall's walkway and figured scaling them would give him some pep. He told me he thinks of the mall's stairs as "Sanford's 'Rocky' Steps," which he knew I'd appreciate, since "Rocky" is my favorite film and the walkway is named after my father.

As my friend approached the bottom of the steps, he randomly picked a song from his iPod. Right on cue, the theme from the "Rocky" soundtrack started coaching his ears. He found his moment and scaled the steps with renewed vigor. I wonder if he gamely jabbed the air with a right hook when he reached the top.

What does all of this mean - - the incident with the bagpiper, first and foremost, but also the episode with my friend, the runner? No idea. None. Who knows how the world works in such cases? I'm just relaying to you a confluence of events, simply because their arrangement quietly amazes me.

But I'll say this. A friend told me that he saw the bagpiper too, and that the man likely was performing in affiliation with the Prince of Peace Church at the lower level of the Midtown Mall. That seems likely to me. I do not require confirmation or more details.

Sometimes, mystery and wonder are enough for me.

The Moment

I put the DVD in the machine last week, pressed "play," and there he was.

Dad.

He appeared on the screen in a tuxedo and stood alongside his friend, Lorraine Masure, on stage at the St. Ignatius Parish Hall. With a nostalgic and funny script, a gift for improvisation and a healthy dose of school spirit, they were co-hosting a multiclass reunion for anyone who attended the former St. Ignatius High School in Sanford during the decades it was open. It was Saturday, Aug. 2, 1986, and the gym was packed with Spartans and their spouses.

Dad was 41 at the time - - the same age as I am now, yet roughly eight months younger. I watched him at the podium, laughing and smiling with ease, delivering his lines perfectly and matching them with just the right heartfelt and comic expressions. I was reminded that he was told more than once in his lifetime that he could have been a stand-up comedian.

"Boy, your father's stomach was upset before the event that night," Mom told me as we watched.

"Really?" I turned to her and asked, not quite believing her. "He looks so natural up there."

Mom had come over that night for dinner. Mom, my wife, Valerie, and our daughter, Madeline, and I all raised our glasses at the table and toasted Dad. That night, Wednesday, Jan. 8, made exactly two years since Dad died after a seven-year battle against amyotrophic lateral sclerosis.

I remember Dad that evening, roughly 28 years ago. I hung out with him in his bedroom while he put on his shirt and coat and fiddled with his tuxedo's bow-tie. I was 14 years old at the time. I don't remember him seeming nervous about emceeing that evening's event. He had always been very adept at making sure his children never saw him worry. He might have said something about the monkey suit, though, and how it was a humid night for such attire.

He definitely made a joke about the heat later that evening. At the start of the event, he and Lorraine Masure addressed the stuffiness in the gym and recommended a way that everyone in the room could keep the warmth to a minimum.

"If you graduated from St. Ignatius High School during an even year, we want you to breathe in. If you graduated during an odd year, we want you to breathe out," Dad instructed the crowd. "Breathe in . . . breathe out . . . breathe in . . . breathe out . . . by doing this, we can cut down on the hot air in the room."

And then, with sharp timing, Dad added, "And for those of you in the room who didn't go to St. Ignatius High School, we prefer that you don't breathe at all."

Every Spartan in the room laughed and applauded.

Strange, to see Dad so young and to hear him in his prime. He had a strong, deep voice that he always maintained was his saving grace because he always had what he would jokingly refer to as a wimp's build and persona. His voice grew raspier during the final years of his disease, and during those final weeks he spoke little. Several months after he died, I woke up before dawn one morning and heard his voice in my living room. At first it startled me and I spent a second trying to make sense of what I was hearing. Then, when the cobwebs of sleep quickly cleared from my mind, I realized that I was listening to the audio book that he recorded for Maddie the day before he died. Perhaps one of our two cats had brushed against it, causing it to open and start the recording.

Two years. That's a long time, yet it's not. It's a long time because I went nearly 40 years either seeing or speaking with Dad just about every day. But it's not a long time because two years is a blink compared to all the time ahead without him.

It gets easier.

That's what I hear Dad say in my head. He said that to me once. At the time, he was telling me about his efforts to try to move forward after his father's death. Now his words echo in my mind every now and then. *You'll never be the same, but you will find a way to move forward.* He said that too. I've whittled that second statement down to a single word: *Forward.* It comes in handy whenever I find myself getting caught up in the sad memories.

As with most things Dad told me, he was right. It does get easier. Not better - - no, not better, because better would be if he were still here, healthy and well. But easier.

For those who might be grieving over the recent loss of a loved one, here's what I mean. Last year, I approached the first anniversary of Dad's death by telling myself, *I just gotta make it through this day.* This year, though, as I approached the second anniversary, I thought, *I can do this.*

There are two reasons I felt such peace and confidence during the second coming-around of the saddest day of my life. One is time, which heals all wounds, just like the expression says. The other reason, though, is perspective. A year ago, I focused on my loss. This year, however, I honored the second anniversary as the day when my father's suffering ended and his peace began. Dad loved life, absolutely loved it, but in his fight against ALS he experienced agony. At the end, he ached for the peace his passing would bring.

"I know you'll be sad when I am gone," Dad told Mom a few weeks before he died. "But when I am gone, please take a moment to be happy for me."

He asked the same of the rest of us. It took two years, but on Wednesday, Jan. 8, 2014, I found that moment.

'An Island in the
Chaotic Ocean of Life'

A few years ago, my father coined a simple but picturesque term that has since resonated with me.

At the time he was referring to his prized chair, an old brown recliner that sat in the corner of his living room. He called this chair an "island in the chaotic ocean of life."

He came up with this metaphor as an explanation, a *defense*, of his long history of booting me out of that chair when I was growing up. As a child or a teenager or a young man home from college, I would relax in that chair and he'd walk into the room and say he wanted "his" chair so he could watch television.

Most times, I surrendered and got up without incident. Once, though, I challenged him. I was relaxing and watching an old movie, feeling quite happy with the world on a quiet summer afternoon. Half way through the film, Dad entered the room and told me he wanted his chair.

"But I'm comfortable," I told him.

He tried a bit of humor to get his way, but I dug in my heels. He persisted, though, and I ended up losing a quick battle of wills. In no time, I found myself sitting on the couch across the room. I sat there and stewed. I lost interest in the movie, got up, told Dad what I thought and left the room.

For me, the disruption of my comfort was not the real issue. I was in my twenties at the time. Getting ousted from the chair had made me feel like a child.

Dad and I looked back and laughed over this episode when I wrote a column about it in October of 2006. That's when he told me that his chair was an "island in the chaotic ocean of life." A man who works hard and raises two children does not have much he can call his own, he explained. He said his chair was one of the few places in this world where he could retreat and feel all his pressures, challenges and responsibilities slip away. He could read the paper in that chair, doze off or watch his favorite shows on television, and all would be right with the world.

This was a more eloquent explanation than the one I heard while growing up. Back then, he used to say he paid for the chair, so he got to sit in it whenever he wanted. One day, he'd tell me, I'd be older and would be able to buy my own chair and be in charge of it.

Not quite. I'm banned from having a Dad's Chair in my household. My wife, Valerie, rejects the notion of someone in the house controlling a piece of furniture.

The truth is, I agree. I had to figure that out on my own, though.

A few years ago, I woke up one Saturday morning and found my daughter, Madeline, snuggling in our chair in the living room. Most mornings, I wake up before Valerie and Maddie and claim that chair without having a problem. It's where I like to sit and read while drinking my first cup of coffee for the day. On this morning, however, I woke up too late and missed the boat.

I looked at Maddie. She sure looked peaceful. I looked at our couch and tried to imagine resting there with my book and coffee. I couldn't picture it. I'm too much a creature of habit. I prefer the chair. It's comfortable, yes, but it's also near two lamps that throw the right amount of light onto the pages I read. And the view out our picture window is a nice one.

In a soft-spoken tone, I told Maddie my hopes of sitting in the chair after I finished making my coffee. Valerie, who was sitting on the couch, looked down at the floor with silent disapproval. Maddie paused and slipped out of the chair without a fuss. It took her a while to warm back up to me, though.

I got the chair that morning, but not its comfort. I read a few chapters and drank my coffee but felt less than serene. I empathized with my daughter because I remembered how I felt under the same circumstances as a son.

I later told Dad that I had booted Maddie from the chair. Dad always takes his granddaughter's side, but on this occasion he held true to his principle of a father's chair.

"You told her you wanted the chair, right?" he asked me. "You didn't *ask* her for it, did you?"

Indeed I *had* asked Maddie for the chair, in an admittedly roundabout and hesitant way. Dad shook his head with the same disapproval most elders show when they think today's parents surrender too much control to their children. He was teasing, of course, but he still meant business.

Valerie and Maddie later chided me about the incident. Maddie, a second-grader at the time, was learning about the civil rights movement at school. On her own time, she had been showing interest in Martin Luther King and the Norman Rockwell painting that shows an African-American girl walking to school under protest and a police escort.

"When you tell someone to get out of a chair, it's like what they used to do on the buses," Maddie told me, referring to what she had learned about Rosa Parks.

I looked at Maddie. I paused and then smiled. *Son of a gun,* I thought. *You know, the kid has a point. When one person tells another to give up their seat and sit somewhere else, that person is attempting to establish or assert superiority.*

I didn't tell Maddie I thought she had a point, but I have not booted her from our chair since. Instead I now find other ways to claim the seat in the morning before someone else can. I put my book on the armrest as a placeholder, for example.

But the truth is that the incident that Saturday morning was probably enough to establish a lasting and unspoken understanding that "Dad likes sitting in that chair in the morning." Valerie and Maddie tend to claim that chair during afternoons and evenings, and I'm fine on the couch during those times.

But I'd like to be clear about something. My father told me his chair was an "island in the chaotic ocean of life." I understand that concept. I appreciate it now. I should have understood it and appreciated when I was younger.

While he and Mom were raising my sister and me, Dad would relax in his recliner and the burdens of bills and parental and professional obligations would be kept at bay. In his final years, he sat in that chair and he was able to escape the ravages of ALS - - in fact, there were some days when he was so content and rested in that chair that he completely *forgot* he had the disease. He'd be cruelly reminded when he tried to rise from his seat.

And here is another truth: When Dad wanted his chair, he was taking far, far less than he had given. He and Mom devoted themselves to my sister and me all throughout our childhoods, making sure we had what we needed and enjoyed our lives. They continued to provide that love when Kelly and I got older and started out on our own, and they extended it generously to our spouses and to their grandchildren. Dad is gone now, but his legacy of love endures, and Mom continues to show her love to this day.

An island in the chaotic ocean of life.

I like the ocean. It's vast and majestic, and it promises adventure and achievement. But sometimes the sea turns choppy and rough. The waves swell and charge you with unrelenting force, and threaten to topple you. For all of its beauty, there are often hardships and challenges out there at sea. There is often pain and loss.

You need an island at such moments.

Dad's island was his chair. My island or yours might be something else.

Faith. Family. Friends. Laughter. Love. Books. Sports. Exercise. Movies. Music. Art. Travel. There are, thank God, lots of islands out there.

For me, my father and his chair provide a true and clear way to interpret the world: all things in life fall into one of two categories.

They're either the ocean or the island. To fully experience life, you cannot choose one and avoid the other. You need both.

ACKNOWLEDGMENTS

First and foremost, I am grateful for my parents, Lorraine and Gary. The scope of their love, support and encouragement would be impossible for me to capture here in writing, but I can provide one example of it: they were the first ones to suggest to me that one day I should assemble my columns into a book.

I would like to thank my former employer, Patrice Foster, for giving this project her blessing. I'm also grateful for the support of my current employers at Seacoast Media Group, which now owns the Sanford News.

I would like to thank a few friends. Brian Boisvert, a professional editor, proofread the manuscript and offered invaluable suggestions and encouragement. Mike Kleinrock and Nathan Saunders also offered encouragement and technical assistance. Fellow writers Gary Sprague, Patrick McGinnis, Sandy McKeon and Jennifer Genest answered a few questions and offered guidance on the subject of self-publishing.

I particularly appreciate everyone who has read my column over the years. I based many of my selections for this book on the positive feedback that I have received from readers.

The one thing I appreciate most about my column is that it gives me the opportunity to put my loved ones into the hearts of readers. Finally, I wish to thank my two favorite loved ones, my wife, Valerie, and our daughter, Madeline, for their support.

Thank you for reading my book. I hope, for you, it has proven an island in the chaotic ocean of life.